CONTEXT
AND
UNDERSTANDING

WILLIAM M. WENTWORTH

CONTEXT AND UNDERSTANDING

AN INQUIRY INTO SOCIALIZATION THEORY

ELSEVIER
New York • Oxford

Elsevier North Holland, Inc.
52 Vanderbilt Avenue, New York, New York 10017

Distributors outside the United States and Canada:

Thomond Books
(A Division of Elsevier/North-Holland Scientific Publishers, Ltd.)
P.O. Box 85
Limerick, Ireland

© 1980 by Elsevier North Holland, Inc.

Library of Congress Cataloging in Publication Data

Wentworth, William M.
    Context and understanding: An inquiry into socialization theory

    Bibliography: p.
    Includes index.
    1. Socialization. 2. Individualism. 3. Power (Social sciences) I. Title.
HQ783.W46   303.3′2   80-11424
ISBN 0-444-99073-9

Desk Editor   Louise Schreiber
Design   Edmée Froment
Art rendered by   José García
Production Manager   Joanne Jay
Compositor   Lexigraphics, Inc.
Printer   Haddon Craftsmen

Manufactured in the United States of America

For Priscilla, Michael and Davy

CONTENTS

Acknowledgments	xi
List of Tables and Figures	xiii
INTRODUCTION	1
PART ONE. HISTORY, IMAGES AND ISSUES	**11**
CHAPTER ONE. AN ETYMOLOGY OF "SOCIALIZATION"	13
Sociology as a History of Ideas: The Concept of Socialization, 1896-1921	14
The Discovery of "Society" in an Arena of Individualism	14
The "Individual" in a Theoretical Limbo	17
The Early Institutional Development of Sociology in the United States	19
Social Structure, Interpenetration and the Birth of the "Oversocialized Man"	21
The Influence of Freudian Psychology and Anthropology on the Concept of Socialization	22

The Dominion of "Society" and the Demise of Individualism: Changing Conceptions of Socialization, 1921-1976	27
The Old Definitions in Transition	27
Toward the Modern Definition: A Passive Individual, A Passive Process	30
Talcott Parsons and the Modern Concept of Socialization	32
Summary and Conclusions	38
CHAPTER TWO. BETWEEN THE OLD COLLECTIVE DETERMINISM AND THE NEW INDIVIDUALISM	**41**
The Undersocialized Conceptualization of the Individual	43
Interpretive Sociology	44
Need Sociology Capitulate?	46
Are Groups Real and Are They Determinate?	48
Models of the Individual in Theory Formation: Situation, Creativity and Uniqueness; Structure, Conduct and Continuity	50
An Example of the Interpretive Approach	50
A Functionalist Account	53
Performance and Principles	55
Summary and Conclusions	59
CHAPTER THREE. A CRITICISM OF MODERN SOCIALIZATION CONCEPTS AND RESEARCH	**62**
The Concepts of Socialization and Culture	63
An Anthropomorphic Model of the Individual	68
Primary and Secondary Socialization Raise the Issue of Sociological Autonomy	70
Socialization Studies as a Form of Explanation	72
Summary and Conclusions	77
PART TWO. CONTEXT AND AUTONOMY IN SOCIALIZATION THEORY	**81**
CHAPTER FOUR. RECONCEPTUALIZING: A SOCIALIZATION-AS-INTERACTION MODEL AND THE CONTEXT	**83**
Redefining "Socialization"	83
The New Definition	85
Superficial Activity in Socialization	86
Ritual, Seriousness and Play	86
Expressive and Instrumental Competence: An Exhaustive Typology of Activity	88
Fundamental Structure in Interaction: The Sociological Context	90
World-Building and Limits	90

Related Concepts	92
Focused, Unfocused, Routine and Problematic Contexts	95
The Rules of Context Construction	97
Superficial and Fundamental Structure	102
Primary Contexts	105
Summary	108

CHAPTER FIVE. CONTROL, POWER, AUTONOMY AND THE SELF IN SOCIALIZATION — 110

Introduction	110
Reality, Structure and Structuration	112
A Summary of the Attributes of Power	112
An Overview of the Theoretics of Power	115
"Aligning Actions" and Control	117
The Margin for Discretion, Respectability and Types of Deviation	119
Levels of Human Behavior and the Relationship of Control with Power	121
A Social Psychology of Control and Power Relations: The Basis of Autonomy	122
Goffman and Mead: Identity, Resource Management and the Self	122
Karl Marx: Rebellion and History	125
Durkheim: Society, Complexity and Sociological Autonomy	126
Conclusions: Control and Power Relations and the Theory of Socialization	130
Context, Control and Autonomy	130
Counter-Control, Resistance, Seekership and Autonomy	133
Stress and Socialization	134
Summary	137

APPENDIX I. A LOGIC OF DEFINITIONS — 141

APPENDIX II. THE THEORIST AS SOCIOLOGICAL OBSERVER: A METHOD FOR THEORY — 147

Analytical Framework	147
Theoretical Methodology Specified	150
References	155
Index	177

ACKNOWLEDGMENTS

This work represents an effort dedicated to the attainment of a fresh look at socialization theory and its subsidiary concepts. It is also an attempt to discover how the process of socialization may be discussed in a way compatible with the theoretical and empirical heritage of sociology, while at the same time avoiding several theoretical deficiencies.

If there is any success toward those ends within, it grows from the extraordinary ability of Jeffrey K. Hadden to create an intellectually stimulating environment. That environment is always free, yet informed by his wide knowledge of sociology. Furthermore, he has managed to sustain an unflagging faith in my abilities. Robert Bierstedt has provided me with the opportunity to develop and hone several theoretical insights. He has shown me the importance of the history of ideas in sociological inquiry. His writing has been a model of clarity and style for me, although I cannot pretend to have approached his ability.

Todd Hanson and Theodore Long have engaged me in hours of conversation, which are reflected throughout my writing. I appreciate the very helpful suggestions given by Lewis A. Coser on a draft of the manuscript.

I owe a tremendous debt to these colleagues and friends for their multifaceted contributions to this exercise in general socialization theory. And because the work was begun under the auspices of the Developmental Study of Medical Socialization in the University of Virginia School of Medicine, there are many others who more indirectly but significantly lent me their support. I would like to thank the following people for their cooperation and assistance: William R. Drucker, Dean of the School of Medicine; James W. Craig, Associate Dean; Ralph Ingersoll, Associate Dean; Harold B. Haley; and Thomas H. Hunter. In addition, I gratefully acknowledge The Commonwealth Fund for its backing of the larger research effort out of which the present study is derived.

Through it all, my wife Priscilla Geier Wentworth has been my editor, an effective critic and my diligent typist.

Clemson University   William M. Wentworth

LIST OF TABLES AND FIGURES

TABLE 1. Significant Trends in the Changing Meaning of Socialization

TABLE 2. Primary Contexts

FIGURE 1. Weber's Conception of the Sources of Social Power

FIGURE 2. A Heuristic Comparison of the Likely Theoretical Balance According to Perspective (Appendix II)

CONTEXT
AND
UNDERSTANDING

INTRODUCTION

This book is not a tract on philosophy. Neither is it a history of ideas. It is a theoretical work that attempts to trace, explicate and expand upon sociological perspectives of socialization. The meaning of socialization is complex; theories of the process are often somehow disjointed; and the concept deeply penetrates the rest of sociological theory. Because of the imbeddedness of "socialization" in what sociologists can say about the world, however, any serious attempt at grasping the sociological position must admit some historical and philosophical discussion to make useful sense of the otherwise intertwining metaphysics and traditions that inform our current conceptions of socialization. The bulk of the philosophical comments will refer to individualism, and to what may be called sociologism. I have chosen the name "sociologism" in place of the more common "collectivism" or "solidarism." By it I wish to distinguish a position that acknowledges historical social structure and not the mere influence of other individuals in social processes.

Much of the theoretical content of modern sociology has been forged in a shifting engagement between individualistic and sociologistic philosophies. Individualism, in its most reduced form, declares that (1) autonomous individuals are the causal forces that create society; (2) the individual therefore has a kind of ontological priority over "society"; (3) socialization renders the individual fit for society through rational conversion and coercion; (4) through their actions people create society; and (5) individuals, or more precisely, the conditions for action, constitute the correct sphere for analysis (i.e., motives are the source of history). Similarly, sociologism may be reduced to a skeletal framework: (1) that the causal flow is from society to the individual; (2) that society has ontological priority over the person; (3) that the societal cause becomes embodied in the personality during socialization; (4) that individuals are products of society, that is, historical social structures; and (5) that society is the correct object of analysis (i.e., the structure of society governs the actions of individuals and therefore the course of history). The historical influence of the two perspectives on sociology has been most evident in socialization theory. This area of theory has sensitively expressed the relative ascendancy of individualism (or sociologism) in our sociological thinking.

Although these philosophies alone cannot be said to have fully shaped the changing concepts of the individual and society found in the history of sociology, they have provided a presumptive framework for our scientific theories. Individualism and sociologism provide metaphysical backdrops against which we judge and make sense of people and society. As citizens of Western culture we depend upon them just as some of us, as sociologists, have relied upon their images in formulating sociological theories.

The primary goal of this book is to use this twin philosophical heritage in the synthesis of a foundation for a more adequate socialization theory. The task is advanced by examining how it is that sociologists have thought about the individual, society and the process of socialization as a function of their philosophical perspectives.

The premises upon which the present endeavor rests are that the images invoked by individualistic and sociologistic theories provide valuable insights into the human sociological conditions; that the images rooted in one philosophy are too extreme when untempered by the other; that these insights and images bear upon socialization theory; that an examination of both positions will afford the critic some detachment from either; that these positions may be integrated to produce an "anthropomorphic" model of the person (Harré and Secord, 1973), that is, one neither "oversocialized" nor undersocialized; and that the integration may be accomplished through a particular understanding of culture associated with a concept of social place—the "context."

The forms in which the concept of socialization has been cast pose the venerable determinism-versus-freedom issue for socialization theory. Early forms of individualism simply took freedom as an intuitively obvious, ontological quality of individuals. It was a self-evident truth. No driving need existed, therefore, to explain its appearance. After the explanatory successes of the sociological model—in which behavior is described in terms of social structures transmitted by socialization and made "determinant" of individual behavior through internalization—the given quality of freedom was called into serious question. Freedom now *required* an explanation. This challenge has been largely ignored in sociology. Rather than accept "freedom" as a serious theoretical problem, brought to light by concepts like "sociological ambivalence" (Merton and Barber, 1963) and intrarole conflict, the short-run solution was denial. Freedom has been characterized as a romantic and unscientific myth from more naive times.

Remember that determinism came to sociology through the door of a now outdated philosophy. It was, along with the corollary of "causality," part of the 18th- and 19th-century model of science that sociologists came to accept as ideal. If we still seek participation in the model of the natural sciences, then the observation has been missed that determinism itself is now passé. Apparently, there is no purely scientific necessity that demands a deterministic position of sociologists.

The choice of either determinism or freedom is not a comfortable one. Determinism is not a flexible philosophy; it requires detailed predictability with no loose ends. An adherence to determinism has diverted us from the basic nature of what we as sociologists have to explain: a crucial intersection of the individual and society. At this intersection, intangible societal structures are given particular form by human actors whose productions of reality are subsequently modified. Accordingly, the task that drives determinists after unfailing prediction is Sisyphean. Sociological determinism must continue to deal in its historical currency of promissory notes—hypotheticals really: *if* all conditions are given (when they so obviously cannot be) or *if* we knew everything (when we so obviously never will), *then* determinism will be proven sound (Barrett, 1961:48). And too, the very idea of free will appears vacuous in light of modern social psychology. Both positions traffic in a clutter of unnecessary contingency.

Despite the dated nature of the freedom-versus-determinism argument, in a special sense it remains a fundamental obstruction in the progress of sociological understanding (Gonos, 1977). As the issue is commonly stated, however, it presents one of the false dichotomies within sociology. It is not a matter of opposites. The crux of the problem is finding the culturally identifiable nature of even novel activity. That is, sociologists do not now have a suitable method of thinking about how *socialized* persons may also be *creative*.

Creativity is the strong card in the individualist's and the neo- or social individualist's suit. Nevertheless, individualist sociologies have not taken the crucial step of going beyond the sociological argument to a theoretical explanation of the possibility for freedom in a sociological world.

But for a paradox, there would be an exception to this description of individualistic sociologies. This near-exception requires examination because it is the major social psychological perspective in sociology. I am speaking of the tradition now called symbolic interactionism and about the work of its foremost founder, George Herbert Mead. The various works that may be identified by this name represent an extensive, systematic and surprisingly consistent study of the relationship between the person and society. And too, socialization has remained a focus or springboard in much of symbolic interactionist writing. What then is the paradox?

It may be called the paradox of mutual indeterminism. Unlike mainstream sociology, which otherwise has freely borrowed insights from symbolic interactionism, the latter position pictures persons and society as mutual emergents (Mead, 1962; Blumer, 1969; Hewitt, 1976; Charon, 1979). That is, the individual and social structure

> depend on and, in some sense at least, control each other. The proportions in which the one controls the other are left undefined by symbolic interactionists (Skidmore, 1975).

Let me elaborate.

The symbolic interactionist perspective holds that "society" can be reconstructed from the acts of individuals: individuals align their actions into joint actions, acting always toward the "situation," based upon expectations about "common responses" under conditions allowing for a correspondence of meaning (Mead, 1962; Blumer, 1967). This is the stuff of immediate reality, and also, somehow, of institutions, organizations and generally, social structure. The symbolic interactionist focus upon the *intentional* act leaves an enormous and unexplained gap between that act and the *unintentional*, structural aspects of the situation. Structural-level entities are said to form nondeterminant frameworks in which people act. It must be conceded that in no small measure these provide the interpretable, and hence, stable building blocks of meaning and the environmental bases of action. There is then that unqualified mutual control, in which interaction constitutes society, yet distinctly sociological phenomena are left disconnected from action but manage to form the context for action. Theoretically, all that exists is flux, designated by the special term, emergence.

The full implications of this image of society are often conveniently ignored by those in the symbolic interactionist tradition who take socialization seriously (and not all do). For the present, however, I will attend strictly to those who acknowledge the process of socialization. Symbolic interactionism, in its steadfast attention to the here and now, has failed to describe analytically that which is internalized in the generalized other. Put simply, it cannot account for the "fixed sets of symbols" that transcend specific interactions and are the source of continuity in the self. Historical social structures are not reproduced by accident or by intention only, although this is what the concept of emergence is often taken to imply.

The "generalized other" is a concept that establishes the priority of society in the formation of the self. The idea of a mature self embraces a recognition of continuity between the past, the present and the future. The continuity of self avoids denying the emergent quality of microsocial situations (Mead would not be caught on so simple a point) and actually arises from the relative stability of social structures. Nevertheless, *the overenthusiastic tradition in the symbolic interactionist perspective of stressing "emergence" has eclipsed the historically powerful, the morally authoritative, the reified and the taken-for-granted facets of society.* It is thus that the mere logical priority of ongoing social process is theoretically incorporated, while the sociological and less tangible priority of one real, constituting entity over another escapes attention. Such an omission should be expected from the hand of a Jamesian pragmatist and self-proclaimed social behaviorist.

There is a way out of the paradox of mutual indeterminism that I believe to be consistent with Mead's perspective. That route lies in examining Mead's idea of internalization in the light of three concepts somewhat rare in the lexicon of social psychology: power, social control and authority. The employment of these concepts has been typically confined to historical, political and macrosociological literature. That precedent notwithstanding, the manifestation of these types of relations in society must have social psychological concomitants. As it turns out, power, control and authority are essential elements in considering the construction of either the self or society and the mutually sustaining connection between the two.

Mead's posited reflexive character of the person allows the individual to attain mind and self in the "organized community." The reflexive ability prevents the complete (deterministic) absorption of the self in a situation. Reflexivity accounts for the creative distance between self and situation that permits the contextual quality of emergence; it allows the self to negotiate through what is sociologically ambivalent terrain. By internalizing the generalized other, mere reflexivity is superceded by the socially sensitive reflexivity (what I will later call sociological autonomy) that Mead described in the interplay of the "I" and the situated "me." And according to Mead, internalization includes more than a cognitive map of the self's place in the larger scheme of interaction. The generalized other provides an insider's feel for the attitudes, values, goals and outlooks that have been part of a person's range of experience in society (Mead, 1962:154−155).

It is that which guides conduct controlled by principles, and a person who has such an organized group of responses is a man whom we say has character, in the *moral* sense (Mead, 1962: 162–163, emphasis added).

This appreciation of the moral order may be seen as reflecting the fundamentally coercive quality of society. Through the mechanism of the self, a heightened susceptibility to the power, control and authority in society is encouraged in individuals.

Because socialization does not abolish reflexivity, but only directs us toward society, our susceptibility to sociological coercion does not become determinant of action. However, the perhaps unconsciously compelling experience of society, which resides apart from a fear of overt sanction, places (internalized) social self-control as the primary mechanism of social order. Members' moral sense (i.e., their socialized feel for the mandate of custom, against a backdrop of the apparent givenness of society) carries forward the historical social order.

I derived this role for these three concepts from two sources. The first is, in essence, a Durkheimian principle stating that *reified social facts have power* (Durkheim, 1964; Berger and Pullberg, 1965). The second is the simple, powerful, and in its context, original insight of Robert Bierstedt:

> Power, in short, supports the fundamental order of society and the social organization within it. Power stands behind every association and sustains its structure. Without power there is no organization and without power there is no order. The intrusion of the time dimension and the exigencies of circumstances require continual readjustments of the structure of every association and it is power that sustains it through these transitions (Bierstedt, 1974b:235).

Here Bierstedt states clearly the pivotal function of power (and powerlike) phenomena for structural stability.

This kind of solution to the paradox of mutual indeterminism is not the complete solution to the problem of explaining creative behavior in socialized individuals who daily reproduce structures. Furthermore, giving society and its agents the reins, in a wholly asymmetric view of control relations does not describe the situationally refracted presentation of society during socialization. Socialization is a species of interaction—not the simple sculpting of a human personality. The novice too may initiate control and power relations, thereby managing the content of socialization but not endangering societal continuity (e.g., Bucher and Stelling, 1977). Properly for an introduction, I have only begun to show that concepts like reflexivity and emergence are not incompatible with notions of historical structure. It is enough for now to indicate that symbolic interactionism has certain serious flaws and omissions. These include its individualistic approach and preclude it from being the correct foundation for the continued development of socialization theory. Its insights are nonetheless valuable.

The inquiry set forth in Part I of this book traces the history of and the issues within the development of socialization theory. The history of the concept of socialization is confined to its etymology in American mainstream sociology. Chapter 1 follows the most theoretically promising path, the one coming to see society in terms of structure and insisting on the priority of historical structures over social psychological persons. In this chapter, such a path leads the reader eventually to a view of the possible excesses of sociologism. These may be avoided; they can be instructive and they do not damage the effective core of the position. I purposefully neglect any historical examination of certain parallel or offshoot perspectives such as exchange theory and symbolic interactionism. However worthy, these have remained frozen in individualism. I hasten to point out that symbolic interactionism is criticized as one of a number of "interpretive" sociologies in Chapter 2 and the work of George Herbert Mead is relied upon heavily in Chapter 5. The field of research is constrained primarily as a means of focusing upon certain issues in the early part of the analysis. Further, that focus provides a baseline for the more inclusive comments found in Chapter 5.

Because concepts are like gateways between philosophical assumption and theory, a parsimonious approach to analyzing socialization theory lies in attending to trends in defining "socialization." From this analysis a type of definition becomes intelligible not only by what it says, but also by what it implies. Definitions of concepts are indicators of the way a problem is framed. Furthermore, definitions suggest which facet of a phenomenon like socialization will receive systematic attention, and socialization has many aspects worthy of extended consideration. For example, a complete characterization of the *process* of socialization might include the following subject areas. (The present book, in taking only the initial steps toward theoretical reformulation, will be restricted to a discussion of the starred items below.)

1. The processes of recruitment and selection for types of socialization experience
*2. The *sociologically relevant* nature of the persons who enter the socializing process as some category of nonmember
*3. The nature of socializing activity (how society is presented)
   a. its contexts of delivery
   b. its content
   c. its (essential) *sociological* qualities
   d. the relationship between the novice and other actors present in the socialization context
*4. The nature of internalization and the change that occurs as novices interact with members
5. The relation of the "product" to the type of socializing experience. ("Product" refers to the relative completeness of the identity typically

emerging from particular socialization experiences. In this respect it may be asked if the new identity is workplace specific or whether it is significant in several social contexts.)

Part I further establishes that most recent theory and research attempts have converged their efforts to explore internalization and the attitudinal or behavioral impact of socialization experience upon the novice (item 4 above). Convergence has been prosecuted to the extreme of confusing, and finally identifying, socialization with internalization. There exist some good historical causes for this focus and confusion; however, there is no sociological purpose.

In fact, that approach nullifies the logic of the sociological paradigm and subverts much of the possible fruitfulness of inquiry. The sociological position asserts that the person is derived from society. This general proposition might even be designated the central tenet of socialization theory. If the sociological qualities of the individual are said to be derived from experience in society, there is no logical sense in beginning serious scientific inquiry into the effect (the role-related, social self), while ignoring the cause (society, and *ipso facto*, socialization). Truism or not, the person and society are inextricably related, but sociology proclaims that "society" is prior to any person. The nature of the "society" presented in socialization must be described. In addition, the usual social power differential between the two suggests that the influence of society on the individual will be greater than the influence of the individual on society. When this relationship is theoretically conjoined with the concept of the self, it means that an adequate description of society logically precedes an adequate description of the sociological individual (item 3 in above list).

Moreover, the species of activity called socialization must be portrayed in sociological terms to grasp internalization as a process and understand the possibility of variable behavioral outcomes from similar socialization experience. The lack of substantial success in socialization research results directly from trying to record the psychological imprint of the sociological environment (internalization) before characterizing the *medium* and *unit of transfer*—or, how it is that society is represented during socialization.

Having raised the basic issues, I attempt to grapple with them in Part II.

More precisely, the second part of the work directly confronts problems with solutions. Producing a theoretical solution here entails concepts that encompass the specific questions of "situation," "creativity" and "uniqueness" versus "structure," "conduct" and "continuity."

In keeping with the idea that the representation of society (significant to the socialization and internalization processes) should be accounted for first, the discussion begins there. Culture, as posed in the latter portion of Part I, is taken as the medium of transfer and the "context" as the appropriate unit of socialization. Admittedly, it is not an entirely new idea to use culture in this relation to socialization. However, attempting to depict culture as a set of underlying principles or rules that help to organize contextually bounded, and otherwise discrete items of behavior is a new approach to socialization theory. That approach allows for the explanation of both the "predetermined" and the "spontaneous" facets of socialized behavior, within a framework sociological to the core.

Therefore, Part II lays the foundation for a socialization theory that can account for both the creative and the routine. First, the nature of socializing activity is given some theoretical substance distinct from internalization in accordance with the concept of the context (list item 3, a through c, above). Then, in the final chapter, a social psychological perspective is drawn (list items 2, 3d and 4 above) to fit the idea of context and the anthropomorphic model of the person implied by the reformulated view of socialization. The purpose there will be to construct the sociological individual as an extension of classical sociological theories, without the deterministic excesses. At the same time, the role of novice is granted the status of a powerful co-producer of socialization realities. Seeing the novice as an active agent of some consequence points to the need for including a discussion of control and power. Society may well exhibit the greatest power overall, but in the specific contexts of socializing environments, novices countervail and refract the superficial effects of society. The *effective* control of society must then be considered in terms of structural continuity and situational power. The conception of culture I will offer here will once again prove useful.

One additional comment remains necessary for this introduction: that is, all theories are written from some perspective. Socialization theory is virtually always written from the point of view of a participant in the process. Inkeles (1968) and Speier (1973) note that the usual perspective in socialization theory is that of the member, or that is, an agent of socialization. Becker et al. (1961) make a significant contribution to studies of socialization by elaborating their description of a medical school from the point of view of the student (see Gonos, 1977, for general comments of the perspectives taken by structuralists and interactionists).

In order to avoid the particular limits imposed upon theory formulation by the participant's perspective while still maintaining the advantages of a constant perspective, an attempt is made here to remain in the role of the sociological observer. Appendix II supplies the details of what I understand to be the characteristics of this role for a theorist. Suffice it to say that this role is in accord with a theory designed to illuminate the structure of socializing activity rather than the intentional properties of member−novice interaction.

PART ONE

HISTORY, IMAGES AND ISSUES

CHAPTER ONE

AN ETYMOLOGY OF "SOCIALIZATION"

In this chapter I examine chronologically the changes in the meaning of the concept of socialization as it was influenced primarily from three sources. These influences were: (1) the inner dynamics of sociology itself as it evolved as a scientific discipline; (2) the concepts and focus of psychoanalytic psychology; and (3) the example set by anthropologists in their attempts to illuminate the cultural antecedents of the personality.

As will be elaborated, orientation provided by the changing concept of socialization follows the relative dominance of individualism or sociologism among sociologists. Thus, early definitions are quite explicitly directed by a concern for the possibility of society among independent individuals. The unit of analysis is, therefore, at the level of society. Later, more sociologistic definitions assume society to be a natural, rather than an artificially contrived condition. The problem of social order was no longer seriously or widely pursued. As a result, the unit of analysis for socialization is at the level of the individual. The interest is not in how individuals create society (an individualistic perspective), but in how individuals are created for roles in society. Table 1 provides a summary of the trends of meaning to be found between 1896 and the present. The information in that table will act as a guide for our discussion.

SOCIOLOGY AS A HISTORY OF IDEAS: THE CONCEPT OF SOCIALIZATION, 1896–1921

The Discovery of "Society" in an Arena of Individualism

Although it is true that nothing derives from nothing, ideas can be said to have their beginnings. Some discoveries, like the idea of social structure for example, are taken over as basic tenets in the pursuit of knowledge. Then, when scholarly discourse sets about to articulate these premises, subsidiary concepts are promulgated as part of an explanatory vocabulary. "Socialization" has been such a secondary concept throughout much of the history of sociology in the United States. In order to trace its etymology within sociology, constant references must be made to the very framework of the discipline: the prevailing images of society and the individual. This particular strategy is derived from the principle that if modifications occur in the fundamental tenets of a conceptual apparatus, these changes will be transmitted to their attendant concepts, which will in turn undergo transformation (Kuhn, 1970: 118–119). In the following brief history it will be shown that this principle is particularly relevant to the career of "socialization." Of course, ideas are explored and promulgated by people in real-life situations. Therefore, the history of a concept is written by linking it to the purposes of those people who have given it serious use.

Like their European counterparts, sociologists in the United States began to be differentiated from other social scientists by a promise to create the science of society.[1] Precisely what this meant in terms of a programmatic approach to the subject matter depended a great deal upon whose designs one followed. However, the scattering of individual explorations into this new territory showed that two major themes were held in common. The first was a desire to say something scientific and the second concerned a hypothesis that "society" existed. "Society," being a new idea, was difficult to talk about. The concept did not immediately point to the correlation of some thing and its physical manifestations; but in this way "society" is no more difficult to comprehend than is "electricity." We can say these words, animate them, anthropomorphize them, but they are not things in the ordinary sense of tangible lumps. Both

---

[1]Following Albion Small (1916: 194; 1924: 333) and Floyd N. House (1936: 294), I will date this emergence as 1883, the year Lester Frank Ward published his *Dynamic Sociology*. This book was "the first comprehensive sociological treatise written in the United States"; but more than that, and in light of the framework of my analysis, "He [Ward] was the first and most formidable of a number of thinkers who attacked the unitary assumptions of social Darwinism and natural law individualism" (Hofstadter, 1959: 67, 68).

concepts, electricity and society, may be seen as relationships, processes or as fundamental events.

If society is taken as a fundamental event or property of the human condition, it steadfastly defies capture by ordinary, ostensive language. We may say that it is an easy idea to use, but a difficult concept to define in a way *useful for sociology*. Nevertheless, as an idea, it persistently remains a valuable and necessary assumption in the explanation of human behavior. The idea of "society," the antithesis of the "individual," became a fundamental category for sociology even as its explication came to be framed in terms of more readily comprehensible processes and relationships.

There is ample evidence to suggest that early sociologists were actively trying to find a "sociology" among the various philosophical structures purporting to lay bare the human condition. And it was true, too, that the first generation of American sociologists were not so casually certain (as perhaps we are today) that society, its internal relationships, and its subprocesses were really "things" that could bear the burden of being labeled as causes. Albion Small (1916: 255–263) states that sociologists felt considerable discomfort with any moves that tended to reify collective concepts. At least part of the reason that sociologists felt an uneasiness with their new concepts was a traditional attachment to individualism. A person was understood as a being with a self-contained nature that was prior to any social experience and as a creature primarily at odds with the requirements of society. Consequently, so the reasoning went, if society is to persist a person must be made fit for society by coercion or attraction, reasoned with, made to cooperate or, if uncultivated, left to follow a naturally disruptive social career. In short, the individual had an egoistic, asocial nature; the so-called Hobbesian question of order was central.

We find that this individualistic conception of society held sway early in American sociology (see Cooley, 1964: Chapter 1; Mead, 1930a,b; Frank, 1962: 211). In such an atmosphere a major theoretical motif concerned the possibility of social order. Looking back, we find that the solution to the problem of order came in the form of a taken-for-granted assumption that individuals were driven together by various "socializing forces," by which term Franklin Giddings designated:

> all forces that act towards social ends, — that create association, perfect social organization and develop a social nature. They may arise outside of society or within it. Soil and climate, for example, and the appetites and passions of individuals are often socializing forces (1896: xv).

"Socialization" was then, at first, defined as a condition of society brought about by people forced into a form of *willing* cooperation among individuals. It led to increased solidarity and reduced the conflict otherwise inherent among individuals in association (see Table 1, Cell I).

TABLE 1. Significant Trends in the Changing Meaning of Socialization

Underlying Occurrence	Theme: How Is Social Order Possible? Unit of Analysis* at Collective Level	Theme: How Do Individuals Become Group Members? Unit of Analysis* at the Level of the Person		
	Socialization as Willing Cooperation, Increased Solidarity or Social Efficiency	Socialization as		
		Training	Becoming Social	Social Learning
The Reduction of Conflict, Aggression and Competition Among Members	I 1896–1921† (Residual use until 1943)			
The Rendering Social of a "Crude and Contrary" Human Nature		II 1921–1940		
The Shaping of the "Personality" (Human Nature Depends on Social Interaction)		III 1942–1976	IV 1944–1950	V 1951–1979

* Unit of analysis relative to use of concept of socialization.
† All dates are approximate, representing published material.

People were assumed to have natures prior to social contact. In accordance with this belief, socialization was seen to redirect an already existing complex of specific impulses rather than in the modern sense of a process during which "human nature" is actually constituted (as in the form of a self). Hence, socialization accomplished "the *moulding* of the individual's feelings and desires, to suit the needs of the group" (Ross, 1896, emphasis added). And similarly, socialization was "conceived of as the development of a *social* nature or character—a social state of mind—in individuals who associate" (Giddings, 1897, emphasis added). Although socialization affected the individual, the interesting effect for sociologists was at the level of society. It was there that the good of socialization was felt, so that "all men may live together as members of one family" (Park and Burgess, 1921: 496).

James Dealey sums up this entire position in a few words:

> The process of socialization is difficult and contrary to crude human nature. Society must build up through social control and education a type of mind that will become individualistic through social service. . . . Men become socialized as they cease to war against society, or to fight for a narrow interest as against a greater. (Dealey, 1920: 385–386).

In modern sociology we take for granted that the self is produced from elements to be found in society, and further, that without participation in society a person would remain socially incompetent. Undoubtedly, early sociologists were not unaware of the effects of simple fostering activity; socialization was, however, something different and something more: it was at root a moral or ethical phenomenon. Socialization put the final touches on individuals, making them fit for an orderly society. Because of this moral tone in the usage, Albion Small could say: "At present we may use the terms 'socialization' and 'civilization' interchangeably" (1905: 363). Within this context, too, sociologists were able to appeal to something like "inadequate socialization" as an explanation of disreputable or dishonest behavior. That is, if an individual's naturally asocial nature were not properly adapted for society, immoral conduct would be the sure result. Today, however, with a considerably less independent model of the person, social scientists seek to understand behavior per se and not a certain presumed moral stage of society. And in the light of the subtleties of current social psychology, the concept of "inadequate socialization" sounds quaint and without substance.

The "Individual" in a Theoretical Limbo

It was mentioned earlier that in addition to the early sociologists' interest in developing the concept of society, they also were concerned about their studies contributing to the birth of a science. That is, sociologists qua scientists were forced to "find" their ideas in the empirical world. This imperative continually exerted its influence. Accordingly, "society" was probed to reveal its internal structure, thereby creating a loose web of less abstract concepts (e.g., group, social control, socialization, association, social structure, telesis, social forces, social evolution, etc.). Following the typical pattern of science, these corollary concepts then became subjects for still more initmate inquiry. Some were dropped and others were added as the 19th-century conceptualization of science worked itself deeper into the substance of sociology. At this point, our model of events in the history of sociology renders the central abstraction (society) in concepts sufficiently close to experience that actual research might ensue (Eubank, 1937). This occurrence corresponds to approximately 1918.[2]

During the early, more speculative stages of sociology prior to 1918, the opposition of the person and society was apparent but not troublesome in general treatises on sociology. After all, it was the individual's first nature to be selfishly quarrelsome. Moral behavior and generosity were only a social laminate. The beginning of empirical sociological research, however, represents a movement down through layers of abstraction and toward potentially observable activity. This was a change that brought less reliance on classical philosophical ideals and more attention to discovering the social-causal explanation of behavior. As a result, ideas were required to have a pragmatic appeal and, in addition, provide useful accounts of an empirical realm. It was also a change that brought sociologists toward a confrontation between their new ideas and the image of the individual traditionally a part of sociology.

The dilemma was that if "society" was a real, determining factor in behavior, how is it that concrete individuals can fit into such a scheme? How does an abstract entity (society) affect a concrete entity (the person)? By introducing the concept of society—expressed more generally by the notion of social structure—as an explanatory tool, the individual had been placed in a theoretical limbo.

A controversy arose, and interestingly, events followed the general outline predicted by Thomas S. Kuhn in the chapter, "Response to Crisis," from his excellent book, *The Structure of Scientific Revolutions* (1970: 77–91). There was a questioning of what has been called the "group hypothesis." There were many attempts at theoretical repair, trying to resolve the relationship between

---

[2]This date follows the suggestion that the publication of the first volume of *The Polish Peasant* by W. I. Thomas and Florian Znaniecki marked the beginning of the epoch of sociology as an empirical science (House, 1936: 283, 294). As with all such attempts at finding beginnings, the exact date is negotiable until fixed by convention. For example, Louis Wirth indicates that 1915 is the year symbolic of this event (Wirth, 1947: 274). I prefer 1918 because it appears more reasonably accurate than merely symbolic and it is aligned with the publication of a work of lasting significance. Furthermore, John Clausen (1968: 29) records 1920 as the year in which sociological studies of socialization began, and this puts 1918 comfortably in between.

the group and the individual. There were efforts to decide finally what a group was. In some quarters there arose an expression of discontent with the "group fallacy" (or sui generis fallacy). The concept of "society" could only be rejected by rejecting sociology itself—something sociologists were not about to do!

The immediate tension of the situation was removed by a growing enthusiasm for a nontheoretical empiricism. This trend was perhaps brought on by the difficulty of the theoretical problems but, more importantly, by a fervant desire to explore society. Whatever might have been the primary motivation, the tendency to operationalize theoretical constructs in terms of their presumed indicators temporarily sidestepped the more fundamental theoretical issues.

In spite of this strong trend, however, there were sociologists who retained a need to deal directly with theoretical problems. As a consequence, another trend began in which a series of subtle changes were made in the prevailing image of human nature. These changes were reflected very nicely in definitions and uses of the concept of socialization.

The individual was being reconceived in the minds of sociologists to fit the prevailing scientific needs (Collins and Makowsky, 1972: 9–17; Geertz, 1974). This was neither an unusual historical occurrence nor the product of some odious ideological design. Whatever human nature might *really* be, its defined nature is always vulnerable to the effects of revised interests. During this translation process, our nature came to be understood as less independent and quarrelsome and much more determined by social experience. However, to describe these changes in any further detail would be getting ahead in the story, because sociology is more than a history of ideas. Several historical events were to play a considerable role in shaping the concept of socialization. Therefore, before continuing with the history of ideas approach, we will digress a moment to discuss some of these events.

The Early Institutional Development of Sociology in the United States

It was not until several years into the 20th century that the sociological mode of inquiry began to attract anything like a professional following sufficient to become a scientific community. Starting with these early days, this subsection reviews some selected details of the institutional development of sociology; after all, in order for the ideas of sociology to change there must be a membership to debate them. Further, if "sociology" is to be influenced by other disciplines, sociologists must explore and communicate the relevance of new ideas among themselves. I only recite these truisms to help usher our discussion from the realm of ideas toward some more concrete occurrences.

According to Albion Small (1916), the first generation of American sociologists (including such notables as: Lester Frank Ward, E. A. Ross, Franklin H. Giddings and William Graham Sumner) had no sense of common purpose. Each theorist of this generation worked within a personal conceptual system and with little formal recognition of the others. Very shortly before the beginning of the 20th century, sociologists were united more by title than by orientation or mutual recognition. Any debates these men might have had were verbal, and largely carried out in face-to-face encounters during meetings of the various historical, economic or political science associations to which they belonged. Indeed, before the 1920s (e.g., Ellwood, 1923; Bogardus, 1924) it was rare to find one American sociologist making direct use of the work of another in print; they could find little common ground upon which to argue.

In such an environment it was with some trepidation that Albion Small published the first issue of the *American Journal of Sociology* in 1895 (Small, 1916: 218). He feared that there was neither the readership to receive the new journal nor a forthcoming volume of articles sufficient to fill its covers. In keeping with these fears for the new journal, Small portrayed turn-of-the-century sociology as more like "a yearning . . . a determination to follow a few promising clues . . . a running advertisement of the *need* of a science than a realized science [emphasis in the original, 1916 (1948): 229]."

There was as yet no real sign of a scientific community of sociologists. Some evidence for this condition of professional isolation lies in the preface to *Pure Sociology* (1907) by Lester Frank Ward. There, he lamented the absence of mutual, substantive criticism among sociologists. It is the opinion of Albion Small that not until about 1905, when the first official meeting of the American Sociological Society was planned, did American sociologists achieve a sense that they were a group with common interests.

The fledgling American Sociological Society held its first annual meeting in December of 1906. From that time the membership grew from "a few men and women, in full possession of their senses" (as Small in 1907 humorously put it) to about 2000 members in 1950. It should be noted that not only was the number of sociologists increasing, it was, as well, a time of great intellectual vigor (corresponding to the period in Table 1 showing the most change in the concept of socialization).

With rather surprising rapidity the American version of the science of society found its focus. The membership that gathered was, by 1920, predominantly interested in a social psychological and process explanation of human association (Small, 1916: 238–240, 255; Carter, 1927; House, 1929: 137–144; Hinkle and Hinkle, 1954: 7–8, 14, 28–33; Maus, 1962: 120; Faris, 1967; see also Ellwood, 1913: 57–58).

There existed in the newly developing discipline a certain fascination for the "mind in action" and "individualistic" or social psychological explanations of "social forces" and processes. There was a very strong bias against hypostatizing sociological concepts such as "the group" or "society." A surety and an appeal existed in the work of George Herbert Mead, Charles Horton Cooley, James Mark Baldwin, W. I. Thomas and Florian Znaniecki that proved to be of significance as the distinctly sociological image of the human condition was negotiated among American sociologists. The direction sociology began to assume seems to have emerged from the previously discussed restless compromise between a taken-for-granted individualism and the foundation stone of sociology: the social structural causation of behavior (or the "group hypothesis"). Thus, the concept of society was first used as a means to understanding the behavior of individuals. In America only much later could the concept be plausibly grasped as standing for a sui generis reality.

Aside from sheer historical interest, I have briefly sketched the institutional development in sociology to demonstrate its ripeness: It had new purpose, new membership and an optimistic outlook; this was the social matrix from which old problems would receive more fruitful and penetrating explanations.

SOCIAL STRUCTURE, INTERPENETRATION AND THE BIRTH OF THE "OVERSOCIALIZED MAN"

The history of ideas sometimes appears to be the history of extremes; that is, it is the story of ideas pushed to their logical, and of course, ragged, limits. The presociological idea of the individual had long been used beyond its ability to explain satisfactorily human behavior and human society. "Society," or more generally the idea of historical social structures had appeared as a kind of theoretical nostrum and as another sort of explanatory approach. It functioned to derelativize radically a history otherwise populated by independent monads. "Social structure" binds otherwise dissimilar people into units that are explanatory of their behavior and circumstances; it is a valuable simplifying concept lending parsimony to social explanation. In short, "social structure" provides a more powerful theoretical basis for order, continuity and explanation than does the "individual." The concept, however, contains within it the seeds of an overdetermined society and an oversocialized conception of the person. With the benefit of hindsight, it can be seen that the discovery of the "social self" (i.e., an historical personality) helped to nurture those seeds of sociological determinism. *The "social self" provided the mechanism that allowed for the determination of individual behavior; indeed, in this now familiar view the very constituents of the self would come from society.*

Later refinements to the concept of the social self were foreshadowed by William James (1890), Charles Horton Cooley (1902) and by James Mark Baldwin's concept of the "socius":

> The development of the child's personality could not go on at all without the constant modification of his sense of himself by suggestions from others. So he himself, at every stage, is really in part someone else, even in his own thought of himself.... In short, *the real self is the bipolar self, the social self, the socius* (Baldwin, 1902: 30; emphasis in the original).

Freud, Durkheim and Mead were later able to impart a depth and subtlety to this concept.[3] And while the psychoanalytic movement was gaining worldwide recognition, the 1920s found George Herbert Mead spreading the word of his formulations from the philosophy department at the University of Chicago to eager sociology graduate students at the same institution. For his part, Durkheim would not for some time become a widely acknowledged authority within American sociology.

Holding in mind the institutional developments and the direction we have described in the trends of American sociological thought, we will now turn to the authority and high visibility of the Freudian movement and its relationship to anthropology and sociology.

The Influence of Freudian Psychology and Anthropology on the Concept of Socialization

A great intellectual force was growing that would be extremely relevant to the history of "socialization." In fact, psychoanalytic psychology (particularly Freudian) may have had the single most significant influence upon the concept of socialization. Certainly, numerous authors have commented on the importance of the Freudian movement for our modern approach to the socializing process (see, for example, MacIver, 1947: 28–29; Frank, 1962: 211; Clausen, 1968: 37–38; and Sewell, 1970: 566). Dennis Wrong pinpoints the key element of influence:

> Freud's theory of the superego has become the source and model of the conception of the internalization of social norms that today plays so important a part in sociological thinking (1961: 186).

In Freud's writings, then, we read an accounting of the psychodynamic effect of society, through a child's parents, on the formation of a new member. According to Freud:

> the superego is the successor and representative of the parents who supervised his actions in the first period of his life.... In the course of the individual development a part of the inhibiting forces in the outer world become *internalized*; we

---

[3] I must note the fact now as later, after the advent of the Parsonian system, the distinction will cease: these six theorists just mentioned all held to the traditional distinction made between the individual and social aspects of the person.

call (this product) the Super-ego (1939: Part III, Section II, emphasis added; see also Freud, 1961: 71–79).

For not only did Freud have a theory of the human psyche and its relationship to experience, he proffered a succinct answer for the question of what happens when persons are socialized. The answer was posed in the form of a tidy physical metaphor: *an aspect of the world of experience is "internalized," and is thereby incorporated as an element determining personality.* I will briefly examine the Freudian revolution for its effect on the course of socialization theory and research.

Sigmund Freud became world-known around 1910. The power of the psychoanalytic movement grew as the names of Carl Jung and Alfred Adler were added to the pantheon during the teens of the century. For many, starting in the 1920s, Freud's influence took on the air of authority. Accepted or rejected, the growing presence of Freudian theory could not be denied. Nevertheless, its primary influence upon sociology was more indirect than direct. After all, sociologists are somewhat shy of psychology—and all forces which might prove reductionistic.

The influence upon sociology was somewhat circuitous, coming as a consequence of the broader impact of Freudian theory upon the developing course of social science theory and research—and perhaps as a result of the adjustments made by Freud's ideas in Western culture itself, although this latter is too general an explanation to have much weight on any particular point. First, experimental psychologists imparted to psychoanalytic theory an air of academic respectability by successfully incorporating analyses of some psychoanalytic concepts into their ongoing behavioral research (Clausen, 1968; Sewell, 1970). Experimental psychology was also able to transmit the rhetoric of behaviorism to the social science language that described socializing experience. Hence, for a time (approximately 1920–1940) it became somewhat common to speak in terms of "stimuli," "acquired behavior patterns," "the conditioning of behavior," "training" (as if people were experimental rats), "the shaping of behavior" and the like.

What about anthropology? Anthropologists in the mid- and late 1920s started to address seriously the psychoanalytic position and began to collect data relating this body of theory to personality formation in primitive societies (Bidney, 1967; Clausen, 1968). As a consequence of the recognition given to Freudian concepts by experimental psychology and anthropology, fundamental changes began to arouse these disciplines. Of the two fields, we will examine, however briefly, anthropology, because within that discipline the overall effect of Freudian perspectives was more profound. Moreover, the concerns of anthropology were of a more manifest influence on the sociological concept of socialization. Prior to the time of this new source of intellectual stimulation, anthropologists were primarily "concerned with an impersonal factual survey of the traits and institutions of a given culture," and only slight attention was given to the carriers of culture (Bidney, 1967: 327). However, the "culture and personality" trend in anthropological inquiry soon became prominent. Its beginning in the United States was with Margaret Mead's highly influential *Coming of Age in Samoa* (1928) and it reached its height during the 1930s and 1940s.

Freud's ideas were present in the substance of the theories that surrounded this research and also in the way attention focused upon the importance of the formative early years. Psychoanalytic assumptions guided those interested in the study of the social person toward (1) child-rearing practices (socialization—rendering the young fit for society) and their subsequent effect upon (2) personality development (internalization, loosely defined). This new research interest in seeking out the cultural antecedents of personality brought the term socialization into the jargon of anthropology. According to Margaret Mead, some time around the mid-1930s the term changed from merely intelligible English into an anthropological concept (M. Mead in Clausen, 1968: 41; and Whiting, 1968: 545).

Freud had coined and defined the concept of internalization and anthropologists, seeing the implications of cross-cultural data for a deeper understanding of our nature (M. Mead, 1928: 1–13), began to trace out in many different cultures the product of internalization: the personality. "Socialization" began to be the term frequently employed to denote the activities that facilitated the stamp of culture upon the individual. (Enculturation, acculturation, assimilation, culturization and sometimes accommodation were others.) This overall trend in anthropology was groundbreaking. It gave impetus and, more importantly, legitimation to the study of personality by those not considering themselves psychologists. The unintended legitimating function which anthropology had accomplished opened another avenue for intellectual exploration by sociologists. John Clausen put it strongly: "Developments within anthropology contributed more to the rise of interest in socialization in recent decades than did any other single influence (1968: 39)."

Sewell (1970) and Clausen (1968) make the claim that the study of socialization came to be one of the principal points of convergence among psychologists, anthropologists and sociologists. They both indicate as well that sociological contributions to this area arrived somewhat later than those from the other two disciplines. Considering (1) the turmoil of institutional growth and development in sociology, and (2) the evidence within the sociological literature of its eclectic grasping for a world view and a subject matter, it would seem that sociology was influenced, in the matter of socialization, by the other two relatively more established disciplines. Further, and very closely related to the form of analysis in this chapter, all three disciplines seem to have been able to merge their efforts in the study of socialization because of the similarity in theoretical problems common to the three modes of inquiry. Clearly, that problem rested in the difficulties of the attempt to establish a plausible relationship between the person and society.

There is very firm evidence, I believe, that this problem was of great importance to all the disciplines concerned with the social aspects of the individual (Park, 1974). For example, note the sheer number of relatively independent efforts to reconcile the individual to society (James, Baldwin, Cooley, G. H. Mead, Freud and Durkheim). These names are all associated with this fundamental social psychological problem and the discovery of the social self.

We are again reminded that Baldwin, with a mixture of prescience, pride and objectivity, declared that the scientific recognition of the intimate social linkage of persons in society was the most impressive achievement of modern social theory (1911: 16). And, too, Talcott Parsons, in looking back over the accomplishments of others (and seeing the direction of his own not insignificant work), deemed the philosophical discovery of the interpenetration of individuals in society to be a landmark in the history of social sciences (Parsons, 1967: 27; see also the authoritative critique of Parson's work in Bershady, 1973). Freud, however, stood out as the most spectacular success in the franchising of his ideas.

What then was the influence of Freud upon the climate of ideas in which sociology was involved? First, there was the new (for sociology and anthropology) focus on the psychodynamic impact of childhood experience for the developing personality. Second, Freud provided the concept of internalization and a theory of socialization in which society was a necessary precursor of the mature personality. Now, it has been said many times that Copernicus plucked us from the center of the Universe; that Darwin took from us our special relationship with the Divinity; and that Freud then proceeded to remove the last shreds of our impertinent dignity—he took away our inherent rationality. For the meaning of Freud's contribution to the demise of our supreme egocentrism, as recorded in this elegy, we must examine the Freudian description of society.

The Freudian scheme carried forward the older motif of the individual in confrontation with society; that is, human nature's impulses were in conflict with social conventions. (We have discussed this before.) The Freudian twist was significant in that the conflict was brought *within* the self (see Rieff, 1961: 28–30). In other words, the parts of the personality stood in representation of the whole person's antagonism with the social principle. The primitive instincts of the *id* were met only by the inhibitions of the internalized *superego* ("the successor and representative of the parents"). The *ego* somehow mediated between these two nearly overbearing forces, and personality was expressed to the outside world as the (mollified) residue of the inner conflict—a product of subconscious psychic struggle. We find no place in this perspective for the rational capability granted to us since the time of Francis Bacon and René Descartes.

Third, in addition to the new focus on psychodynamic development and the significance of "internalization" in linking the person to society, the overall effect of the Freudian scheme was to weaken considerably the image of human nature by the philosophy of individualism. More specifically, Freud put the responsibility for any apparently rational behavior onto the logic and conventions of society. In short, the "individual" had been decapitated, leaving a still active viscera; sociological repair was the only hope. What the person lost in the Freudian interpretation only "society" could replace.

As we turn back again to the sociological enterprise, we will see the growing post-Freudian tendency to view socialization from the new developmental perspective. In this vein, but long after the acceptance of these new views, Lawrence K. Frank looked back to describe the changes he had witnessed.

> Indeed, the genetic approach [i.e., the *socio*-genesis of the personality] to the understanding of children and youth, so strongly emphasized by Freud, has become almost universally accepted as essential to the understanding of human behavior and personality. . . . This re-orientation becomes increasingly remarkable when we recall that not long ago it was believed that the baby started as a small homunculus, who grew in size until ready to be born and that the individual was endowed at birth with his personality. Here we see how the concepts of development . . . have had an enormous impact on all of our thinking and research (1962: 211).

Closely related to this conceptual alteration is the gradual disappearance of the connotation of "moulding" and "conforming" carried by the scientific concept of socialization. Instead of *con*forming a preexisting entity (i.e., human nature) to social acceptability, the personality came to be thought of as actually forming in social interaction.[4] Furthermore, (1) the personality was now thought of as coming into being only through the individual's relation-

---

[4] As I have tried to show, sociological thinking (vis-à-vis socialization) was bound up with an extensive and new interest in child development. Frank (1962) discusses the massive nature of this movement, especially after 1920 (see also House, 1936: 355–366). Wolfenstein (1955) examines the different conceptions of human nature as presented in *Infant Care* bulletins of the United States Department of Labor Children's Bureau. Her study indicates that the changing image of human nature that I am tracing in sociology was taking place on a much wider scale. Wolfenstein contrasts primarily the different socially acceptable images of infants in these bulletins for the years 1914–1942. The overall trend in these changing images, although not without some discontinuity, depicts an increasing belief in the basic passivity and harmlessness of babies. The 1914 "child" had "dangerous impulses," a "sinful nature" and was pictured as "rebeling fiercely" against social control. The 1942 "child," on the other hand, had a curious, harmless, more diffuse and moderate character—one more open to guidance and love.

ship with others; (2) the individual—society conflict had been removed to the realm of the psyche, and (3) a person no longer had the benefit of an inherent rationality. It seemed that the very foundations had been removed from the traditional image of the individual.

Prior to the Freudian revolution the "individual" was not terribly problematic. There were, of course, many inquiries regarding the mechanisms of human nature, which may be generally subsumed under the question of the subject—object relationship, but that we actually *had* natures was rarely questioned. Controversies of the "nature-versus-nature" type simply could not be sustained before the coming of Freud; there were no assertions that the "object" was in fact mediated by social relationships that contributed to the very formation of the "subject." The Freudian revolution left the individual with a much more plastic nature; what was left was suitable for mutation and further degradation "beyond freedom and dignity." Let us watch this trend as it works itself out in definitions of socialization.

THE DOMINION OF "SOCIETY" AND THE DEMISE OF INDIVIDUALISM: CHANGING CONCEPTIONS OF OF SOCIALIZATION, 1921–1976.

The Old Definitions in Transition

The famous *Introduction to the Science of Sociology* (1921) by Robert E. Park and Ernest W. Burgess represents perfectly the old-style definition of socialization (Cell I, Table 1). In the view of these sociologists, socialization is a condition of society in which a particular reciprocity of influence leads to social unity. Socialization is similar to an esprit de corps or a condition of patriotism among adult members of society:

> Socialization is thus the form, actualizing itself in countless various types, in which individuals . . . grow together into a unity . . . . (1921: 349).

And continuing this theme, Park and Burgess write that:

> . . . [socialization] sets up as a goal of social effort a world in which conflict, competition, and the externality of individuals, if they do not disappear altogether, will be so diminished that all men may live together as members of one family (1921: 496).

The authors add some refinement to their meaning of a socialized society in a later discussion of assimilation.

> The unity thus achieved is not necessarily or even normally likemindedness; it is rather a unity of experience and of orientation, out of which may develop a community of purpose and action (1921: 737).

Although this type of definition was used until 1943, for example, in new editions of older books or in the writing of those sociologists as yet unconvinced by the developmental model of socialization, the majority movement was toward inquiry into early socialization and becoming a group member.

The first evidence of these changes vis-à-vis "socialization" started in 1921. In that year Edward Hayes published *Sociology and Ethics*. His use of the term "socialization" appears as a link between the old and new perspectives. Hayes uses socialization to refer to the "social conditions necessary to human welfare" and the "intelligent utilization of the tendencies of human nature" (1921a: 264)—this last definition qualifying for inclusion into Cell II of Table 1. Hayes continues by saying that "childhood and youth are the time for acquiring a socialized personality (1921a: 266)." Additional changes and considerable continuity with the past are found in Franklin Giddings' conceptualization of the process of socialization (*Studies in the Theory of Human Society*, 1922). There he says that the socialized person has an "acquired nature" that "mingles with his inherited characteristics and this is the source of his uniqueness" (1922: 288), but further that:

> socialization is the opposite of mutation and supplementary variation. It is an aggregate of acquisitions, in distinction from native traits. It cannot be transmitted through heredity, but by teaching it can be handed on with compounding interest from generation to generation (1922: 287).

In the writings of both Hayes and Giddings, then, we see mention of the intergenerational transfer of the ability to make society; socialization is no longer a process of reciprocal accommodation among adult members. Importantly too, the text surrounding these passages indicates a lessening of the moral elements formerly linked with socialization; and, too, the focus has shifted somewhat from the effect of socialization on society and more toward an account of individual changes.

Individualism is not dead, although the "natural" struggle between the individual and society seems to have subsided. As further evidence of these as yet miniscule changes, we examine an article written by Hornell Hart. It was titled "Research Possibilities with a Socialization Test" (1923). Hart demonstrates a paper-and-pencil test for differentiating between socialized and unsocialized persons. According to the author, the test shows "striking differences" between "a highly socialized man" and a "thief." Hart views successful socialization as dependent upon the "sublimination of *social* emotions into intellectual assimilation of group interests" (1923: 164, emphasis added). Socialization itself is described as certain "conditioning factors" that affect "personality and character." In Hart's contrast of the "highly socialized man" with a "thief," the moral aspects of socialization once again become apparent. However, the use of such words as "sublimination," "intellectual assimilation" and "conditioning factors" represents the newly pacified confrontation between an individual and society. Hart also emphasizes changes in personal qualities as opposed to the older societal aspects of socialization. What this means is that the moral concerns with socialization are now set into another context, and thereby given another meaning. The interest here is no longer with the moral condition of society; instead, the morality (or criminality in this case) of the individual is now the new focus of sociological attention.

These are the barest beginnings of differences in conceptualizing the fit of the individual in society. There has not yet been a full break with the past in regard to the imagery and content of definitions; however, a clear shift is evident in the unit of analysis. Examine the following definition, for example:

> The socialization of the individual is, then, to be viewed as a continuation of the parental and other instruction under which a child learns to observe the various taboos and acquire an ability to use the institutional practices as the group-sanctioned patterns for tension management (Frank, 1928: 725).

In the above definition socialization is characterized as a process *beyond* the initial training provided by parents, a process functioning to *reduce social tension*; such thoughts are clearly holdovers. Be that as it may, the author's main concern is not with the collective product of socialization, as would have been the case in earlier definitions, but it resides instead with the effect of the process upon *individuals*. Dating from the 1920s, the new genre of definitions was oriented to the recognition of either the (active) training of individuals for social participation (Table 1, Cells II and III) or the (passive) acquisition of social attributes by individuals (Table 1, Cell IV).

While describing these the first changes wrought by the developmental perspective, I should note the single thread of continuity, running from 1896 to the present. These definitions on the whole contain a supposition as to what *ought* to be the final outcome of the socializing process. Cell I-type definitions take the final and desired outcome of socialization to be a condition of moral unity and social solidarity based on willing cooperation. Definitions from the other four cells in Table 1 make the assumption that socialization produces a social acceptability *or* functionality in individuals. Such definitions are, as Alex Inkeles expressed it, "inherently forward looking" (1968: 77). That is to say, the final outcome of socialization is taken to be its defining characteristic. Understanding socialization by its outcome has drawn sociological attention away from the interaction that in fact constitutes the process.

This observation bears directly on the meaning granted to the concept. For one thing, it demonstrates that the new developmental framework did not simply pass over into sociology unaffected by the existing system of sociological thought. For another thing, it points to the distinction between those investigators only alleging to be interested in process while in actuality focusing on outcome, and those persons engaged in attempts to see process in social reality. W. I. Thomas is an instance of the latter. Quite early in the century, he viewed the individual from a developmental standpoint. Furthermore, he retained a long-standing interest in the child and in "situations" that orient personal becoming. He was deeply interested in the interactional construction of personality; nevertheless, he did not find the term socialization appropriate, so strong were its other Cell I-type meanings.

In this respect, it is interesting to observe that Baldwin, Cooley and Mead, men whose names sociologists frequently associate with "socialization," rarely used the term. When the term was used by them, it takes on the general meaning indicated in Cell I. Baldwin, Cooley and Mead are famous as "social psychologists," and yet so firmly established was the Cell I type of meaning that "socialization" bears no social psychological connotations in their writings.

In addition to this lack of a true process orientation in mainstream sociology, our continued tracing out of the evolving imagery surrounding "socialization" will show that eventually the "individual" lost the qualities of robustness and independence. And while the idea of sociology as a science grew more evident in the writings of sociologists, the moral implications of socialization simply vanished. While these changes were taking place, the concept of socialization became more and more established as the social psychological concept par excellence. Generally, during the next several decades after the 1920s, the tension slackened and the color faded from sociological reports of the now more passive socializing process. The individual and society were no longer locked into an eternal antagonism.

The process came to be seen as passive because the individual was being taken as more malleable. This is quite clear in a sentence written by Robert Sutherland and Julian Woodward: "Socialization can make many sorts of models out of the same human material" (1937: 156). Human nature is losing its battle with society. In fact, it is becoming fairly common to consider socialization as the process "whereby the individual is *converted to a person*" (Ogburn and Nimkoff, 1940: 131, emphasis added). Even though human nature is no longer specific, sociologists at this time still grant a degree of efficacy to the fuzzy notion of a "dynamic biological heritage" (Ogburn and Nimkoff, 1940: 159–160).

Toward the Modern Definition:
A Passive Individual, A Passive Process

The *domestication* of the "individual" is no longer required during socialization. In fact, along with an increased stress on the priority of society, "human nature" became understood as a metaphysical concept to be replaced in the interests of science by the concept of the self, an entity constituted through potentially observable experience in society (Young, 1942: 375; an example of a Cell III definition). The moribund status of the "individual" brought passivity to the socializing process and the passive voice to the use of "socialization":

> the process of socialization, that is, the taking over of another person's habits, attitudes, and ideas and the reorganizing of them into one's own system (Young, 1944: 170).

Young's definition (a representative of Cell IV, Table 1) equates socialization for the first time with *becoming social* rather than with some form of social nurturing activity.[5] At this juncture the pacification of the individual is nearly complete. It was mentioned earlier that the idea of the self and the Freudian concept of internalization provided the mechanism to claim the person entirely for society; Young has nearly accomplished the claim. Sociology and social psychology, Freud and the influence of George Herbert Mead, all meet in Young's once frequently cited transformation of "socialization" (e.g., Cuber, 1947; Dawson and Gettys, 1948; Sargent, 1950). In this definition we find that becoming social—attaining selfhood (Young, 1942)—means acquiring the social attributes of members. Although Young's conception of internalization required the *active, selective, dynamic* organization of others' characteristics within one's psyche, it is society that supplies the constituents of the self. With the exception of some small changes Kimball Young produced the prototype for what will become the dominant species of definition: the socialization-as-internalization model. Although the concept of socialization as training shows no signs of disappearing, and in spite of the fact that it is linguistically less awkward, it does not reemerge as the dominant style of definition in sociological theory of research.

Once the necessary conceptual and linguistic transformations (equating "socialization" with a hybrid form of "internalization") were completed and accepted, apparently without objections, more of the important Meadian subtleties were injected into later definitions. Stansfeld Sargent, referring in the surrounding text to both Mead and Young, gives the following definition:

> This role-taking, with its internalized conversation, or 'conversation in the inner forum,' to use Mead's own term, is the essence of socialization, since the child is

---

[5] It may be getting somewhat ahead of ourselves to refer to a definition written in 1968; however, the contrast it provides shows how the elements of the definition have been exactly reversed, transposed in the drift from Cell III- to Cell IV-type definitions. John Clausen (1968: 4) writes that "the process of socialization includes patternings of social learning transmitted through child care and training. . . ." In other words, instead of socialization being a form of training that induces social learning, socialization is here defined as social learning brought about by training activity. Except that the mention of training is in ellipsis, the definition devised by Young (above) demonstrates this curious reversal.

learning to make the speech, habits, attitudes, and behavior of others a part of himself (Sargent, 1950: 53).

The significance of this definition lies in its tying the concept of role to the term socialization. Sociologists will only a little later take advantage of this connection to generalize the concept of socialization beyond the limits of childhood to include any role-learning. Hence the distinction will arise between primary and secondary socialization or, stated another way, between childhood and adult socialization.

Talcott Parsons and the Modern Concept of Socialization

Talcott Parsons was the first to take full advantage of the possibilities that have evolved in the conceptual apparatus surrounding the modern understanding of socialization. However, Parsons did not merely accept the mainstream position. Parsons (1951) defined socialization:[6]

> The acquisition of the requisite orientations for satisfactory functioning in a role is a learning process, but it is not learning in general, but a particular part of learning. This process will be called the process of socialization . . . (p. 205).
>
> [Socialization is] . . . the learning of any orientations of functional significance to the operation of a system of complementary role-expectations . . . (p. 208).
>
> [Socialization is] . . . the internalization of certain patterns of value-orientation. This result is conceived to be the outcome of certain processes of interaction in roles. (pp. 208–209).

In a footnote to the introduction of *Toward a General Theory of Action* (Parsons and Shils, 1951), Parsons wrote that he considered his standpoint on socialization only to be an extension and a clarification of some already existing definitions. On the face of it, his definitions appear similar to those we recently quoted by Young and Sargent. There are profound differences beneath the surface. Let us examine his position at some length.

Rather than continuing piecemeal repair, Talcott Parsons had the rare energy to address the whole search for a comfortable relationship between collective and individual entities (Bershady, 1973). Surely, part of the brilliance of his work lies in its apparent compatibility with developments in the culture of American sociology. For at least a decade prior to the 1951 publication of Parson's two major works, ever less attention had been given to what must be *done* to socialize a person and correspondingly more attention paid to

---

[6]All definitions of socialization from this point onward to the chapter's end, whether devised by Parsons or not, are representatives of the Cell V type in Table 1.

how the person could *learn* to be actually human at all. In some respects his work was like a lens through which the light of the discipline's culture became focused. However, the lens is not a neutral instrument. Parsons created what has been called a "grand synthesis" by implementing a systems theory perspective as the matrix for his unique, American blending of several classical theorists (Parsons, 1951: vii, 3; Swanson, 1953; Bendix and Berger, 1959).

That Parsons could create "society" in its purest form—as a system—meant that he had taken the next step along a path partially cleared by the work of others; he had discovered a scheme whereby the individual could be dissolved into the system. The concept of socialization was a major link in his grand synthesis (Parsons and Shils, 1951: 227). Socialization (now thought of as internalization, social learning, role learning or the acquisition of value-norm complexes) provided the means to bring the individual under full social control—a job made easier because the official position in sociology now held that human nature was subsequent to experience. Following this line of development, Parsons' writings lack virtually all hints of the uncertainty of outcome or the work that must be done to produce actors capable of fulfilling social roles. By the time Talcott Parsons was contributing to the history of ideas the individual was no longer outside and warring against society.

But in *The Social System* (Parsons 1951), even the stress of inner conflict, of contest and collision between basal impulses and superego controls, so central to the Freudian scheme, had been removed from consideration (Wrong, 1961: 187). Freud's "id" and, for that matter, the concept of the impulsive "I" in George Herbert Mead's theory of the self, became obsolete and uninteresting in one stroke. Parsons, remember, considered his concept of socialization to be an extension of work already accomplished, and he was correct to an extent. However, it seems that he did not understand the profound difference it made to consider the individual against the background of (and as an element in) a *system* rather than as a "member of society."

Parsons provided more than a simple extension of the sociological tradition; it was in reality a qualitative change. *He produced a "society" with more integration, order and consensus than can be found anywhere outside the writings of the various utopians* (see comments by Dahrendorf, 1958). The individual actor is portrayed accordingly: the actor's survival is possible in such an "overintegrated" system only because it is no longer necessary to mold, domesticate and render human nature fit for society; all that is needed is to learn proper role expectations to become a functioning element in the social system. Such role learning is what Parsons calls socialization, but it is more. Just as the cog only exists for the machine after it has been put in place, the actor really only exists in the Parsonian system's framework as a properly functioning element. Socialization brings actors into existence, or that is, constitutes them according to socially sanctioned expectations and need dispositions. Without the proper "articulation," as Parsons put it, of actors, based on consensual values and reciprocal motives, there is simply no system per se and anomie prevails.

Parsonian sociology gives us no serious reason to consider social conditions similar to anomie; his is a sociology of order, of institutionalization and of normative patterns (Parsons, 1951: 552). Parsons' theory was motivated by the "problem of order" in society; but rather than producing an actual solution, his design is a denial of the problem. David Lockwood makes an astute observation when he says that "the process of *exploitation* in the Marxian theory represents a radical conceptual antithesis to the social process which has a central place in Parsons' analysis: that of *socialization* (Lockwood, 1956: 138)." I understand this insight to mean that in Marxian theory the natural relationship between the establishment and the weaker classes is inherently conflictual and degrading; while for Parsons the relationship is one of grooming and interdependency among individuals who share master symbols of legitimation, but whose stations in life have been granted different values according to the functional requisites of the system. Actors, then, are either appropriated by the system as they are constituted by it (socialization), or else they are, by definition, external to the social system (socialization failure). Parsons makes no real provisions for socialization failure; therefore, deviance and conflict are nearly incomprehensible conditions (Lockwood, 1956). Indeed, Parsons has been severely criticized for creating the "oversocialized conception of man" (Wrong, 1961).

The work of Talcott Parsons leads his readers to an overly simple statement of the human being's fundamental ontological condition. To wit, human being is unavoidably social and successive generations inherit ongoing social conditions and systems of meaning. Such a statement, while true, is misleading if left unqualified. It reifies the social system, thereby distracting sociological attention from the discovery of the manner in which people sustain their structures and their realities even at the price of conflict, sometimes stepping far beyond "their roles" to do evil, perform saintly acts or even acts of genius. Peter Berger and Stanley Pullberg have come up with a succinct negative critique of such reifying sociologies. When our imagination is informed by the categories of these sociologies,

> the world is seen as inhabited by people who not only perform but are embodiments of roles. To put this a little facetiously, *role-playing precedes existence–or, even better, replaces it* (1965: 206, emphasis added).

Parsons did no less than find a (temporary) solution to the sociological and epistemological problems of integrating society and its elements, of joining the "individual" and "society" (Bershady, 1973: 20, 79–81). His work was from the first controversial, often receiving criticism for its nearly impenetrable prose and its vocabulary laced with eccentricities. Nevertheless, beneath the level of style lay an attractive conceptual apparatus—one to be reckoned with for at least several decades. *The Social System* especially has a sense of completeness about it that was attractive in many respects to contemporary sociologists. It was, in Parsons' own words, a "statement of general sociological theory"; it was a disquisition thoroughly informed by the sociological tradition and the product of a careful meshing of insights acquired over the years since the publication of *The Structure of Social Action* (1937). Parsons considered the concept of the social system to be a major integrative device ("the core of human action systems") that linked culture and the individual—something he thought "culture and personality" theorists had not adequately accounted.

In the case of *The Social System*, Parsons' prose achieved infamy, but there were many criticisms based on more than mere style. In general, the complaints objected to the overall tidiness of the social world as depicted by the systems approach. And, too, his construct was a world of equilibrium, not one of change and strife as Marx, for example, had described it; change, if it could be described at all in Parsonian terms, was more like a series of still photographs than a moving picture of history. Faults and criticism aside, Parsons' scheme struck a responsive chord in the discipline and his influence was powerful.

The effects of this influence in studies and definitions of socialization are quite marked. In the first place, there have been few references by sociologists writing in the area of socialization that go back beyond 1951, the date when both *Toward a General Theory of Action* and *The Social System* were published. To this point, the obvious exceptions to this barrier (e.g., Cooley, Mead and Durkheim) have all had their models of the individual emasculated as part of their induction into current American sociological literature. In other words, the important distinction these older theorists made between our inherited nature and our social nature is no longer ever conceived of as more than an interesting curiosity (e.g., Mead, 1962: 173–178; Cooley, 1964: 423; Durkheim, 1965: 29). The feeling seems to be that any reference to a phenomenon's nature is prescientific philosophical speculation and hence not within the purview of social science (for a statement on this, see Bierstedt, 1974a: 521; and also Joseph H. Fichter, 1965: 112). Therefore, direct descriptive characterizations of our genetic disposition have disappeared. In addition to this evidence, examination of the content of definitions of socialization since 1951 indicates that: (1) the prevailing type of definition depicts socialization as a form of internalization; (2) our social aspects are all that is deemed interesting and these are fully determined by society; (3) sociologists have not made any basic changes in their definitions of socialization since the Parsonian version was written; and (4) Parsons gave further legitimation, shape and direction to the continued framing of the socialization process in terms of social psychological problems. This last point is implicit in his work where it is not directly commanded. For example:

> One cannot effectively study the family as a socializing agency without an understanding of the process of socialization itself in its psychological aspects, i.e., the process of development of the personality of the child (Parsons and Bales, 1955: v−vi).

And again:

> The central focus of the process of socialization lies in the internalization of the culture of the society into which the child is born (Parsons and Bales, 1955: 17).

The focus was to be upon personal change and that is where attention has remained in studies of socialization (Inkeles, 1968).

Parsons did not only write of childhood (primary) socialization, he also discussed so-called secondary socialization (Parsons and Bales, 1955). Parsons felt that primary socialization was the relatively nonspecific process of personality development in children. It was also taken to be the basis for the transition to the roles that are to be encountered in later life. Secondary socialization is, on the other hand, specific (adult) role-oriented learning of functional utility for the system. Whereas the "actor" is the significant unit for the personality system, the "role" is the basic unit of the social system; during secondary socialization they meet and become one.

Fully aware of this distinction, Merton et al. in *The Student Physician* (1957) managed to design a definition general enough to encompass both categories of socialization. Merton writes that:

> socialization designates the processes by which people selectively acquire the values and attitudes, the interests, skills, and knowledge—in short, the culture—current in the groups of which they are, or seek to become a member. It refers to the learning of social roles (1957: 287).

Merton then speaks specifically of secondary socialization as the development of a role-related self whose content is an internally consistent set of behavior-governing dispositions.

This account of socialization is interesting for reasons other than its attention to the rather new idea of secondary socialization. It seems that in incorporating the phrases "selectively acquire" and "seek to become," Merton is granting a degree of autonomy or at least individuality to his actors. This appearance is erroneous. Although the evidence for my understanding is not readily forthcoming in *The Student Physician*, the definition found there closely reflects Merton's famous concept of anticipatory socialization: "those men who, through a kind of *anticipatory socialization* take on the values of the nonmembership group to which they aspire" (1949: 265, emphasis in original).

The context in which anticipatory socialization is discussed relates the concept to reference group theory. Merton says that while an orientation to a nonmembership group *appears* to be an instance of nonconformity, it is in reality simple conformity to another group. Merton attempts to explain how "group alienation" and conversion to another group occurs on the grounds of "a deterioration of *social relations* within the membership group and positive *attitudes* toward the norms of a nonmembership group" (1949: 270, emphasis in original). The "convert" is pushed from one group, while being simultaneously attracted (and perhaps pulled) to another group. Merton does not try to frame the conditions that lead to group alienation or the elements behind a new positive orientation to another group—but that is a deficiency that does not concern us.

What is important for our etymology is that the "individual" has not (once again) been granted autonomy in either *Social Theory and Social Structure* (1949) or in *The Student Physician* (1957). The "individual" was too recently submerged to be raised again by a sociologist in the forefront of the discipline. Instead of an autonomous person, Merton presents the actor as helplessly driven by needs to conform and to belong. Consequently, while socialization may be "selective," what is acquired in the process is limited (by definition) to potentially functional role characteristics that become fused to the role self. The emphasis is placed upon a plastic quality of the actor much more similar to malleability than to a purposive adaptability. This quality is like water conforming itself to a container, and after being poured into another container is still able to conform perfectly again with no residual effects from the first container. At least this is the logical extreme of this position.

The social psychologist Orville G. Brim gets as close as anyone to this extreme. In a chapter titled "Personality Development as Role-Learning" in an edited collection of studies in socialization, he defines socialization as

> a process of learning through which an individual is prepared with varying degrees of success, to meet the requirements laid down by other members of society for his behavior in a variety of situations (1960: 128).

He explains that given this position, the mature adult identity expresses itself socially only through strictly compartmentalized, role-defined activity. The existence of an overarching personality is taken as a residual contaminant in role behavior. Brim later (Brim and Wheeler, 1966) backs away from this extreme perspective and says that the "acquisition of roles is not the entire content of socialization," but that he merely wishes to explore the potential degree of human plasticity. Although most sociologists have not gone so far in this matter as Brim, an extreme case helps to highlight the assumptions beneath the surface of current usage.

The most frequently taken perspective is that primary socialization forms a relatively stable emotional and social matrix that affects (in some unspecified way) all later role learning. Conceiving of primary socialization in this way functions much like the belief in an original human nature. Thanks to the passage of Freud's influence into our culture, however, our "nature" consists of the "personality" constituted within the strongly emotional setting of childhood. Our meshing into the requirements of adult roles is understood as the result of a laminate of role learning laid upon and eventually worked into the fabric of our personality. This overall position is preferred (to the extreme view proffered by Brim) because it accounts for our experiential sense of continuity—that is, we feel we are the same person at whatever age and in whatever role. Although I believe this latter position to be more existentially comfortable (and in my opinion, but for different reasons, more correct), it is not faithful to the principles of relativity and human plasticity that were evolved in the social sciences over decades. The immoderate, albeit heuristic, position taken by Brim, however, is true to this tradition.

There is very strong consensus in modern sociology that socialization is associated with "deep rather than superficial influence" on the individual (e.g., Broom and Selznick, 1968: 99). This distinguishes socialization from the mutual influence exerted in any interaction. However, there is a major difference of opinion as to whether to define socialization as a form of teaching activity or as a special kind of learning. There is little doubt, however, that the socialization-as-internalization model is dominant (Berger and Luckmann, 1966: 129–163, and 205, ftn. 2; Inkeles, 1968: 76–77). For example, even if socialization is defined as training, the discussion of the process that follows is usually focused upon the psychological events of social learning. For another thing, the taken-for-granted quality of the socialization-as-internalization model is hard to deny, even for those taking the concept to mean a fostering activity. As an example, Robert F. Winch (in Smelser, 1973) clearly defines socialization as education or teaching, and then, unable to control himself, writes that "socialization refers to a more general process (than education) and embraces all manners of *learning*" (1973: 204, emphasis added). And finally, demonstrating the thoroughgoing consequences of socialization, Perry and Perry write that it is the learning process "by which a biological organism becomes a human being, acquires a personality with self and identity, and absorbs the culture of his society" (1976: 162).

SUMMARY AND CONCLUSIONS

This chapter has been devoted to an analysis of the changing meaning of the concept of socialization and the manner in which definitions of socialization reflect the prevailing images of the individual and society. The primary assumption in this particular form of analysis was that a contradiction existed between the image of the individual spawned in the philosophy of individualism and the concept of society. The emerging discipline of sociology had inherited the traditional, individualistic conception of our nature. However, in creating a "science of *society*" from the extant scientific ideology with its one-dimensional emphasis on cause and effect, "sociological determinism" came to be the principal corollary of the concept of society. "Society" was understood as an efficient determinant in the explanation of human behavior—and this was the foundation stone of sociology. However, the traditional image of the individual included autonomy. Therein lay the contradiction: both sides of the cause-and-effect equation were deemed causes. Something had to give.

An ever more sociological portrayal of society, spurred on by the Freudian revolution and the new developmental perspective, produced a progressive enfeeblement of "human nature." This new perspective indicated to social and behavioral scientists that as the child matured into an adult, society became an internalized constituent of the personality. This discovery worked heavily to help recast our conceived nature and what were taken to be the necessary bonds between members of society. It gave "society" the edge in the theoretical and causal contest and redirected the focus of scientific attention from "society" to the social psychology of group life. As the sociologistic ideas took deeper hold, socialization came to be seen as a much smoother process in which the person's nature (or self, or personality) was constituted entirely by social processes. Human nature per se became a metaphysical concept, not to be called upon by a self-respecting social scientist. Consequently, conceptions of socialization now refer to what the person can *learn* to be even thought of as human, and not what must be *done* to make the individual merely acceptable. The side of society won the theoretical battle, making human beings much more plastic creatures for social scientists to work with.

From the beginning to the end of this long struggle between the "individual" and "society" the one consistent thread was that definitions of socialization were "inherently forward looking." That is to say, the principal object of interest was the *outcome* of the process rather than the process itself. The socialized condition was what made a person acceptable to, or in recent times, *useful* for society. The socialized person is the functional person, one easily compatible with a tidy deterministic explanation of behavior. After all, the individual's ("scientifically" recognizable) qualities were constituted by society, and therefore, rightfully appropriated by its system of stable relationships and consensual values.

The modern sociological perspective on socialization is a compromise position that has grown out of a long tradition. What has it brought to sociology? There are five parts to the answer. *First*, the evolving imagery has left us with a conceptualization of people that emphasizes our plasticity. Along with this plasticity came the idea that socialization implied increased conformity and a decreased ability to vary willfully from the norms and values of society.

Individuals were left without the ability to create and to sustain the society in which they live. *Second,* sociologists are thoroughly persuaded by a highly legitimated, albeit subtly disguised, psychological interpretation of socialization. For years, the research in this area has concentrated on isolating one, two or more independent variables from the social environment and watching their effect on the individuals in a group of subjects. Similarly, theories and hypotheses are almost entirely confined to accounts of personal change in social attributes. *Third,* work has been directed away from research attention to and systematic conceptualization of the actual process of interaction that constitutes the socializing environment and developing methods of depicting the sociological substance of what is presented to the novice during socialization. *Fourth,* the problematic character of the socializing process has long since been removed. It has been conceptualized as though replaceable parts were being machined by a machinist never known to fail. Present-day theories allow no logical connection to mistakes, failures, misunderstandings, personal preference, balking or simple refusal to be an eager learner. For that matter, an active and eager learner is not a real possibility. *Fifth,* the modern concept of socialization is defined in a way that is grammatically awkward. The standard English definitions have always defined the term in the active voice, as an overt activity. By contrast, however, the current definitions in sociology define it in the passive voice as a process of learning, internalization or acquisition. The problem related to this change of voice is clarity of expression and precision of meaning. There is a considerable difference between teaching and learning. There should be an immediate and obvious difference between socialization and, say, "social learning," or else we have no general term for the interaction in which culture is presented to a novice.

If the legacy of the sociological tradition has a subtle psychological bias, a criticism levied numerous times by leading figures in the discipline, it is nowhere more clearly demonstrated than in the sociological approach to the area of socialization (e.g., Wrong, 1961; Homans, 1964). We have engaged in forms of collective psychology more often than in a sociology of member replacement. The questions in the area have been directed more toward personal change than toward characterizing the medium of interchange between member and novice.

Perhaps one of the first redirected steps that might be made is to keep a clear distinction between socialization (taken in the active voice) and the concept of internalization. A next step along the path is once again to give the individual more credit for an ability to create society. Certainly we conform; certainly we keep to routines and habits; certainly we can be moved by the coerciveness of social institutions; but we are more than norm followers—we are rule-and-system *users* and rule-and-system *breakers* as well.

CHAPTER TWO

BETWEEN THE OLD COLLECTIVE DETERMINISM AND THE NEW INDIVIDUALISM

In the previous chapter we saw individualistic conceptions of socialization superceded by the sociological account of the process. It was emphasized that sociology promised a more powerful explanatory tool, although it too had faults in its particular historical manifestation. This chapter will follow through with the major dimension of the analysis begun in the first chapter. Here individualistic and sociologistic approaches will be examined—first in the negative critique of a revised form of sociological individualism and second, in a comparison designed to expose the specific sociological issues arising between them.

Contemporary individualistic sociologies emphasize the situated, unique and episodic qualities of human social encounters. By contrast, in my examination of an example from this school of thought, I stress the requirement of viewing the continuity of life events. Sociologistic functionalism portrays society and careers as ongoing and structurally continuous. My brief examination of this perspective tries to show the need for a sociological theory capable of explaining the discontinuous, unique and creative side of life. Not wanting to present a paradox and then run, I attempt to provide an introduction to a way of understanding both structure and uniqueness in a single framework. The concept conveyed by this introduction is a very important substratum for a later discussion of culture (Chapter 3) and the "context" as both a natural unit of culture and an appropriate organizational unit for understanding socialization (Chapter 4).

A few words of clarification are necessary. I will hereafter refer to pertinent individualistic sociologies as "interpretive sociologies." The change in name is intended to exclude from consideration a class of deterministic, behavioral sociologies also oriented to the individual actor. This excluded class originated with George C. Homans' attempts to wring a drop of sociological importance from behavioral psychology (1958; see also 1964, 1970), and is closely linked by orientation and determinism to several later individualistic perspectives (Webster, 1973). I exclude these sociologies because they are a peculiar hybrid of sociology, individualism and determinism—a combination producing a kind of collective psychology. They are not, therefore, a new assertion of individualism within sociology, growing instead out of Watsonian psychology.

I am using "interpretive sociology" as a name for those branches of sociology that explicitly grant a person engaged in interaction credit for a *skilled* performance, achieved through interpretive ability and uniquely adapted, or innovative responses to the developing situation (see Wilson, 1970; Giddens, 1976). In varying degrees, this rubric includes the dramaturgical school, symbolic interactionism, ethnomethodology and labeling theory. For a good idea of what this aggregate position has to offer, the following works provide excellent insights: Becker et al., 1961; Becker, 1964; McHugh, 1968; Blumer, 1969; Cicourel, 1970b; Douglas, 1970, passim; Lyman and Scott, 1970; Wilson, 1970; Ellis, 1971; Schwartz, 1971; Harré and Secord, 1973; Hewitt and Hall, 1973; Goffman, 1971, 1974; Skidmore, 1975; Mehan and Wood, 1976; Hewitt, 1976; Stokes and Hewitt, 1976; Turner, 1976; Charon, 1979; Handel, 1979. I base the observations I make in the next section regarding interpretive sociology and the undersocialized version of the person on my reading of the above and other books and articles.

Later in the chapter some essential features of interpretive and traditional sociology are demonstrated. The vehicle supporting this demonstration is a comparison of the theoretical views found in *Boys in White* (Becker et al., 1961) and *The Student Physician* (Merton et al., 1957). These two works are not reviewed for their worth as studies of medical education, but because they are unusually careful reports whose focus and findings are thoroughly permeated by their competing theories. Further, they are examined solely for the manner in which their approaches impinge upon socialization theory. These specific studies were chosen for two reasons. First, due to their similar subject matter and the proximity of their publication dates, the socialization research reported on in each volume lends itself to comparison with the other. Secondly, the different theoretical positions that infuse each piece of research are fairly pure representatives of two extreme schools of thought still at oods today. Their uniquely suited comparison demonstrates two theoretical lineages. The one, Merton's study, represents the traditional functionalist school and proffers the "oversocialized" conception of the person. The other study represents several schools of thought that are in many ways writing in the shadow of functionalism, but certainly presenting an equally lopsided alternative at the opposite extreme, and therefore, picture an "undersocialized" version of the person (Broadhead, 1974).

THE UNDERSOCIALIZED CONCEPTUALIZATION OF THE INDIVIDUAL

There seem to be two ways of understanding human identity: the person apart, independent and significant; and people a part of some larger order that both humbles their individual beings and provides them with participation in something powerful, more lasting than themselves. The contrariness of the two views may not be apparent in the everyday application of opinion to circumstance. Yet, they stand as two distinct pillars of Western culture: supports for political, economic, religious, legal and social scientific intellectual frameworks, the bases of "self-evident truths." In the sphere of judicial decisions alone, such questions as responsibility, motivation, justification, diminished liability and other categories of evaluation are dealt with regularly. Legal opinion on these matters seems to be very much related to the contemporary wisdom of who we are in relation to society. Individualistic climates have offered a person with "inalienable rights" and "equal opportunity." More recently sociologism informed us that "separate is not equal," thereby legally establishing the existence of a social environment that systematically structures and qualifies life's opportunities. Sociologism speaks of an environment capable of molding people and behavior, an environment, therefore, of reduced personal responsibility.

Rarely are these two positions presented in such purity as they are in the theoretical models of the social sciences. And when it becomes apparent that the current model has been explored, expressed to the fullest, and still the serious questions remain—no matter how many answers have been given—thinkers turn again to the other obvious, available alternative. Progress has been made while spiraling between sociologistic and individualistic perspectives. However, there is also an unnecessary repetition of past controversies over perspectives and sentiments. The worn standards are taken up as if they had never before been in battle.

Interpretive Sociology

Chapter 1 followed the transformation of a rather feisty, individualistic version of the individual into an "oversocialized" component of a social system. With the peculiar alchemy of ideas, that "oversocialized" person has spawned an "undersocialized" conception. The very mention of these two antipodean adventures into the metaphysical fringes of sociology—the former somberly achieved, the latter sometimes evangelically espoused—brings us immediately to the crux of socialization theory. That is, the sociological heritage offers an invitation to understand the person as derived from society. Interpretive sociologies decline this invitation through the images they offer, while accepting its reverse. However, the proposition that the person is derived from society is the central tenet of socialization theory, and for that matter, of the whole deterministic position. It is the foundation for both traditional sociology and its particular understanding of member replacement. Without this assumption, as is the case in interpretive sociology, there can be no socialization theory, only a theory of an intersubjective world stratified according to interactional competency. In this latter framework, "socialization" has come to mean a study of the child's practice of various language categories and conversational gambits in a way which: (1) points to the perspectival differences (i.e., the axis of differentiation in stratification terms) between children and adults; (2) tends to highlight the situational uniqueness of meaning; and (3) attends to the moment-by-moment emergence of interaction rather than the process of, or stages in, social careers (e.g., Speier, 1970; Fuller and Jacobs, 1973; Mehan and Wood, 1976: 37–59).

It was the ratification of our derivative status through years of sociological endeavor that led to the oversocialized conception of the person. The faultiness of that image *does not lie in the fundamental assumption that the person is derived from society, but rather in the way that assumption became manifest.* The fact became clear that the sociological imagery involved the theft of our freedom and even our responsibility. In the functionalist model, the representation of individual existence was a picture of the person as almost an automaton, driven by the springs of deeply internalized and anonymous value-norm complexes. Objections to the functionalist imagery are simply too obvious; it treads on cultural ideals, the apparently solid experience of our daily lives, and carefully gathered evidence. But there is no real news any more in saying that the functionalist position deals in faulty images; the admission of such inadequacy is now a commonplace (e.g., Wrong, 1961; Gouldner, 1970; Fichter, 1972).

Functionalism is on the wane. My repeated criticisms attempt neither to whip nor to revive the proverbial dead horse. However, functionalism is not departing without progeny. Functionalism, or more precisely, the contradiction within functionalism has already generated its literal antithesis: latter-day individualistic, interpretive sociologies. The contradiction is that the fully determined person must also be the creator of society.

Taken en masse and reduced to an ideal type, interpretive sociologies stand in opposition to the principal elements of the mainstream sociological credo: that the person is derived from society; that society is best understood in terms of historical structures, not as just a collection of individuals; and that the concept of internalization—*how* a person is derived from society—is the key to understanding the influence of abstract structures on a concrete person. Accordingly, the extreme proponents of interpretive sociology deny the existence of historical social structures, the priority of society, sociological determinism, the deep internalization of social values and norms, and in some cases they rightly deny even that they are a form of sociology (on this last, see Mehan and Wood, 1976: 6). Interpretive sociologies *offer in place of functionalism, what can only be taken as a neo- or social individualism.*

Because they deny historical social structures and reaffirm the "individual," interpreters no longer see society as "ongoing." Society, rather, is an accomplishment of individuals who must ceaselessly bring order and meaning into an otherwise absurd world. The order that does exist comes about of the moment and through the skillful negotiations of "individuals" completely uncontaminated by that intimate linkage of internalization, which was, remember, heralded by Parsons as a landmark development in the history of the social sciences. Having cast this discovery aside, it is now the individual's reflexive ability that attracts celebrants (Giddens, 1976: 19; see also Mead, 1962: 134, for the original statement on reflexive behavior). Some of the interpretationists have even returned to the notion in the original individualism that conflict is an intrinsic, therefore constant, if frequently *sub rosa* quality of human relationships. Karl Marx and not Thomas Hobbes is often cited in this respect, but the effect, in their translation, is roughly equivalent.[1]

The new scheme of things does not admit a conduct-governing, deterministic role-self that emerges from socializing experiences in society. Action—true action—is the vehicle of expression for the undersocialized individual. As a result, interpretive sociologies shun the suggestion that values, norms, routines and habits contribute to the content of social activity. Instead of internalized routines grounded in consensual values, the undersocialized individual has a stock of knowledge.

It is instructive to see Freud's physical metaphor of internalization jux-

---

[1] Marx was not, of course, an individualist, although he made certain concessions to individualism. In the veiw of Michael Harrington (1977: 150), Marx's work is partly a negative critique of individualism and its legitimating function in the rise of capitalism.

taposed with the new physical metaphor of a "stock" of knowledge. Freud's concept pointed quite clearly to the symbolic removal of some part of society from the "outside" and the placing of it on the "inside." By contrast, the stock of knowledge concept implies that the individual approaches supermarket shelves of knowledges, picking and choosing at will for the recipe that should be brought to the social occasion at hand. The metaphors are most agreeable complements to the rhetorics of their origin.

The undersocialized person chooses tools for interaction like an artisan of social realities. This person learns from society, but is not society's creature:

> Thus humans are not necessarily the creatures of social and psychological forces—class, caste, race, or deep-lying unconscious states—which *determine* their behavior in the situation (Lyman and Scott, 1970: 4, emphasis in original).

Lyman and Scott are stating here their thesis from A *Sociology of the Absurd*: that apparently enduring structures, definitions and conditions do not strictly determine human behavior. They use the word "necessarily" to juxtapose their position with that of traditional sociology. They are doing more than quibbling with the semantics of determinism. The apparent reasonableness of their statement is considerably diminished when placed in context.

Lyman and Scott are claiming that the world is meaningless prior to the act. That is hubris, not sociology. The world is not born anew with the call of each human action. Individuals are born into a structured and meaningful world—a world shaped and constrained by definitions and demographics. Conduct and action may well maintain, reproduce, change or crush societal realities, but in fact, an act is meaningful only insofar as it signals its sociological origins. An absurd act is one that cannot be related to its origins. The very basic sociological task is to discover the way preexisting structures and meanings are made to count in situations put together by persons capable of creative involvement with their environment; we are not, after all, protohuman creatures on the historical verge of reality, but fully selved and cultured beings.

Need Sociology Capitulate?

From the tone of criticism I have set thus far it must be clear that I will answer the title question in the negative. There is now no good reason to swap a less than satisfactory position for an unsatisfactory one. Earlier students of our societal life were driven away from individualism by grave inadequacies: originally, its inability to explain history, and later, its impotence as an account of our conduct in groups. With good reason, and after much consideration, they turned to a more sociological form of understanding. Interpretive sociology offers a larger, more focused and powerful descriptive capability than its presociological counterpart while still maintaining the old explanatory deficiencies. Why, therefore, should this whole cycle be repeated? Is the new "person" of interpretive sociology worth the trouble of rehashing old disputes disguised in new trappings? Let the argument be cast first in the categories available within interpretive sociology.

In arguments for the new person, the abiding conviction among interpretive sociologists is that the "problematic" has replaced the "deterministic," presaging a renaissance of concern for human volition and thereby reuniting the doer with the deed and the thinker with the thought (e.g., Poole, 1972, Mehan and Wood, 1976: 198–207). On the surface, this appears to be a moral concern, but the person of interpretive sociology is not true to traditional humanistic ideals. The older version of the "individual" was a kind of fallen Adam who received his morality from society once he had learned its ways. Today, however, scientism is considerably more advanced. Hence, we are now less prone to view the effects of original sin in our own offspring, so that even from the humanistic point of view, there is no compelling cause to embrace the new "individual" who is born, and remains, amoral.

Now, a moral act is one that ultimately grants the worth of others in society. There are two sources from which a person can attain worth as an individual, either as the creature of a divinity or as a member of society. Outside of these relationships, and that is where the pure interpretive sociology would put us, the celebration of the individual can only be for the sheer sake of individuality. In this analysis, interpretive sociologies represent an areligious humanism wherein the individual becomes the ultimate value. Too often, the theoretical and empirical observations of this perspective are surrounded by a halo of rhetoric that clearly projects what amounts to a form of collective narcissism. It is perhaps for the reason of this last characterization that an undisguised zeal sometimes walks boldly astride accounts of the new perspective (e.g., Lyman and Scott, 1970; Mehan and Wood, 1976).

Considering the two sources of individual worth mentioned above, it may be said that there is more than enough in the world to understand by way of physical relationships and emotional ties to warrant the invocation of a methodological atheism by sociology. This leaves sociologists free, if they are of a mind to do so, to discover how it is that individual worth or dignity can arise in a society. Many sociologists have considered the question of personal integrity, but their answers are too often derived from an overly simple determinism, similar to the position discussed in the first chapter regarding Merton's ideas of group alienation, shifting conformity and anticipatory socialization. In spite of a similar weakness, Robert Bierstedt (1974a: 522) phrases the correct question succinctly:

> Where, in this welter of processes, in this structure of norms and statuses and groups, is there room for the person, what guarantees his integrity as an indi-

vidual, what confers upon him the irrepressible and unrepeatable character of his own personality?

Although he is not advocating change, Bierstedt is describing the inability of sociology to express the personhood of individuals. As long as the sociological perspective is applied to the so-called micro level, as it must be in studying socialization, and not only to macrostructures, then the qualities of personhood are integral to its theoretical statements. However, traditional sociology has advantages that cannot be denied. Reform, more than capitulation to the new individualism, is prescribed.

Are Groups Real and Are They Determinate?

It will be remembered that early in this century sociology expressed a concern with the individual's place in society and the attendant distrust of collective concepts brought about a long controversy over whether groups were real. The late "sociology of sociology," heavily frowned upon by many as idle navel-gazing, was in many respects a resurrection of the old controversies. The sociology of sociology was an outburst that began in part as a celebration of the person's reality and efficacy. As a movement, it questioned the status of sociological discourse, which was at that time based almost entirely upon the supposition that collective entities were a sui generis reality.

The sentiments voiced by this movement were worthy enough, but its analysis lacked sociological depth. Collective entities such as structure, group, class and society form a powerful set of *theoretical* determinants, and I believe they have meaning for us at the level of everyday experience.

Considered as theoretical determinants, the question of whether collective entities are real—real like the human body is real—may not be so important as the explanatory power they lend to sociology. This point of view grows from the operative philosophy of 20th-century science regarding the relationship between theories and phenomena. The current assumption in science is that science *constructs* a reality (which can, I may add, be invested with considerable ego attachment) that either works as an explanation of certain questions or it does not. If a once-fruitful explanation falls before new questions or new visions, no one suspects the laws of nature to have been violated.[2] This is in

[2] For example, Albert Einstein described theory as a workable knowledge of a subject field from some perspective (Einstein, 1961: 123–124). The same sort of pragmatic grasp of the ontological status of theory is quite openly displayed in the two highly theoretical areas: subatomic physics (dealing with quark theory) and astrophysics (in accounts of "black holes" in space). Thomas Kuhn (1970) tells of this attitude in the sciences he scrutinizes in his account of scientific revolutions (see also Toulmin, 1961). The new philosophy in science does not, as some have said, claim that the world is an illusion and thereby deny the existence of phenomena. It simply does not accept "brute fact" in scientific discourse; a fact is a proposition about phenomena, having been abstracted from the realm of phenomena according to the rules of some conceptual scheme.

stark contrast to the 19th-century philosophy which, along with a faith in individualistic perspectives, fueled the original "Are groups real?" controversy. Nineteenth-century scientists believed that their theories were in some way duplicates of nature.

To the present point, the modern philosophy acts to dissolve the meaningfulness of the inquiry into the reality (or ontological status) of groups. The question resulting from the new perspective is, "Does the group hypothesis supply a fruitful approach to problems of understanding our behavior?" To my mind, the answer is unequivocally, yes.

An alternative but related means of allaying an inordinate fear of groups among certain social scientists grows out of everyday experience, or perhaps, common sense. We may ask the question, "Are groups real to individuals in society?" This can be divided into three more specific questions.

The first would ask if people ever bestow allegiance on or act in the name of collective entities. Certainly the answer would affirm the existence of such things as team spirit, the bureaucratic official, patriotism, fighting to protect one's family, and the profound difference between an ideologue and a liar.

The second question is immediately apropos to sociology and social psychology. Such a question would concern the contingency that observable patterns of relationships, meanings and experiences effect a kind of subliminal seduction upon the individual, thereby forming the (prearticulated) basis for what is known to be self-evident in the world. Thus, the individual's relationship to the group and what it stands for sustains the capacity to believe or act in a particular fashion. As a consequence of experience with the patterns of the social world, people "grow into their ways." There is a point—the taking on of the generalized other—in the dual processes of socialization and internalization where people can be trusted to carry themselves without the benefit of constant supervision. This can sometimes be carried to the point of being "old fashioned," acting like an "American" when visiting abroad, or in simply "being one's self." And so to the second question, we can also answer, yes, groups are real for people in society.

The third question would be whether persons ever experience collective entities apart from the individuals who form the membership. Another way of phrasing this concern would be to ask whether people can grasp the abstraction of an "external" institution—to use the Durkheimian term. It seems that we have no trouble in saying "the barbarians," "the enemy," or in feeling oppressed by "the bureaucracy." What undergraduate has not felt something dire in the pit of his or her stomach on returning after a vacation to "school"? Once again the "group" hypothesis can be sustained on the level of experience. This has been a commonsense apology for the reality of the group in everyday experience; however, the history of systematic research in sociology has done no less than confirm the results of this thought experiment.

This section condemns the undersocialized conception of the person for the reason that it offers no humanistically appealing or sociologically efficacious explanation of the human social condition. However, as a reaction to the functionalist imagery, it provides an equally extreme but opposite description of our nature. Both the functionalist and the interpretationist positions belie the experiences we have of people in our everyday lives. Perhaps people can, but rarely do, live as exemplars of either position; our habits and sociological constraints easily mix with our freedom. In any case, it would seem that some synthesis of these images would give a better starting point for sociological theory than either could do by itself. Before attempting a synthesis of any sort, more must be learned about the concepts engendered by reference to the unadulterated images at both extremes.

MODELS OF THE INDIVIDUAL IN THEORY FORMATION: SITUATION, CREATIVITY AND UNIQUENESS; STRUCTURE, CONDUCT AND CONTINUITY

Internalization is a useful explanatory concept when stripped of its deterministic trappings. Likewise, there is no scientific reason to reject evidence to the effect that individuals can be autonomous and creative, as claimed by the interpretive school. The urge to push our creative side to a theoretical extreme is, unfortunately, only too apparent in interpretive sociology. If the functionalist model stresses that the past is forever realized through normative behavior in the enactment of roles, then surely the interpretive model locks interaction into the eternal present. In this view, characteristics of the situation emerge and are interpreted in the light of a stock of knowledge. Social behavior then becomes a skill as people ceaselessly construct performances on the basis of their interpretations. And because behavior is not seen as the result of previously imprinted societal dicta organized into a personality system, actors take on a quality of flexibility quite impossible in functionalist thought.

An Example of the Interpretive Approach

Howard S. Becker (1964) puts the fluidity of the self beyond the point where performance can be guided by historical social structures. He writes that the "individual turns himself into the kind of person the situation demands," labeling this type of behavior "situational adjustment (1964: 44)." The reader is left somewhat confused by this concept, wondering how it is that situations can "demand" anything or even be intelligible if everyone is creatively adapting to the immediate exigencies of the milieu. It sounds more like chaos. The question also arises regarding the origin of situations and what stable, cultural qualities they could possess in a world of flux. Without addressing these dilemmas and without explanation, Becker offers an apparently contradictory concept: "commitment." According to Becker:

> A distinguishing mark of commitment [is] that the actor rejects other situationally feasible alternatives, choosing from among the available courses of action that which best suits his purpose. In so doing, he often ignores the principle of situational adjustment, pursuing his consistent line of activity in the face of a short term loss (1964: 50).

Closer examination and some effort on the reader's part reveal that commitment is not contrary to situational adjustment. It turns out that the actor has a "purpose," a "responsibility," and has made "side bets," or has taken some "actions which commit him more or less permanently to a given line of endeavor." These conditions that lead to "committed" action merely indicate that the actor has defined the situation in terms of a more inclusive context. Because both "situational adjustment" and "commitment" are behavioral adjustments according to the actor's definition of the situation, they are not contradictory after all. However, the formulation is not without immediate deficiencies.

Becker (1964) does not use the "definition of the situation," but instead implicitly relies upon the more complete concept of *perspective*. The notion of perspective is taken from George Herbert Mead and was the guiding idea for *Boys in White*, a major study of medical education (Becker et al., 1961). Becker and his colleagues write that they:

> use the term perspective to refer to a coordinated set of ideas and actions a person uses in dealing with some problematic situation, to refer to a person's ordinary way of thinking and feeling about and acting in such a situation (p. 34).

Just as Becker's notions of situational adjustment and commitment depend on the more fundamental idea of perspective, so did their conceptual prototypes in *Boys in White*. (These conceptual forerunners were labeled "immediate and long-range perspectives" [1961: 35].) Perspectives represent adjustments on the part of the actor, and further, are developed collectively during interaction with those who confront similar circumstances. A perspective is the guide to action that actors bring to situations, despite the emergence of the perspective's precise character in and through situated interaction.

A grave difficulty arises when it is realized just how thoroughly Becker's thinking is tied to the "situation" and just how little work he has done to elaborate this concept.[3] Somehow situations arise and are without meaning until they are defined, yet they are sufficiently recognizable to be defined; people face and adjust to many situations, but we are given no idea of con-

---

[3]Becker is not alone in his inattention to the "situation"; see Goffman (1964) "The Neglected Situation."

tinuity between situations. On the one hand, situations are said to be emergent and unique, while on the other, role learning (Becker, 1964), roles and organizations (Becker et al., 1961) are possible. *Becker's notion of the situation presupposes social structure, but his description of situated interaction denies its possibility.* These contradictions are not merely seeming; they are real and cannot be reconciled within Becker's theoretical framework.

Becker's own formulation of symbolic interactionism concentrated on definition and perspective and is distinct from the theories of George Herbert Mead. Mead showed a great concern for the *consequences* of action upon participants in social encounters. Although deeply influenced by Mead, Becker has conceived of a theory that is oriented toward, but stops short of, elucidating *the conditions of action from the standpoint of the situated actor.* His attention is upon the present and upon response, not upon the contribution action makes to the environment. As a result, a socializing environment cannot be pictured as having a deep psychodynamic impress upon persons engaged in it. Socialization, if such a notion can exist at all in Becker's formulation (the word does not appear in the index of *Boys in White*), would not be cumulative; it is situationally specific and, therefore, has virtually no relevance for activity, say, outside the bounds of the medical school organization. Put another way, from Becker's "perspective," medical school experiences do not provide students with the resources to manage the transition between the role of student and the conduct suitable for a doctor's role.

Becker et al. cannot find in the content of medical education any principles by means of which professional medical situations are organized, that would be applicable in both the life of a student and the various professional encounters for which physicians are responsible. In such a close study of the trees, the forest becomes invisible. In the absence of some actual underlying continuity between situations, the social world would dissolve into chaos. Without the idea of an underlying continuity the practice of a generalizing sociology would be impossible.

Certainly we are adaptable in situations. That we can adapt at all implies some transsituational continuity and the applicability of some interpretive schemes, the scope of which are at least sufficient for us to feel the sometimes subtle hints that our conduct is inadequate and to learn what does pass for adequacy. Conversely, the myriad possible events, topics and personnel encountering one another to create the conditions for situations, even within one culture, *must display some basic organizing principles beneath the surface variety.* That is to say, once the norms and conventions are established, their observance is structured in a way that allows these discrete items of behavior to be related to the setting and understood as a whole.

With no concept of rule-based structural continuity, Becker's theoretical position offers two logical possibilities regarding interaction. Either a four-year-old child (because she is human and therefore adaptable) could muster the social resources and skills necessary for a respectable adult performance in any role, or there is no possibility of human situations, roles or society. The notions of structural continuity must be a part of any general explanation of social life.

Despite the preceding criticisms, the situation Becker has given to the situation as the locus of interaction must not be overlooked. For without a doubt the actor's "situation" must be included as an important element in the explanation of social behavior. Recognizing this, a detailed elaboration of the "situation" must lie at the heart of any account of socialization theory. The discussion of situation, uniqueness, continuity, action and structure has not taken us as far afield as it might seem. Socialization is, after all, a species of interaction that has elements in common with all interaction.

It was just stated that an account of structural continuity was a necessary element in any general sociological theory. Nevertheless, there is a discontinuous or episodic quality to social careers and encounters. Because of this, I feel obliged to present and declare the theoretically contrary desideratum. That is, discontinuity, or more specifically, situational uniqueness must also be accounted for by sociological theories. As has been suggested, Becker and his colleagues consider medical education to be an idiosyncratic experience with few lasting effects on the conduct of future physicians. In making the second desideratum, I wish to recognize, along with Becker, the sociological chasm between studenthood and membership. But unlike Becker, I take the chasm itself to be a valid problem for sociological theory. Functionalism does not approach the problem head on, but instead assumes socialization produces continuity. The issue is worthy of further examination.

A Functionalist Account

It is the question of discontinuity that brings *Boys in White* into the most serious disagreement with its important counterpart, *The Student Physician* (Merton et al., 1957). Whereas *Boys in White* is an investigation of student culture and the problems accommodated by students as they face the challenges of attaining a medical education, *The Student Physician* concerns itself with socialization per se.

The point of contention extends the earlier discussion of continuity into the empirical realm. The previous discussion centered solely on theoretical perspectives. Here, however, the same conflict arises out of empirical investigations of grossly similar educational environments.

Merton states in *The Student Physician* that the medical school infuses students with the orientations, the knowledge and the skills fundamental for living the life of a physician. As a comparison of the two titles alone would indicate, Merton, unlike Becker, is not struck by the great differences in status and other attributes separating students from faculty. It is possible, of course, that this alternative finding is merely a function of the style of education offered in the relevant medical schools. However, a very strong case may be made for another interpretation.

Hanson and Long (1976) argue persuasively that dissimilar theoretical and methodological approaches led the two research teams to different conclusions. *The Student Physician* exemplifies a clearheaded and thoughtful use of the predominant functionalist understanding of the socialization process. Its theoretical basis is virtually identical to the Parsonian scheme. That is, socialization is taken as *a smooth change in absolute personal qualities*. The change is from an undifferentiated condition of individual potential toward role-specific orientations and functionality. It is assumed that the root of this change lies in the deep internalization of particular values and norms that become the relatively permanent governors of behavior. From a larger perspective, the individual is being incorporated as an element in the social system.

This being the dominant viewpoint in sociology, one may even say that current socialization theory, seeing only continuity in the process of status mobility, cannot recognize the significant difference between socialization experience and life as a member lives it.

In contrast, the interpretationist theory that animates *Boys in White* views social life in terms of situational discontinuity and can offer only a view of the gap between the studenthood and the role of the physician.

Combined, the two positions tell us that although the world of socialization fulfills its membership-replacement function, it is indeed a different world from the one that members inhabit. Consider socialization directly for a moment as an example of the need to account for the relationship between uniqueness and continuity.

The human activity that constructs socialization realities is not a replica of the world the novice will inhabit as a member. During any typical day of socialization, the emphasis upon and sequencing of certain tasks, the rhythm and segmentation of time, and the patterns and kinds of social relationships may be quite different from life as a member lives it. In other words, socialization presents a world, but it also constructs a world. The world of socialization is a model, or even better, a caricature of the world of membership and not a replica. Not only does socialization present a mere model of life, the status of "novice" is different from that of "member." Even the most congenial relationship between a novice and a member cannot finally dissolve the meaningful distinction in status between the two. The achievement of membership is a distinct change in identity in that membership entails a new pattern of rights, responsibility, accountability and sanctioning (Hanson and Long, 1976:24).

Socialization succeeds when apparently distorted sets of information are converted (by the novice) to the social competence of a new member. The sociological perspective must be that socialization, in spite of its superficial distortion of the member's world, presents the rules whereby "respectable" behavior might be constructed. "Respectable" in this case is an entirely relative term referring to life as it is lived by members, whether they are thieves or saints.

The comparison of *Boys in White* with *The Student Physician*, even though these studies are two decades old, points toward still relevant and undecided issues in socialization theory and research. The problem once again is to discover the medium of continuity between the worlds of socialization and membership and the means whereby socialization does lead toward or produce social competency, but at the same time allowing for the variation and flexibility common to human interaction. The issue of situational uniqueness versus structural continuity is in question here; these are the sociological counterparts of the psychological processes of creativity and habit. The means to embrace the several sides of this issue is the concept of sociological autonomy. That concept will receive detailed elaboration in Chapter 5. For the present, the groundwork must be laid that will allow us to conceive of structural continuity, situational uniqueness, conduct and routine, and creativity within the same framework.

Performance and Principles

A sociology of language, for example, is possible because certain classes of English speakers have established an acceptable mode of speech. These classes of people have negotiated the norms and conventions of their speech, and these features may or may not be identical to "standard" English (e.g., Bernstein, 1966). What is spoken by all classes is recognizable as English despite its regularly situated use. In other words, the patterns and structures of life circumstances affect speech performance in such a way as to create differences in dialect. In spite of the differences, each dialect participates in the institution called "the English language." From another perspective, furthermore, within the bounds of usage produced by one of these classes, an incredible variety of sentences can be produced and understood. These speakers can say and understand new sentences never before spoken, at the same time observing the conversational style of their class.

Noam Chomsky has postulated that this can only be possible in the light of both the surface conventions of language (performance) and a related set of underlying principles (deep structure) through which language is made intelligible (Chomsky, 1965: Chapter 1; 1968: passim.; 1975:3–134). This, Chomsky's basic position, is a powerful explanatory device and has become a widely accepted conceptual tool in the explanation of human linguistic capabilities.

Acts of speech display the inherent principles of organization that people use to produce conversation. Similarly, social activity, including socialization, is a demonstration of the underlying rules that make human interaction possible. Granting this, it may be said that situations can be only partially understood as unique events occurring as a result of the reflexive behavior or creative involvement of the participating actors. Situations display a structural continuity as well. It is a continuity based upon cultural principles of organization.

The game of chess may be used here as an analogy to help elucidate the relationship between institutionalized performance, creativity and underlying organizing principles. In this analogy the rules of chess should be understood as if they were the principles organizing any life situation. Strategies (norms) and the legitimate relations among the pieces (the "social structure" of who does what to whom, and how) are the institutional aspects of the game. A norm is a pattern of conduct considered to be a standard for behavior. "Social structure" describes a persisting pattern of relations that can be resolved into components called roles, and that can be made meaningful to the participants. Any legitimate individual move is made according to the rules, perhaps as part of a strategy, and it might evidence a novel or creative exercise of the rules within the structure of relations among the pieces.

The game of chess is contained by its rules. They govern the initial organization of the several pieces on the board and all lawful moves made thereafter. The rules are constantly apparent in the organization of play. Without chess rules the sliding and hopping pieces on a checkered board could be part of a game, but no move could be recognized as a move in the game of chess. Because of the rules, any move, however novel, is intelligible as part of chess, or it may be deemed illegitimate. The quality of moves and of play in general may even be judged by the rule-defined object of the game. However, the rules are permissive; they indicate which moves a player *may* make; none of them dictate what he *must* do (Wittgenstein, 1958: 80; Goffman, 1961a:17−81; Harré and Secord, 1973; Chapter 9; Weizenbaum, 1976: 48−72). It may be said, therefore, that rules guide but do not govern conduct (Blum and McHugh, 1971:104). Rules lend organization to the play. In fact, they are the basic instructions on how to integrate all possible repertoires of moves. To state the obvious, in order to play the game at all, one must know the rules.

Conventional or "classical" strategies are normative procedures in chess. They are rule-constrained in that the implementation of a strategy may not violate chess rules without, that is, being deemed deviant and outside the game. Nevertheless, the principles upon which chess strategies rest are sufficiently open to allow for a literally incredible variety of offensive and defensive strategies. These procedures are recognizable to practiced players and may be passed on to the novice. Accordingly, strategies make up the specific institutional content of chess.

This equation of game strategy with social institutions is founded on the definitions of norm and structure supplied above, and upon Berger and Luckmann's definition of the institutional process: "a reciprocal typification of habitualized actions by types of actors" (1966: 54). Strategies, like norms, are permissive. A strategy opens up a specific range of possible actions, but only commitment to the object of the game constrains a player to invest his game with strategy. Norms, then, are both constraining and enabling. They provide a framework within which certain moves have more value than others, relative to the rules.

A game is a social encounter. In this case that means an opposing player is also making moves—and hoping to win. Carrying a strategy out is directly affected by the interaction of the players' pieces. Strategies help to add a *savoir-faire* to the play and a sense of "long-range perspective" or "commitment." A player about to move faces a certain "situation" of the pieces upon the board. (Goffman defines the "situation" as an "environment of mutually monitoring possibilities . . . occurring when two or more individuals find themselves in one another's immediate presence . . . [and establish a] shared current orientation") (1964: 135). Because the "situation" of each move changes by turns, a strategy requires constant "situational adjustment." The requirement of novel or creative situational adjustment holds true in spite of the unchanging rules and the perhaps centuries-old strategy and counterstrategy that the players evolve on the board.

Without any easy (internalized) grasp of the rules the game proceeds only haltingly. In the absence of strategies, and some practice in their implementation, as in the case of novices, all moves may be made for the expediency of the moment. With experienced players, however, each move is less an episode unto itself and more a part of the institution of chess. In almost paradoxical fashion, the greater a player's participation in institutional chess—or, stated differently, the more internalized the game—the less dependent that person is upon any one situation for the raw material of play. Consequently, the chess master's creativity becomes more profound. The primitive, situation-bound creativity of the novice is eventually transcended by the sociological autonomy of the master. That is, the master gains an ability to adjust that is closely associated with an increased sensitivity to the requirements of the game.

For chess, it is the very nature of the rules and institutions that calls forth creativity, giving chess its profound quality. Not all board games encourage that sense of profundity. Checkers exhibits a highly superficial similarity to chess, yet its rules do not present the same opportunity for institutionalizing so many or such complex strategies. Further, checkers has a reduced potential for mature creativity.

Similarly, the places where actors encounter one another in everyday life do not all offer the same openness to creative actions. The casual greetings of passersby and highly circumscribed religious ritual do not admit much innovation (Turner, 1962). Creativity in such places is a breach of the rules (Garfinkel, 1967). Sometimes respectable activity is so narrowly defined that only a degree of personal style can be injected; at other times the social context allows great freedom. The organization of NASA, for example, promotes directed creativity.

There are several reasons a game analogy is not complete or accurate. The "game" is itself only one form of life (Goffman, 1974). If the rules of a game are broken, the essence of the game disappears. If cultural rules are broken, life does not disappear; either a new "game" can be established or "accounts" (Scott and Lyman, 1968), "disclaimers" (Hewitt and Stokes, 1975), and other "aligning actions" (Stokes and Hewitt, 1976) help to reestablish the old context. Games are entered voluntarily and are for fun. The game analogy does not then point up any morally constraining aspects of life (e.g., Durkheim, 1964), but instead emphasizes rules of practice (Mulligan and Lederman, 1977). Knowledge of the rules of a game is usually explicit. Life's rules, on the other hand, are more often tacit than not. Therefore, "knowing" the principles of organization that contain other social encounters means knowing their application and not their abstract formulation (Giddens, 1976: 124). (This last statement can be applied to games: the rules of *a* game may be explicit, but the rules of gaming encounters lie in the usually tacit realm of culture). The lack of explicitness, or the prerational nature of life's rules allows for the possibility of ambiguity, contradiction and the so-called negotiated basis of social order. Furthermore, games overemphasize the rational, win-or-lose, conflictual aspects of human encounters. In spite of the various flaws in the game analogy, it does provide a simple and good heuristic vehicle—even criticism of the model is instructive.

The theoretical frame of reference I am attempting to establish here does not take the basis of society to be either conflict *or* consensus. Instead, I understand "order" to be the fundamental concept. People encounter each other, recognize each other's presence, interact and discover in the ensuing context the rules that can guide their conduct. The result of the encounter might well produce degrees of cooperation, competition, conflict and consensus. Barring these outcomes, the encounter might remain ambiguous and therefore continually in the process of negotiation. That is to say, people attempt to establish an order—they introduce one another to the situation by making its possibilities apparent—to draw upon for their continued definition of the situation. Conceptions of order and personal resources are the origins of continued participation in a given context. Most of life's contexts are "preexisting"; the territories we traverse have been walked before; and the rules for our passage are already in the culture. Either personal experience can be relied upon, or as in the case of socialization, more experienced individuals show novices the way.

Analyzing the game points to the bounded nature of all interaction. That is, actors place limits on the range of appropriate topics and behavior and even on the physical requirements of encounters. Another way of viewing such social boundaries is as natural units of activity, organized by rule and in terms of the concrete activity of actors. The game helps to demonstrate the relationship among the principles organizing encounters, conventions and the creativity necessary for situations to evolve. Further, the way preexisting rules and norms may guide and not determine actions is perhaps clearer now.

Organizing principles relate otherwise separate behavioral events (as if they were the words of a sentence or moves in a game of chess) into a meaningful whole. Because of rules any "move," however original and related only to the immediate situation, retains its identity as a move in a given frame of reference. Likewise, an actor retains a specific cultural identity while moving sometimes creatively, sometimes in stereotyped fashion through life's variety. Once the rules are presented (socialization) and then grasped (internalization), the game, no matter how unique in a given manifestation, may be played virtually anywhere the conditions of play are met. A situation, however, can only be constructed as a context for conduct on the basis of its organizing principles. Without rules, continuity is lost to chaos and all action becomes quite literally absurd.

SUMMARY AND CONCLUSIONS

Some comments on the themes of this chapter might be useful in lodging it in the foundation of the chapters that follow. I have just explained what I believe to be the basic issues for socialization theory. These issues are actually specifications of long-standing general arguments for and against deterministic images of the individual.

The chapter is intended to phrase the general problem of determinism in terms analytically derived from the approaches to the sociological understanding of the individual. Sociologistic functionalism offers a determined description of the person. Consequently, the person's absolute dependence upon routine is emphasized along with the smooth intrasystemic continuity of the individual's career. Individualistic interpretive sociologies make de facto declarations of our freedom. The routine and continuous aspects of life are ignored to portray the person's autonomy from a deeply internalized behavioral and attitudinal repertoire, a creativity in interaction and the discontinuity of uniqueness of each situation.

The underlying assumption of the chapter is that neither functionalist nor interpretive sociology presents an adequate characterization of the individual and society. Everday experience suggests that a given interactional encounter exhibits continuity and elements of discontinuity. Certainly, too, each of the two forms of sociology discussed here has been able to ground itself in observations of social reality. It seems that the person is both a function of society and relatively autonomous. A plausible account of human social activity cannot be purchased from either school alone.

Individualism, sociological determinism and neoindividualism are all artifacts of the history of ideas. "Determinism" is no more a scientific necessity than the idea that "autonomy" must be denied by a scientific explanation of the human condition. Both our cultural and our unique, personal identities require consideration, and neither has a more fundamental ontological status in society. But ontology may be left aside. By recognizing the relativity of knowledge, the newer philosophy in science must show more concern with the fruitfulness of explanations than with ontology. In respect of what experience suggests and with some sanction from philosophy, it was intimated that functionalist and interpretive descriptions may be used as complements instead of viewing them as contraries. Out of such a position could issue a more rounded image of the person and a perspective able to account for structural continuity and episodic discontinuity, for institutionalized conduct and creativity.

No current theory reconciles freedom with determined behavior. No natural, ready-made connection exists to unite what has been separated into opposing facets of life. A theoretical device, a bridge, must be built. At one time, the discovery of the concept of internalization filled a corresponding, if different, role.

Internalization firmly spanned the seeming chasm between the subjective and the social, between the person and social structure. So great was the power of this concept that our understanding of people and society has not been the same since its inception. Society can no longer be viewed as an artifact contrived out of convenience and fear. The intimate ties postulated by internalization will not allow observers to see humanness only in terms of our organism and its evolution. What had been regarded as a chasm was in some cases closed.

The problem today is not once again to establish the necessity of internalization within the sociological form of explanation. The problem is, instead, one of characterizing the substance of the link among persons. Given such a direction, sociologists should attempt to provide a theory of *what* is passed from member to novice during socialization and internalization.

It is clear, I believe, that the social is neither an aggregate nor a herd. The essence of the social is the symbol. Or, as Durkheim said, society "above all is the idea which it forms of itself " (1965: 470). Society is thus a reality sui generis existing in our consciousnesses and expressed in action. A symbolic representation of society is usually said to be *what* is presented, passed and received during member replacement activity. Sometimes it is said that the symbolic transfer occurs as the novice reconstructs the "generalized other," as a cognitive abstraction of community structure, function and attitude, during socializing experience. Or again, the novice might take on need dispositions and functional patterns of value orientation. These suggestions for *what* is passed between member and novice may be correct, but they are not sufficient. What is lacking is an explanation of the means whereby behavior and interaction are organized.

The game analogy was introduced to depict a theoretical device capable of dissolving the meaningfulness of the freedom—determinism polarity, capable of retaining the concept of internalization, capable of using insights rooted in sociologistic and individualistic philosophies, capable of considering society in terms of structure (but not denying autonomy), and providing, at the base of all this, a description of what socializing activity transfers to the novice during internalization. The primary medium of transfer is a unit of rules that ultimately functions to organize and contain behavior, perception and interaction.

CHAPTER THREE

A CRITICISM OF MODERN SOCIALIZATION CONCEPTS AND RESEARCH

This chapter is intended as an epilogue to my observations about the historical development of socialization theory. I seek to criticize some accepted concepts and a number of attitudes guiding socialization research. There is no intention to write an article-by-article review of the literature. Instead, the chapter summarizes and appraises the style of thinking somehow informed by the dominant sociological tradition. Therefore, that which follows should be regarded as a conceptual analysis rather than as an exegesis of various prominent studies in the field.

Several seemingly diverse topics are discussed here. The underlying and unifying theme, however, is the need for redefinition. In the previous chapters I have offered a critique of the changing theoretical interpretations given to socialization as the process linking individuals to society. This chapter focuses upon the nature of that link, particularly upon how socialization is currently defined. The socialization-as-internalization model of definition is taken to task for the inadequacies of its definitional form and content—and as a catalyst for empirical research. Just as I criticize the form of the definition of socialization, I criticize the form of socialization research as a model of explanation. I want to show that the need for reformulation does not exist only at the remote level of theory or the even more distant realm of philosophical imagery. Redefinition is necessary at the level of the *concepts* sociologists actually "mouth" and work with in their inquiries, and at the level of defining tasks for empirical research.

Weaknesses in an accepted definition of a concept often relate to fundamental theoretical issues. I believe this to be true for "socialization"; a concept is, so to speak, the tip of an iceberg of thought. And too, concepts are the fundamental tools of science. Surely, we explore the world with them. As our understanding of the world changes, we must seek to rearrange our conceptual apparatus. At some time we must assess and criticize what has already been done. We reforge these conceptual tools with thanks to their designers, but with no regrets. Their effort is not lost; the rethinking of concepts is necessary in the evolution of a science (Toulmin, 1961: 101–102).

THE CONCEPTS OF SOCIALIZATION AND CULTURE

Alex Inkeles (1968) has intentionally constructed a typical example of the dominant socialization-as-internalization definition. In addition, Inkeles provides a glimpse at how sociologically constraining and deeply ingrained is the pattern of thought that underlies this style of definition. Because Inkeles can show us so much in so few words he is worth quoting.

> Despite a good deal of incidental variation, almost all the current definitions of child socialization describe it as the process whereby a person acquires the attitudes, values, ways of thinking, need dispositions, and other personal, yet social, attributes which will characterize him in the next stage of his development.

For its type, Inkeles's is a very common defintion with nothing unusual in its content; then he goes on with more about the matrix of thought that bore it:

> The social scientist is not alone in his sensitivity to the implications of current childhood experience for the subsequent organization of the personality and the public behavior of a social member. In their interaction with the child, parents and other socialization agents generally have in mind some conception of what the child is "supposed to become" and of the role which any particular child-rearing practice may play in achieving or hindering the desired outcome. In other words, both the practice and the study of child socialization are inherently "forward looking." It seems obvious, furthermore, that of the various later stages which socialization looks forward to, it is the personally relatively enduring and socially important adult stage which is the critical one to consider. Therefore, a central task of the study of socialization is to inquire into the effects which the experience of the child has on the shaping of the adult.

We should note here that there are two elements in the common definitions of socialization. One focus is on the input side, on the *process* of acquisition, and refers to what is "done" to the child; the other element stresses the *results* of the processes, or the output side, in the form of the adult person. Many students of socialization feel it necessary to add a third element . . . the social relevance of the acquired adult characteristics . . . the specification that it deals mainly with the acquisition of those characteristics which have major relevance for the particular social roles which a person must play in his status-position as a member of a given society with a specified culture (1968: 76–77, emphasis in original).

What can be learned from Inkeles? Inkeles himself makes the first criticism: such definitions are from the point of view of the initiate; they are, in his words, "forward looking." That is, these definitions focus upon the intended, ideal or hoped-for outcomes of socialization. Inkeles does not then follow this through with an analysis of how such a bias limits understanding and research by diverting analysis away from sociological process per se; he merely acknowledges the particular perspective. Then, in an almost Freudian slip, he demonstrates the bias as self-evident. Inkeles tries to say that the common definitions of socialization talk about what is done to the child, and how that then forms the adult. He labels what is done as the "process of acquisition" or the "input side." However, the process of acquisition is not what is done *to* the novice; it refers to what the novice does to *accept* experience. (The dictionary definition of "to acquire" is "to get or gain by one's own efforts or actions, as in to acquire an education.") It may seem that I am quibbling over minutiae. However, this confusing of social-nurturing activity with a cognitive process is a common error in sociological thinking. The error is related to the ambiguity associated with the term socialization since its transformation from active to passive voice. Sociologists appear to think of socialization as something done to novices by members, and simultaneously, as the changes—becoming social—a novice undergoes. A definition cannot be effective if its ostensive function includes or implies two classes of referents.

A related criticism is that what Inkeles calls the "input side" could just as easily be understood as the output side for society. Putting it in different terms, society is investing emotional and economic resources in an effort to convert certain raw material into more usable form. Inkeles thus unwittingly adds force to his descriptive criticism concerning the "forward-looking" quality of the common social psychological paradigm that generates interest in the psychosocial impact of experience and virtually ignores the structure of socializing activity. Although Inkeles does not seek the cause of this conceptual and research deficit, he tells us it exists and insists, moreover, that the situation is in need of remedy (1968: 76).

Clearly, the social scientists have not sufficiently abstracted themselves from a member's perspective. As a consequence, the viewpoint of the observer—where the social scientist should at some time take up watch—is obscured. The "observer" may see society's investment and understand it as an access procedure that opens the secrets of society to prospective members (*or to observers*).[1] Once socialization is comprehended as an access activity, the relative independence of socializing activity (socialization) from internalization becomes more intriguingly apparent.

Because so little in the way of a conceptual apparatus has been constructed thus far to illuminate socializing activity per se, and because the focus of thought is "forward looking" or that is, upon effect, the indirect relationship between "what is done" and "what results" is not often made problematic. Society does not, and cannot, rubber stamp perfect ladies and gentlemen. Quite obviously, the old stereotype portraying the sinful nature of a pious minister's children can hold true.

The second point of criticism concerns the form of Inkeles' definition but leads into deeper analysis. Socialization is commonly depicted as a process in which some social aspects of the environment are acquired by the person, and some of those aspects are listed in the definition. Inkeles included such things as ways of thinking and need dispositions; Merton et al. (1957: 287), as another example, decided that skills and knowledge were worthy of mention; both definitions admitted attitudes and values; others have thought of such things as beliefs, habits, expectations and norms. A clear objection to the form of this definition is that the length of the supposedly constitutive list is arbitrary. There is no theoretical directive that discriminates between what should and what should not comprise the list. Moreover, the items that are incorporated have no unifying theoretical substrate and no explicit interrelationships. There is a very real family resemblance between these lists and the 19th-century nontheoretical taxonomies of "culture" so arduously constructed by contemporary anthropologists. At that time culture was considered in terms of discrete material and social artifacts. The fate of these definitions was obsolescence.

Currently in sociology, it is intimated that the lists defining socialization somehow depict the stuff of culture. The ancestry of these definitions is never revealed; it may not be recognized. However, various authors may sense their definitions' arbitrary quality at times. This seems most true whenever the listing exercise ends rather ignobly with such devices as "and other," or "in short, culture." "Culture" is an important part of conceptualizing socialization theory. Nevertheless, an adequate grasp of it cannot be delivered up as a list.

The third and final point of criticism bears directly on the concept of culture as implied by the typical definition of socialization. This third point

---

[1] Appendix II provides a detailed description of the "observer's" perspective.

concerns the meaning and content of such definitions, and not their form. As mentioned, culture is implicitly, or sometimes forthrightly, represented as a conglomeration of ideas, or as ideas, norms and artifacts. Most often, the sociological perspective takes a culture to be composed of ideas—the things we can carry in our heads—and separates it analytically from behavior systems (Kroeber and Parsons, 1958). The difficulty is that these various ways of stating that "understanding guides behavior" do not offer a scheme for grasping "culture" as a practical whole. That is, how it is actors move across the social landscape and through their biographical careers in a way that suggests a continuity or organization among otherwise discrete behaviors and events. Conversely, because in experience culture appears as a practical whole, actors can judge some things to be "out of place," "unreal" or fallacious without having to memorize, in advance, all possible permutations of authentic situations. Therefore, this common definitional style does not live up to the requirements of and is disassociated from the functionalist theory that supposedly cradles it. Let us consider the problem for a moment with a different understanding for culture.

Clyde Kluckhohn defines culture as "an historically created system of explicit and implicit designs for living . . ." (Kluckhohn, 1967: 75; see also Geertz, 1974). The notion of "design" is quite helpful, especially when compared to the learning of discrete items or behavioral sequences (recall the chess analogy in the previous chapter). Take, for example, the well-documented cognitive rigidity of children about two years old. Their rigidity is a part of the syndrome known in the textbooks as "the terrible twos." Children in this age group have learned specific ways of doing parts of the daily routine and are insistent that the procedures be followed. This rigidity is reduced later in their lives. The usual explanation for the change is that when they grow older, they have been exposed to more alternatives. But what do alternatives mean vis-à-vis the cognitive organization of children? This is largely an unanswered question—perhaps especially so in sociology. However, intriguing avenues are open for exploration. For example, it may be that continued experience with the content of alternative behaviors exposes the *design* of the behavior in question. (This would be similar in terms of cognition to what L. S. Vygotsky saw as the superordination of categories of experience, or to what Jean Piaget termed a logical structure. Further, the idea of design corresponds to what I called in Chapter 2 the rules or principles organizing social encounters.)

The rigid young child has managed to decipher and then learn a discrete behavioral sequence or *a* correct *form* of behavior. The older child, on the other hand, has internalized the *rules* (design, blueprint) by which respectable conduct can be constructed. As a result, variations in discrete items become less disruptive to the child's appreciation of a situation.

Taking this explanation a little further, it might be profitably suggested that some juvenile misbehavior can be accounted for as a natural "breaching activity" (to employ a now little-used ethnomethodological term) leading to a firmer grasp of rules already possessed, but which become more apparent through the activity of their negation. Durkheim implied the same relationship when, in a social rather than a psychological context, he said that deviance functions to outline the boundaries of moral behavior. However we may wish to extend the original example, it is assumed that the rules are "out there" and further, that what "seems to happen is that the child processes what he perceives of the behavior of mature members of his society in such a way as to extract the rule systems implicit in it. This process is not a simple 'passing over' of the systems from one generation to another" (Brown, 1965: 195).

I am not saying that the learning of discrete information is not an important part of becoming a full-fledged member of society. It is extremely important, analogous to the importance of observation and data for science. Just as theory serves to organize and integrate discrete facts into a meaningful whole, so culture organizes the actor's perception of reality. Another more anecdotal example may help to give further distinction to the relationship between learning and the internalization of culture.[2]

A situation nearly everyone has encountered is the conversation in which we are left sputtering without an appropriate "comeback." We really wanted our retort to be clever and properly crushing, yet it sounded flat. Later, as is so often the case, when the time is no longer correct, a truly remarkable reply comes to mind. Wishing fervently it had been thought of when it was relevant, we save it, waiting for the first opportunity that can be construed as perfect for unleashing our newly acquired wit.

Despite this situation's commonplace character, it has some noteworthy aspects related to the distinction between internalization and learning. First, as a result of internalization, we are fairly adept at recognizing the features of situations that allow joking. Second, an internalized grasp of social situations allows conversants to know when good-natured verbal jousting, and not anger-instilling insults, is intended. Out of context, the spoken words alone might be highly insulting; however, the paralinguistic tone of the situation

---

[2]Talcott Parsons (1951: 203–205) found it necessary to prosecute an analytical distinction between learning in general (any change of state in the personality system brought about by the acquisition of "new elements of action-orientation") and internalization ("not learning in general, but a particular part of learning": "the acquisitions of the requisite orientations for satisfactory functioning in a role"). For my part, I can only agree with the wisdom of the *distinction*, if not its precise formulation, which by fiat unduly narrows the scope of that which may be learned. The distinction that I intend between learning and internalization is based upon the assumption that culture is primarily a design or blueprint that locates and organizes discrete events and activities. This is a discrimination that presents a fruitful theoretical device for clarifying the conceptual jumble surrounding socialization.

produces a joke. Third, the internalized understanding of timing allows speakers to know rather precisely the time limits allowed for a reply. We sense where and how to place our words in a conversation. Fourth, as a result of internalization we can discriminate among poor, good and remarkable requitals.

What of learning? A particular "comeback" has been learned. It is a behavioral sequence that can be woven into an appropriate future situation according to cultural prescription. The meaning and impact of this device will depend upon its sensitive insertion into the correct context. The comeback can be considered a content item made sensible by its location in a social situation. We learn the content item, but use and appreciate it as a result of internalized cultural rules.

An Anthropomorphic Model of the Individual

Springing from this perception of culture as the deep structure of society is a redeemed image of the individual—one who is neither over- nor under-socialized. There has not been a rejection of the sociological perspective wherein the person is the product of society, and just as surely persons are not viewed as independent agents whose sheer, perhaps innate, craft allows them to escape the deep influence of an internalized representation of society. In the place of either of these dichotomous versions of the individual, a dialectical tension is conceived as existing between the individual and society. This view places the burden of producing respectable activity upon the individual (in specific situations) and upon past individuals for having sustained the patterns of recognizable situations. Society is "ongoing" in the sense that its culture serves to organize patterns of relationships and events in intelligible ways. On the other hand, the behavioral events of society may also appear as episodic or, that is, taken up and reproduced during any particular interaction. The actual theoretical division creating society as either ongoing or episodic has been removed. "Episodes," "situations," "encounters," "frames" and the like may now be seen as natural cultural units rather than as unique events.

Socialization and internalization cannot be pictured in this framework as a simple, mechanistic "passing on" or transfer of discrete packages of information between the social system and the individual (personality system), almost as if parts were being assembled within a machine for its drive mechanism. Here, socialization is taken as an actual interactional display of the sociocultural environment. Internalization may be taken as an active abstracting of the cultural design and the cognitve organizing of discrete items of experience within a personal representation of the cultural design.

Socialization, therefore, is first a presentation (to the novice, through interaction and by others) of the *rules* whereby "respectable" behavior might be constructed. Secondarily, it is a presentation of techniques, maxims, trivia and all those other discrete items of information that sociologists may have listed in definitions for socialization. (It should be noted here that I intend to give final form to the definition of socialization in Chapter 4.) Implied by these two pieces of definition is that socialization is also a process occurring over a period of time. During this time the presentational activity takes place and the novice has the opportunity to practice, make mistakes and behave in a manner unbecoming a member. The socialization process is an opportunity for the individual to discover personally the design of respectable conduct and begin building his repertoire of actual content.

The linkage between the individual and society entailed by this view of culture, socialization and internalization may be illustrated by analogy. A proper analogy might depict the relationship of a mother with her child in the womb. Early in the pregnancy the child is utterly dependent on its mother, the very constituents of its body come from the mother through the umbilicus; and yet the child is an independent life. The child is genetically related to its parents and yet unique; it is virtually helpless, but its very existence (not to mention its physical requirements and growing size) has the power to change the life of its mother—and perhaps others. While the pregnancy proceeds toward birth, the child's life, as a life in a separate body, grows more able to sustain itself outside the womb. In purely biological terms, gestation is a process of physical individuation and growing independence. The mother is the source and sustenance for this life; however, the social reality of the pregnancy, with all that it might mean, is dependent on the child's being in the womb.

Similarly, during socialization there is that quality of dependence and independence in the relationship of the member to the novice. The novice can be relatively powerless in an ultimate way, yet actively influence the face-to-face process of socialization. The novice then may also inject control and power into the socialization relationship. This is to say the members' culture is not presented in a vacuum. It is presented *to* someone so that its precise quality is historically and concurrently modified in the interaction between member and novice. The content of socializing activity is thus modified by the very structure of the interaction situation. Socialization is then related to the context of its presentation.

Socialization continues and the novice comes to take on a unique identity. The novice is ever more able to reproduce a plausible version of the members' historic roles: motives, preferences and abilities become more defined. Socialization from the outset leads to individuation and autonomy, that is, an independent *ability* to participate in the construction (or disruption) of particular versions of social reality. Whether a person's activity is routine, habitual and boring or novel and constructed for a particular occasion, it bears the stamp of its cultural origins.

The underlying issue here is the notion of sociological determinism. To the extent that determinism intrudes upon socialization theory, the position holds that internalization necessarily decreases autonomy. That is, an individual's behavior becomes less random (vis-à-vis the system's expectations) as a result of the individual's internalization of a behavior-governing "program" of norms and values. By contrast, the view that one internalizes the design of culture carries the idea that culture is the basis for suggested patterns of action that may be changed, but always in reference to what has been.

PRIMARY AND SECONDARY SOCIALIZATION RAISE THE ISSUE OF SOCIOLOGICAL AUTONOMY

Discounting the functionalist's failure to cope with instances of creativity, deviance, alienation and revolution, there are times even within a "social system" when an actor is between statuses and out of roles. Recognizing this, American functionalism has attempted to come to grips with the necessity of the actor's having to manage transitions between institutions. Two major examples of such status—role changes are the youth's biographical movement from the family into an occupational role, and later, career changes between occupational roles. The socialization problem, in short, is related to an examination of mobility.

Parsons and Bales (1955) discuss what they call training for autonomy. Despite the sketchy quality of their argument, it is quite clear that they are not discussing autonomy at all. Rather, they address what the family does in order to minimize the transitional aspects of the status passage. In so doing, they attempt to show the functional continuity existing between primary and secondary socialization. They surreptitiously back away from accepting that there *is* a transition. Certainly there is the guiding thread of continuity that partly accounts for such transitions. However, it is the disruption of continuity in such transitions that originally bred the distinction between primary and secondary socialization.

For most sociologists the problem remains camouflaged either by the superficial quality of the theory in mobility research or by an intradisciplinary division of labor in which specialties do not often cross the common distinction of childhood and adulthood.

In light of what "primary" and "secondary" socialization say about the discontinuous aspects of the world (and in acknowledging what is a happenstance lack of a recognized sociology of autonomy, which could otherwise complement socialization theory), these readily accepted concepts should be examined briefly on their own terms.

In a typical example of still current usage, Berger and Luckmann speak of primary socialization as the route to membership in society (1967: 130). Secondary socialization, in turn, is "any subsequent process that inducts an already socialized individual into new sectors . . . of his society (1967: 130). A little later they relate these concepts more firmly to an established theory when they tell us that "primary socialization ends when the concept of the generalized other (and all that goes with it) has been established in the consciousness of the individual" (1967: 137). And in regard to secondary socialization, "secondary socialization requires the acquisition of role-specific knowledge . . . vocabularies, [and] . . . at least the rudiments of a legitimating apparatus (1967: 138).

A simple thought experiment can expose the paradox concealed within the apparently quite reasonable scheme Berger and Luckmann present. For instance, if parents send their toddler off to a day-care center, and the child is exposed to that "institution based sub-world," is the experience primary or secondary socialization? The generalized other is probably not present in the child's consciousness and neither is the child ready to be declared a full-fledged member of society. Still, there the child is experiencing "a new sector of society" and "acquiring role-specific knowledge," and so on.

And, in looking at a later part of the life cycle, it could reasonably be said that membership in the United States upper middle class requires a college education. Does it mean therefore that class membership in this case is not complete until graduation? That would be an unsurprising enough stance in view of the rites of passage imposed by many societies. But how then does this coincide with the appearance of the generalized other? The genrealized other, as it is usually understood, would be present before graduation; yet contrary to the theoretical wisdom, these students are not members of their class until the academic degree is conferred.

"Childhood" and "adult" socialization are used quite interchangeably with primary and secondary socialization. Still, in this context, the use of these seemingly more descriptive terms leads to a similar condition of ambiguity. When used as concepts they are nearly impossible to define. Childhood and adulthood are social statuses defined arbitrarily by tradition and convention. A search of Western history alone will show the highly variable way childhood has been defined and will even lead us to discover the invention of the intermediate state of adolescence in response to the surplus of material goods in and increased differentiation of modern societies (see Philippe Ariès, 1962, *Centuries of Childhood*). If a social scientist should attempt to ground the definitions of these terms in an established scheme of biological development, then there arises the real problem of reductionism. That is, biological development, a process with a relatively constant rate, is being used to explain the culturally arbitrary variation of an ascribed status. There is something that helps this problem but, of course, one must not claim that a change in reference, even if it is plausible, will suddenly make all things lucid and pure. However, a significant part of the problem lies in not thoroughly separating "socialization" from "internalization."

The specific difficulty is that the concepts of primary and secondary socialization are mutually defining. While there is nothing intrinsically wrong with that, in this case it encourages a sense that it is desirable to think of a type of socializing practice (e.g., child-rearing, occupational training, etc.) in the same thought with the presumed psychological condition of the novice (e.g., his consciousness does or does not contain the concept of the generalized other, or he has not internalized a set of role-related expectations, etc.) Put differently, both terms are descriptive of the stage of social psychological development on the part of the novice, while at the same time referring to the content of socializing practice. If, however, socialization (the interactional presentation of culture) is kept conceptually distinct from internalization, and the actual processes are seen as having a problematic rather than a narrow cause-and-effect relationship, then simple noncontradictory descriptions may be applied to socialization.

I conceive of these descriptors as adjectives, not as technical concepts. I propose further that sociology abandon the concepts of primary and secondary socialization. Thereafter, when socialization needs to be described within various institutional settings, it could be called, for example, family, educational and occupational socialization or, more generally, formal and informal socialization. When internalization requires some specific characterization, adjectives should be chosen to refer to the life cycle of the individual: early and late; or childhood, adolescent and adult.

These recommendations help to clarify usage at the conceptual level. They do nothing toward a theoretical solution for a theoretical problem, for, as I have alleged, these concepts are tied up with a sociology of autonomy and the mechanics of interaction. But before continuing the pursuit of this theme, the subject of Part II, some attention will now be given to the formal aspects of socialization research as it is most often carried out.

SOCIALIZATION STUDIES AS A FORM OF EXPLANATION

Empirical research in the area of socialization is done in a number of fields and with a variety of perspectives. This section, however, is devoted to an examination of socialization research only as it is carried out by sociologists, and in particular the most abundant species of that research. The interest here then is in empirical sociology wedded to the statistical exploration of the central tenet described earlier as being the foundation of mainstream sociology: that the person is determined by society.

The rhetoric and assumptions that empirical researchers commonly employ contain images of the individual and society similar to those usually associated with the functionalist school. For example, until recently it has been assumed that the regular use of physical or otherwise severe punishment on children led them toward aggressive behavior. Research consistently showed a strong correlation between punishment and aggressiveness. The causal flow from parental sanction to an aggressive dynamic in children "proved" the determining nature of society in relation to the malleable personality of youth.

It is now clear, however, that the direction of causality can be reversed. That is, aggressive children can bring harsh strictures upon themselves (Skolnick, 1978). The earlier correlations were suggestive of a deterministic model of socialization, but only because no other alternatives were explored. No one thought mere children could help to create the "society" in their lives. The child's power in this regard is now recognized (e.g., Bengtson and Black, 1973).

The overall weakness of empirical socialization research lies in the tendency of investigators to choose variables and index them without a theoretical justification beyond simple deterministic assumptions. This has led to the portrayal of a complex activity (socialization) in terms of a perplexing array of ungrounded variables, such as warmth, permissiveness, class, race, authoritarianism, father's education or occupation and many others. The choice of the word "ungrounded," means that there is no theoretical mechanism that explains how society, as represented by these variables, actually comes to bear upon the novice during socialization.

The concept of "differential association" accurately captures the researcher's style in describing socialization and in reckoning outcomes. Even though this concept is now somewhat out of date, the essence from which it is derived survives in socialization research. The concept of differential association is a perfect deterministic model for statistical measures based upon some form of correlation. Explanations of this genre attempt to show that categories of people who have been exposed to similar types of interactional experience tend as a result to produce similar behaviors. To do so, variables are created from constructs of the socializing environment and correlated with variables relating to the individual. This is accomplished in order to predict clusters of people matched more or less well along some behavioral or attitudinal dimension. Behavior is said to be "explained" by a combination of variables thought to indicate significant features of the environment. This way of thinking may be reduced to "the more people have been alike, the more they will tend to be alike." The "school effects" literature can serve here as a representative illustration.

A recurring presumption in the sociology of education has been that quality differences among colleges affect the socioeconomic and educational attainment of their students (e.g., Collins, 1971; Milner, 1972). The attainment differences have been attributed to the impact of the not easily separable effects of both "socialization" (learning and psychodynamic change) and the relative prestige of the school (Kamens, 1971; Meyer, 1972). Thus far, only small college effects have been demonstrated (Astin, 1971), if they can be found at all (Wright, 1964; Spaeth and Greeley, 1970). A welter of variables (e.g., faculty prestige, number of library volumes, liberal arts curriculum, *Chicago Tribune* prestige rating, etc.) have been sifted to discover even those small effects that have been established. Research has been driven on by the notion that college *must* have an effect, but no one really knows precisely what questions to ask of the college environment.

The power of the "college effect" and the sheer validity of previous research into that effect has recently been called into question. This development came about through investigation of what amounted to a revelation: that individual students are not randomly distributed among our centers of higher education. Accordingly, the processes of "selection" and "recruitment" can be used to explain well over half of the variance previously explained by school effects (Alwin, 1974). The recruitment and selection variables may be exogenous to a given construct of the academic environment, relating to students' socioeconomic background; or they may be linked to such interwoven exogenous and endogenous factors as ability, academic performance and motivation.

The lack of conclusive fruitfulness in these researches is underscored by results that indicate unexplained variance in socioeconomic achievement and educational achievement is much greater within college types than it is between them. This style has afforded no explanation. It is a search for regularities and a mere comparison of exquisite typologies arrived at by a laborious reshuffling of types—all toward the end of reducing error. The point once again is that the idea of "differential association," no matter how disguised in regression coefficients and path models, represents a straightforward sociological determinism embodied in a noncumulative empiricism.

As socialization research has been conducted so far, it represents an infirm grasp of the logical maxim that the inductive accumulation of knowledge cannot proceed prior to establishing some explanatory framework. A framework in this sense is a generative core of theoretical knowledge that serves as an organizing principle for research activity. Full awareness of the need to organize investigations around theory has been largely subverted in empirical socialization research by a naive belief in induction—that simply "more research" will reduce statistical error and begin to make findings cumulative. As a result, the history of socialization research has been characterized by a frantic effort to get more data and to find the *key* combination of variables (Frank, 1962; Danziger, 1971).

So too, only the inner relations among the chosen variables are considered, and this fragment of knowledge, this datum, is rarely reintegrated and made meaningful in terms of more complete theories. In practice, findings are only legitimated as they relate to other findings; they are not made meaningful by a logic of nexus with theoretical knowledge. Instead, the induction of data is received and ordered by mathematically generated models as part of the data analysis process.

Some of the purest examples of this highly inductive approach to socialization research can be found among "socialization and mobility" research. This area of research is preoccupied with the methods of constructing mathematical models and the subsequent creation of those models. Models of mobility produce macroscopic views of socialization insofar as that process affects mobility. Thus, so-called social structural variables such as father's occupation and race are related by correlation with such intervening social psychological variables as self-concept, occupational aspirations and personality. These structural and social psychological variables are assigned causal priority and their effects are measured on educational and occupational attainment (e.g., Duncan, 1966; Featherman, 1972).

The basic socialization theory contained in this modeling approach is simple: a class of experiences, indexed, for example, by father's occupation and race, lead to a certain psychology in the novice; this in turn influences the "socioeconomic life cycle" of the novice (Blau and Duncan, 1967). As simple as it is, that is the theory behind this extensive body of research. The research itself does not seek to articulate the theory further. The research merely rearranges the path models according to different values of its variables (e.g., Blau and Duncan, 1967; Sewell and Shah, 1968; Sewell et al., 1970). Methodological sophistication sometimes obscures the thin line between the parsimonious and the simplistic explanation, thereby making it difficult to say on which side a piece of research belongs. In any case, there is a poverty of theory to be found in these empirical studies.

The fault is not to be found within the *internal* logic of particular research projects. In fact, any one study may produce very nice results, clear and compelling by themselves, yet difficult to interpret or step beyond. The fault is one of the genre. The studies have tended to be overly empirical. By this I mean the same thing that Robert Merton (1957: 33) conveyed when in another context he characterized raw empiricism as guided by a "let's try it and see" attitude. Researchers have been data gatherers, not interpreters. At the expense of theory, they have sharpened their techniques of analysis. Trends and fashions have appeared in socialization studies that have centered around technique more than upon a programmatic pursuit of long-standing, clearly defined sociological issues.

A certain provincialism is created in this concentration on technique and by the sway of fashion. It is apparently uninteresting, judging by the lack of mutual citations, how the various "childhood," "school effects" and "professionalization" studies all relate to an overall understanding of socialization. Moreover, there seems to be nothing much in common between the "socialization and mobility" studies (e.g., Porter, 1974; McClendon, 1977) and those on value and political socialization (e.g., Orum and Cohen, 1973; Orum et al., 1974; Bengtson, 1975). Research activity is conducted as if researchers had forgotten that the socializing process itself should be the object of explanation rather than the relationship between variables. So long as theory, and hence the very object requiring explanation, is kept at the periphery of research, it will never be effectively recognized that research is only cumulative insofar as it is informed by and serves to refine theory. When theory is not an operative part of the research enterprise, there can be no accretion of "explained" phenomena, and importantly, no recognition of what is as yet unexplained, or which findings may be deemed "unexplainable," that is, anomalous (Kuhn, 1970).

Concerning the severe limitation of the core ideas utilized in research, various critiques have suggested two general directives for future effort, both of them primarily theoretical. The first is a call to give more attention to specifying the nature of socializing interaction (Sewell, 1970: 582–583; Speier, 1973: 138–142). Secondly, socialization research has been said to have neglected setting forth the environmental "demands" that converge during socialization (Wheeler, 1966; Inkeles, 1968). Specifying "demands" here means the careful weighing of the social forces focused upon individuals during socialization. It means determining what it is that the various structures, situations and attributions demand of the social novice.

Although these several criticisms were made some time ago, they have apparently not been seen as challenges and have themselves been neglected. Taken together, however, their worthy suggestion is that it is time to better define what "society" means when it is said that the person is a function of society.

In sum, the empirical study of socialization proves its worth but rarely as part of an accumulating body of evidence. There has been a demonstrable failure in these studies to attain clear, consistent and cumulative results. This is in fact one of the prominent findings of *Socialization* (1971) by Kurt Danziger, a book described by Hans Peter Dreitzel as "what we know about socialization." (It is a short book!) Since the time of Danziger's survey of the field, there has been little sign of improvement. (For exceptions to this rather sweeping generalization, see Bucher and Stelling, 1977; and in particular, Swanson, 1974. Both of these studies are sufficiently attentive to previous theory and research to have ferreted out crucial sociological issues in need of exploration.)

Without an available, empirically suggestive theory to reveal the potentially important aspects of society as they are manifested during the socializing process, research simply cannot proceed, except by accident, beyond the point of achieving correlations between ungrounded environmental variables and the "determined" attributes of individuals. Certainly, excellent ethnographic materials may continue to be compiled from intriguing institutional and subcultural settings. Fred Davis (1968), for example, offers an interesting qualitative description of "doctrinal conversion" among student nurses. And too, more sheerly quantitative verifications of our derivative status may be repeated forever. However, there is no inherent reason "empirical" studies should be cumulative. The links that would suddenly give a full picture of "society" are not manufactured in research; those links begin as ideas and must ultimately be dealt with according to their own logic, whether for further articulation, modification, rejection or replacement.

Where there is no explicit theory, private assumptions grow in its place. Without an explicit, public theory the readers of abbreviated journal articles cannot be told in a profound way why certain variables were chosen. With no articulated theory upon which to base an investigation, there is no public medium to convey the exact meaning of variables; too much remains unsaid. In the absence of a theory there is no objective procedure to determine what relationship one variable might be expected to have with another, or why. *Ad hoc* and *ex post facto* justifications are supplied and there comes to be no compelling reason to try to replicate another investigator's findings. Research in such an environment becomes mere data gathering; facts and findings are reports to oneself; all this effort is then justified primarily by its historicity—that is, for its own sake as a part of doing sociology.

Theories are the public guides to research and should supply a logical and plausible source of control for those who employ them. Without that control no manipulation of a precise methodology can be turned into a coherent body of knowledge. Inconsistency and confusion are the inevitable results when everyone asks slightly different questions about socialization. Concrete reality is an inexhaustible medium for exploration; as such it is a constant reminder that one cannot merely observe; the question of what to observe requires prior serious consideration (cf. Bierstedt, 1974b: 133–149, 309–321).

SUMMARY AND CONCLUSIONS

Part I has depicted some problems in the conceptualization of socialization theory in terms of the historical development of ideas relating the individual and society. The major framework within which this development took place was the continuing engagement of two competing philosophies—individualism and sociologism.

Some of the major events in the development of socialization theory were brought out in Chapter 1. These events include the discovery of the concept of "society" (or social structure); the discovery of the concept of internalization that explains how abstract structures affect concrete individuals; the appearance of a psychological focus and a stress on the outcomes of socialization rather than the process itself; the diminished importance of human nature as a source of behavior and a correspondingly increased significance attributed to the "personality" or "self"; a growing conviction as to the plasticity of individuals in the face of persistent social forces that work to shape the self; the appearance of the "oversocialized man"; and, finally, a dogged belief in sociological determinism.

Chapter 2 was devoted to exposing some theoretical issues brought to light by an individualistic reaction to the image of the individual associated with a narrow determinism and functionalist sociology. In essence, those issues revolve around the inability of all present sociological theories to explain autonomy (or creativity) without denying the concepts of social structure and internalization.

Chapter 3 was built upon the two previous chapters, but emphasized some different dimensions of current difficulties in socialization theory. First, it was said that the present definitions of socialization are inadequate or, more precisely, the concept of socialization is ill-conceived. The socialization-as-internalization model of the concept directs attention away from process and toward outcomes (i.e., internalized values, norms, etc.). Put in a different way, this model confuses socialization with internalization, a linguistically awkward position at that, and contributes to deemphasizing the study of socializing activity. The model fails to provide a vocabulary for making the process of socializing activity distinct from the internalization of culture. It was also argued that the socialization-as-internalization model typically implies a deficient concept of culture. This conception of culture proves faulty because it demonstrates no unifying theoretical tie among its components (e.g., values, beliefs, expectations, skills, norms, etc.).

At this point it was suggested that a more adequate idea of culture would define it as a "design for living," or as a system of rules that suggest routes to producing respectable behavior. This definition of culture was intended to tie in closely with the chess analogy and the discussion of rules earlier.

Culture is thus displayed in social activity—including socialization. It is by abstracting and internalizing this infrastructre that the novice can organize discrete items of behavior, take on an identity rooted in the culture, and reproduce society.

Such a concept of culture allows for the retention of "social structure," "internalization," and the position that "the person is derived from society." The resulting theoretical individual is neither under- nor oversocialized, but is instead "anthropomorphic." That title would certainly be redundant in the absence of the previous extremes; however, it now signifies an actor capable of "sociological autonomy."

Chapter 3 stressed the need to redefine and reformulate our present approach to conceptualizing the problem of socialization. The chapter ended on the note that pure, hard-nosed empirical research will not, because it cannot on its own, bring about progress toward redefinition. A devotion to technique, method and research for their own sake reduces the researcher's ability to be equally creative as a theorist. The role of research is to discipline theory, not to overwhelm it.

Both the empirical and the theoretical approaches to inquiry in socialization have failed to delineate the *medium* through which the ability to produce society is transmitted from member to novice. I have suggested in Part I that the first steps toward portraying the medium of transfer lie in taking culture as a design (or system of rules) for living.

Part II, which follows, seeks to take lessons from the past. The concept of socialization presented in Chapter 4 turns the focus of attention toward the process of socialization as seen from the perspective of an observer.

As the observer's perspective is assumed, three things are accomplished with one effort. First, the relative independence of socialization from internalization is highlighted. Second, the "forward-looking" bias of the definition of socialization (as given by the socialization-as-internalization model) is dropped as socializing activity becomes the object of interest. Third, the perspective of the sociological observer offers a stable reference point for theory formulation (see Appendix II).

Socialization is defined to keep it distinct from internalization, and my theoretical argument is presented as a solution to the major issues in socialization theory. Therefore, the concept of culture as formulated in Part I is brought forward as the basis of the theory, but modified in terms of the "context" as a natural unit of culture. The "context" then can also be understood as a unit in the *medium* (culture) through which the ability to reproduce society is transferred from member to novice.

Chapter 5 works out the social psychology of the "anthropomorphic individual" implied by the understanding of culture as a rule system with units called "contexts." Chapter 5 then produces a lengthy discussion of "sociological autonomy" and the related concepts of social power and control.

PART TWO

CONTEXT AND AUTONOMY IN SOCIALIZATION THEORY

CHAPTER FOUR

RECONCEPTUALIZING:
A SOCIALIZATION-AS-INTERACTION MODEL AND THE CONTEXT

REDEFINING "SOCIALIZATION"

In cognizance of the demonstrable problems of past efforts, the general goal of this book is to achieve some initial steps toward a reorientation and reformulation of socialization theory. Now that the foundations have been laid, this chapter will inaugurate that process.

To begin, a new definition for socialization is needed (see Appendix I for a logic of definitions). The current socialization-as-internalization model offers too many weaknesses. I propose to relocate by definition the area of concern for socialization inquiries. The new definition will suggest a socialization-as-interaction model. That model directs inquiry toward the interaction that constitutes socialization, rather than continuing to encourage attention to the psychological outcomes of the process. The model will be oriented by the revised definition of socialization, the perspective of the "sociological observer" (see Appendix II), and the theoretical relationship between activity and culture. Three principal ideas are illustrated by this model.

The first idea is that "society" is displayed to the novice during interaction, that is, *mutually influencing activity*. The point is that, to the observer, all individuals "count" as producers of society.

Second, this display functions, with or without conscious intention, to promote change in the novice, who helps to forge the socializing experience. It is the case that society cannot replicate itself precisely within the novice, because at the least the novice's own frame of reference plays upon the meaning of interaction. The personal perspective, at a given time, limits how the novice is *able* to grasp "society."

Only recently has there come to be a recognition of the relative power and control the novice also brings to bear in managing the content of socializing interaction. Certain empirical studies have found that each participant is influential in lending content to the interaction constituting the socializing process. This particular reciprocity between member and novice is observable in all phases, from family to occupational socialization (see, for example, Bucher and Stelling, 1977; Skolnick, 1978).

Apparently, not only does society impose itself upon the person; each of us is part of society in the making, just as our perspectives and capacities inevitably color what we internalize. Society does, nevertheless—through its members, by its culture and with its resources for power—present the novice with a ready-made and perhaps the most obvious form of society.

Owing to the complexity of human-situated activity, it is curious that members' reproductive ability can be accomplished without the advance rote memorization (learning) of all possible permutations of an authentic situation type and all likely situations. Faced with explaining the possibility of concerted action by actors within a complex environment, individualists, however modern, tend to rely upon the metaphysics of "freedom." That is, the complete responsibility for achieving culturally recognizable order is laid upon the skill of the individual. This is an unexplained feat, beause it does not fully admit the aid of preexisting cultural structures that would otherwise relieve some of the burden from the individual.

It is at this point that the "context" becomes an important consideration. The context is a simplifying and limiting mechanism in interaction (and therefore in socialization) that lends parsimony to any attempt at making sense in a situation. So then, the third idea underlying the socialization-as-interaction model is that the content of interaction (what it is participants actually do) makes up the surface structure of society. The surface structure is, in turn, informed by and displays the fundamental cultural design in society. The position will be developed that the content of interaction is organized at a deeper cultural and specific contextual level. The context is a fundamental quantum of the social order, and as such it has a special relevance for socialization theory: the context is the organizing unit of the culture presented to the novice. Elaboration of the concept "context" fills the principal part of this chapter. However, let me first broach the new definition of socialization.

The New Definition

From the point of view of the "sociological observer," socialization is a non-random access activity to historical society. Granting this, the new definition of socialization is: *socialization is the activity that confronts and lends structure to the entry of nonmembers into an already existing world or a sector of that world.* (See Appendix I for a logic of definitions.)

A new world so entered does not exert an irresistible hold on the novice. Perspectival differences, outside influences, creative skepticism and limits to the socialization process itself may act to limit or reverse entry. The anthropologist need not "go native" to gain deep insight; the "society of captives" can hold greater influence than the prison chaplain's lectures; the rebel can work out a system of unbelief; the Azande child thrust into the modern world because of a missionary's zeal for enlightenment; and a tutor in the French language may just barely point out the design of life in France. The possibility of resistance, misunderstanding, nihilation or alternation always exists.

This definition portrays socializing activity per se as establishing *a tension between two social types:* the *member* and the *novice.* This is intended to imply five things. First, there are relative power, prestige, status and other social differences existing between the "member" and the "novice." Second, the novice is somehow within the sphere of influence of the member's world. Third, a variety of "others" may intervene in socialization. This qualification incorporates particularly the important and often powerful function peers of the novice (and others) can have as value makers, deflectors of members' purposes, clarifiers, and as subjectively valuable measures of cohort progress. Fourth, there is a high degree of asymmetry between objective (the member's world) and subjective (novice) versions of reality (Berger and Luckmann, 1966: 163). Fifth, that social learning, internalization, self-formation, identity construction and the like are not confined to socializing contexts. They may also occur in so-called *norm-building* institutions. Norm-building institutions simultaneously create members and the institutional relationships. Berger and Kellner (1970) discuss "marriage" as a norm-building institution, but the concept applies in any case where several individuals encounter one another as "strangers" and rather naively enter into a persisting relationship. A developing institution requires that a structure of reciprocity be established and that participants negotiate their roles in relation to one another, that, in short, membership be constructed. Norm-building institutions can thus be contrasted with ongoing historical institutions, the structure and roles of which preexist a new generation of potential members. Members are added to a historical institution by socialization and by the novices' personal accommodation to its conditions. By definition, the process of socialization requires a historical institution and, *ipso facto,* the tension between "member" and "novice." Once again the distinction between socialization and internalization facilitates discussion of empirically available processes.

I believe the new definition avoids the faults and perspectives associated with the socialization-as-internalization model, in addition to encouraging my intended orientation. The definition retains the logical grammar of the English word "socialization" by defining it again as a concept in the active voice. The active voice is achieved without any of the older "shaping" and "moulding" connotations; that is, socialization is not depicted as either mechanistic or deterministic. The new definition points to socializing activity and process, and is not "forward looking," focusing on outcome. In fact, outcome remains problematic because socialization is taken as *interaction* and the novice is therefore granted a certain efficacy in constructing the content of the socializing experience. Importantly, the new definition does not attend strictly to formal or intentional socialization; it allows as well for casual, incidental socialization. Thus, the realization is encouraged that socialization contributes to the formation of society as well as the individual. In addition to these attributes, socialization defined in this way suggests the theoretical elaboration (and empirical investigation) of the way society is presented by socialization. I also believe that such theoretical work stimulates the development of a social psychology equal to understanding the "anthropomorphic individual" (e.g., see Chapter 5).

SUPERFICIAL ACTIVITY IN SOCIALIZATION
Ritual, Seriousness and Play

The new definition of socialization suggested that interaction with a socialization content structured the entry of a novice into a world. This is not to say that the welcoming structure need be purposively devised. Human social life is naturally structured; it is a nonrandom, if arbitrary, construction maintained very simply by living. Typicality greets a person on all sides and it is this natural structure of life's conduct that allows the novice to gain understanding and a faith in the normative order.

Socializing activity, like all interaction, requires a standard definition of the situation and concentrates the attention of participants upon the objects to be held in common. Emile Durkheim in his concern for the development of the mind (1965, 1974) and George Herbert Mead with his interests in the interactional antecedents of the self (1925, 1962) visualized the interpersonal and physical environment as tied together in a structure imbued with commonly objectivated meaning. Both theorists saw the environment quite literally as a conversation of mutually orienting activity carried on via gestures, symbols, representations, concepts and emblems. Socialization is no different except, once again, that the social types of member and novice are involved and the canopy of standard definitions is being extended to cover potential members.

Some modes of socialization occur more obviously than others. The most obvious socialization occurs when a degree of ritual is injected into the interaction between member and novice. These occasions are the more formal and purposive aspects of socialization such as can be found in schools, religious groups, vocational training facilities and in "the family." Here focused attention is demanded, versions of reality are vouched for by members and a certain degree of conformity (or "success") is expected. These expectations are carried forth as sanctions intended to correct the novice's reproduction. It matters little whether the sanctions correct table manners, spelling, titration procedures, general comportment, or a formula for the trajectory of a moon vehicle in an engineering sciences class. In any of these cases a subjective version of reality is doubted, corrected, and directed toward "ritual purity," that is, symmetry with objective reality.

Demands for ritual purity and corrections of attempted reproductions of reality evoke strong sentiments. Indeed, any time realities are tampered with, protests are sure to follow, whether such cries come from the Jews attempting to repress and murder St. Paul for his proclamation of Christian theology, Albert Einstein in his heated quarrels with the probabilistic statements of quantum theory, or our own vexation at being told we are wrong or have been misunderstood. Disputation of subjective or objective taken-for-granted reality is emotional. Similarly, if we discover that a reality of ours is based upon lies, either a mere lie or the more deeply invested world projected for us by interaction with a con man, the jolt of discovery provokes emotion.

However, these are only the serious forms of emotion: those generated by coercion, necessity or our collision with others. Play and joking evoke emotion, but tend to vent the tension of serious endeavor. Their reality in the human world is a sign of creativity; they are also situations so defined that activity does not have its usual consequences. In play we can try out behavior and roles without the import associated with serious life: name calling can be fun. Joking is similar. If examined closely, joking, or more precisely a "joke," is much like a lie. A story is told, or a sentence or word is used with intent to deceive. A certain view of reality is constructed. Unlike the lie, however, the jolt of discovery comes with the punch line and brings laughter rather than anger. The punch line tampers with reality by rapid switching or distortion (Wentworth, 1976: Appendix), yet because the situation is defined as a joke, insult is averted. Some jokes can, of course, go too far. They are thought to be *out of place* due to the extent they blaspheme respectable realities or because of their injurious "practical" consequences (e.g., the practical joke). In these cases, the definition of "joke" is simply impossible to apply because activity *oversteps the bounds of acceptable interaction.* I believe "play" and "joking" to be sufficiently similar to capture both behaviors under the title of play.

The status of the novice has its specific aspects of seriousness and play. Stages of attaining competence, comportment and demeanor or other requirements that demonstrate the engagement of novices may often be seriously watched and enforced by members' expectations. Overall, however, novices live in a play world. The responsibility of novices for their acts is diminished; and their individual stature as a full person is not recognized. Accordingly, for example, children may wander across property lines and around neighbors' houses without invading that territory. The juvenile court system is an institutionalized recognition of the diminished responsibility of childhood. And generally, members allow the novice of whatever age to practice and make errors in a way disallowed for those with assumed competence. Play can then be seen analytically as a prelude to the ritual of serious life (cf. Mead, 1962: 144–147, 149–173; also see Piaget, 1948: 1–3, 95–103).

Emotion is no doubt an important ingredient of the socializing process (Brown, 1965; Berger and Luckmann, 1966). Out of that emotion strong ties are forged and order emerges; the order may be one of conflict or of solidarity, but it is order. This is in keeping with Durkheim's important analysis of ritual activity (1965). Durkheim claimed that society is "made and remade" periodically through ritualized conduct because it affirms the ideal, evokes strong sentiments and creates social ties. Durkheim is pointing out that "common action" creates social reality; therefore, that society is above all "the idea it forms of itself"(1965: 470) and a unique synthesis of particular consciousness (1965: 471). I generalized the Durkheimian position by finding ritual in other than religious settings (see Goffman, 1967; Collins, 1975: 161, 162). "Ritual" in this broad sense happens when mere social reciprocity is transformed: "This is how these things are done" (Berger and Luckmann, 1966: 58–61). Types of socialization can thus be said to approximate ritual in act and function.[1]

Expressive and Instrumental Competence: An Exhaustive Typology of Activity

"These things," as Berger and Luckmann referred to the superficial content of socialization above, can be discussed in general terms. Max Weber, the sociological typologist par excellence, was one of the first to offer an analytical

---

[1] Berger and Luckmann (1966: 58–61) make the intriguing claim that the (ritual of) socializing activity is a vital constituent of the legitimation and objectification of the social order for *members*. Subsequent to acting as agents of the social order during socialization, members stand as committed to the order they have just, perhaps repeatedly, affirmed and explained.

description of socialization content (1958: 426). He wrote of two "pure" educational models at opposite ends of a continuum. At one pole he placed education that "awakes charisma." Granting the cultural distortion that must come as I "disenchant" the concept of charisma, education toward charismatic awakening can be understood as a communication of the qualities of a certain type of character—a character suitable to a particular status group. Charisma amounts to a capacity for social grace or individual felicity of self-presentation. This type of education provides the novice with tools for developing *interactional or expressive competency* (vis-à-vis a particular social location). By interactional competency I mean the use of customs, habits, subtleties, nuances (both verbal and nonverbal) in the activity by which we naturally express the qualities of our relations with others. Relative to the next type such expressive activity is *unspecialized* interaction.

Weber's second type, at the opposite extreme, was *specialized*, expert training.

> Specialized and expert schooling attempts to *train* the pupil for practical usefulness for administrative purposes—in the organization of public authorities, business offices, workshops, scientific or industrial laboratories, disciplined armies (Weber, 1958: 426).

This is socialization toward the acquisition of *technological or instrumental competence*; it is training in which the novice is expected to learn to manipulate the hard and soft elements of a society's technology. Instrumental competence then relates to the task of marshaling the means to achieve some end.

Weber says of these two educational ends:

> Between them are found all those types which aim at cultivating the pupil for a *conduct of life*, whether it is of a mundane or a religious character. In either case, the life conduct is the conduct of a status group (1958: 426).

As is usual with Weberian "pure" or "ideal" types, they are constructed for the reason of radical contrast. He does not insist they exist, only that they each embody the essential aspects of some real-world activity. Furthermore, the continuum represented by the polar types is intended to be exhaustive of human activity. Socialization or any interaction strikes some balance in its content, but contains elements of both types. And, too, as is not unusual with Weber, the empirical typing of a given instance of activity depends upon the observer's empathetic understanding (*Verstehen*) of the actors' intention. This is true because meaning is not obvious. A single activity may carry several meanings. For example, the "natural" expression of our relation to others may be interrupted, and used consciously, instrumentally, in some task of persuasion such as diplomacy, bullying or the "wiles of feminine charms." Likewise, the unadulterated use of procedure or technique may in certain contexts convey that our relation to another is cold, distant or one of "detached concern" (Merton et al., 1957: 74; Lief and Fox, 1963). By treating an actor instrumentally that person is reduced and acknowledged only as an object.

The chameleonlike nature of Weber's two concepts make them analytically useful to us for several reasons. We are reminded that no human act in a natural setting carries an obvious and necessary meaning apart from the context of its presentation. Social objects and activity become meaningful as they are interpreted in a process of objectivation (see Sorokin, 1943, for an enlightening early discussion of meaning in society and sociology). A conversation of activity weaves social reality from the threads of the externalized intentions and relevancies suggested by participants. Certainly too, Weber indicates that respectable conduct is always a synthesis of the tasks we pursue (instrumental activity) and the qualities of our interpersonal relations (interactional or expressive activity). Given that Weber's two types make empirical sense (and I believe they do), a recognition of the inherently ambiguous nature of activity and the virtual inseparability of instrumental and expressive conduct plunges us directly into the complex relativity of reality construction. We are thus led to wonder how meaning-producing activity finds sufficient anchorage in the inescapable seas of relativity for *shared* meanings and institutions to emerge.

The transfer of shared meanings is clearly the essence of the dual processes of socialization and internalization. Meanings emerge from the fundamental structure of society: culture as displayed in instrumental and expressive activity. The ability to produce objective meaning, and therefore reproduce society, is transferred through the medium of cultural rules. Activity becomes meaningful in interaction, even in the face of the relativity of knowledge, simply because it is securely rooted within such a framework.

To summarize, instrumental and interactional competence is an expression of culture in activity. Socialization as a form of interaction presents the rules for context construction. Internalization is the process in which the novice actively extracts the rule systems implicit in that interaction. As a result of internalization and the ongoing negotiation of interaction, instrumental and expressive activities can be woven together into the fabric of a reality cradled by macro- and microstructures in an unfolding location between a past and a future.

FUNDAMENTAL STRUCTURE IN INTERACTION: THE SOCIOLOGICAL CONTEXT

World-Building and Limits

The concept of the context starts with the obverse of Max Scheler's assumption that human being begins in a condition of "world-openness" (1976: 39). The other side of this supposition is that our survival is dependent upon world-building. We replace world-openness with a cultural closure. This latter position echoes the common phrase that we are creatures of meaning—creatures who demand meaning from our environments. The sociological twist avers that human existence is cultural. That is to say, the production of reality takes place in localized environments composed of social groupings in particular physical settings. The physical world and its inhabitants are transformed into a sociological place by the production of a structure of meaning.

Reality is not only here and now. Durkheim was mindful that reality exhibits the qualities of historicity and geographic transcendence (1965: 29). That is, the immediate situation is the site of reality construction that joins the past to the present and reaches out to include the cultural residue of interaction in other places. Moreover, the implications of activity for the future condition of persons and institutions may also contribute to the construction and negotiation of reality in the here and now.

A world, or a culture, is vast and provides the general boundaries and design for the lives of those who participate in it. The limits of a culture extend beyond the limits available to the individual by introspection and beyond the routine, immediate needs of any particular individual life. With respect to individuals, the limits of a world are typically framed by their direct participation in specific institutions. But even many of the institutions common in the daily lives of individuals have larger scopes of relevance than required by the individual's roles. Be this as it may, however, the subworlds inhabited by individuals are not precisely coextensive with their institutional roles and role expectations. These are more like simplifying devices and resources than they are perfect boundary markers.

A role may suggest the value of certain lines of activity at particular times, but the limits of roles are not necessarily the limits of realities, even when we face actors in reciprocal roles. Accordingly, a "boss" and his "secretary" can interact as man and woman, as sexual partners, and discuss Beethoven or the price of tomatoes on "company time," all the while retaining the authority and deference relationship of their formal organization and, in between, accomplishing their expected tasks. This is, of course, obvious common sense, yet the concept of role does not strictly admit to out-of-role behavior while actors are in role relationships.

Life is lived within the realities created by interaction and draws on a variety of social resources, including roles. Interaction creates a version of reality that participates in the larger world. Realities nest within larger, mediating realities, thereby demonstrating a fundamental cultural unity in life. Larger worlds encompass and make intelligible potentially innumerable reality productions (Giddens, 1976: 144).

"World-building" at the philosophical level describes the production of a cultural habitat. World-building actually occurs in the highly circumscribed situations lived through by individuals who are related to one another, sometimes immediately and sometimes distantly across space and time. However, we simultaneously participate in and produce the macroworld by our activity in the microworld. Our activity is thus an expression of the culture we bring into interaction and the version of reality actually produced in a specific place.

Context is the term I have chosen to use in connection with the activity of world-building. The context could be variously described as a "zone of relevance," a "semantic field," "semiotic space" or a "system of references" that mediate activity. That is, at any one time we limit the range of likely perceptions (and activity) according to the rules whereby contexts are organized. The context is not, however, a subjective view of reality; rather, it is the version of reality created by the interaction of individuals in the total environment. That version of reality may be the very real context of a battlefield or may be an "experientially real" fantasy produced by storytelling or a stage play. In these latter cases we willingly move into the fantasy, laughing and crying, loving or hating *as if the fabrication were real*. The literary description of this contextual phenomenon is the "willing suspension of disbelief." The context is the world as realized through interaction and the most immediate frame of reference for mutually engaged actors. *The context may be thought of as a situation and time bounded arena for human activity. It is a unit of culture.*

As a concept, as opposed to its empirical manifestation, the context is a unifying link between the analytical categories of macrosociological and microsociological events. Aspects of the macroworld are drawn upon by individuals (often not in a conscious fashion), in constituting the reality of the microworld and so tend to reproduce the larger world. Likewise, the concept of context accounts for both structural continuity and situational uniqueness. Institutional roles, discrete items of knowledge, and the like, are treated as available resources, rather than as determinants of conduct, in realities constituted according to the internalized rules of context construction. Stated differently, situations are produced that are both representative of institutions and idiosyncratic in terms of the motives and capacities of context constructors.

Related Concepts

Ideas similar to but not identical with the "context" have been available to sociology for a long time (e.g., Baldwin, 1911: 29; Malinowski, 1923: 306; Znaniecki, 1925: 79–80; Thomas and Thomas, 1932). In fact there have been numerous attempts to speak of the organization of elements of experience. The "social situation" is probably the root concept in these matters. This concept has been used in many ways but the original and core meanings take two things into account: (1) that the situation is based upon the *mutual understanding* of participants:

> the situation is social not in virtue of . . . external relations, but solely in virtue of the understanding of the place and function—the desire, the opinion, the purpose—of all the actors by each, (Baldwin, 1911: 29)

and (2) that actors in a situation *selectively* draw upon, perceive and define prior statuses, meanings and physical objects for incorporation into the situation:

> The concrete milieu in which the action begins furnishes only the raw material upon which the subject draws to shape his own practical construction and interpretation . . . taking practically into account only that aspect of them (i.e., the raw materials) which . . . is apt to affect the course of action . . . . (This process) is seldom a reflective, conceptual one, usually it manifests itself only in the practical meaning which the elements of the situation assume for the subject (Znaniecki, 1925: 79–80).

The first point, that regarding mutual understanding, is too restrictive. It defines out of existence contexts that may well be bathed in ambiguity, distortions of reality and misunderstanding. The concept of context includes both mutually understood and confusing constructions of reality. The second point concerned the selective and "created" nature of situations, but failed to emphasize the interactional and negotiational qualities of such reality construction. Most of the early views of the "situation" were conceived from the point of view of the actor. For example, "the definition of the situation is the *subject's* organization of experience" (i.e., act of interpretation). By contrast, the context is about the organization of society.

Goffman (1961a; 1964; 1974) has worked out some excellent extensions of the important idea of situated selectivity. By design, his useful work is oriented mostly to describing what he calls "focused interaction," or the activity of people who acknowledge one another as mutual participants in a face-to-face encounter that sustains a single focus of cognitive and visual attention (1961a: 7). The kernel of his work on selectivity in focused encounters is directed toward elucidating the notion that interaction frames its own small world in the midst of the larger environment. Interaction, Goffman says, creates a "cell membrane" that contains and preserves the integrity of meaning and activity within that membrane. The membrane "not only selects but also transforms and modifies what is passed through it" (1961a: 33).

Goffman's attention to "focused interaction," however, excludes the analysis of contexts in which all participants are not mutually available to the "naked senses"; tends to omit consideration of happenstance, unfocused encounters (1961a: 7); and treats a good many activities that disturb the "focus" as "out of frame" (e.g., the "flooding out" of laughter; the recognition of the unintended second meaning of double-entendre or "leaky words," allowing attention to run through the membrane; and "collusion" or temporary huddles by some participants). The context is a more general concept than "focused interaction"; it includes an encompassing system of rules that make their fundamental division between contextual definitions of respectable and deviant reality-producing activity rather than activity that is merely in or out of "focus."

A "respectable" context begins when interaction begins, but ends when activity becomes apparently "deviant" relative to the prior definition of the situation. At this time the situation is redefined, once again establishing a context. (Other "natural" terminations occur when the rules of a context suggest that it is over, i.e., the conventions of time limitations have been exceeded—see Hall, 1959—or when the correct conditions are no longer present, e.g., the participants are no longer active or present.) This does not mean that a similar context cannot be reestablished once the deviance is removed, controlled, or when participants reunite. In any case, *some* context will ensue so long as people interact. The point, however, is that a "context" mediates much of the activity Goffman considers to be disruptive of the narrower "focused gathering." Goffman's concept fits inside the "context" as a special subset of reality-producing behavior.

And as a final note in differentiating "context" from other similar concepts, I will mention that it is more inclusive than the "awareness context" used by Glaser and Straus (1967). Their notion refers only to particular, mutual biographical knowledge in a situation, and not to the full array of constituents that may be seen as significant in situated reality construction.

Quickly summarized, a context, however rich or poor in content, arises whenever people act toward one another as social objects. The context is a concept concerned with the social organization of situations and is presumably universal in social gatherings. By referring to "situations," I intend to mean that interaction creates a bounded, or partially segregated social place that is the immediate frame of reference for participants' activity. The notion of a "focused gathering," so perceptively studied by Erving Goffman, is an important subset of context activity because the continuum represented by unfocused to focused gathering points to a range of increasing responsibility of mutually engaged actors for their context of activity.

Although the context is a *sociological* artifact, a context is appraised from different *individual* vantage points as well. We cannot think of the objective context as deterministic of subjective experience. It is suggestive of experience. If experience is considered as attention directed upon (apperceived) objects, the relationship between the subjective perspective and objective contexts may be understood as problematic and never deterministic. The constitution of subjective experience depends upon what may be called—in a very appropriate and self-explanatory metaphor—the "attentional ray" (Schutz, 1970b: 4, quoting Edmund Husserl). Within and outside an objective context many events are occurring simultaneously. The context guides attention toward its evolving themes but the imagination and senses *can* range beyond its boundaries: sometimes we would rather think about lunch than attend to our business.

Empirically, however, we do not experience the absolute freedom in our everyday lives to "leave" the contexts in which we find ourselves, directing our attentional ray willy-nilly according to passing fancy. Once we present ourselves in a context, we assume a socially recognized responsibility for its coproduction. Thus, we can be urged by social control to issue an acceptable presentation. It is usual then that the conversation of activity furnishes ongoing support to the social world being realized within the context. A given context ends when it is redefined, whether because of unaccountable deviance, by rule, or for the reason that actors are no longer socially present.

Focused, Unfocused, Routine and Problematic Contexts

The mere coming together of individuals is sufficient to provide a context, *if* there exists a coercive or morally influential *sense of mutual presence*. People oblivious to one another do not form a context. On the other hand, even so unfocused a gathering as people together in a full elevator is the site of people concertedly producing a respectable version of that reality. Riding in elevators is socially uncomfortable because of the crush—the public invasion of personal space—but the occupants do their best to keep the situation respectable by avoiding insulting, unwarranted touching. The individual occupants of the elevator are responsible to the situation—hence, to a group of strangers. It is possible for a gathering to be without "focus" and still generate a sense of mutual presence. The gathering, therefore, serves as an immediate context for the activity of individual participants.

Routine unfocused gatherings evoke typical definitions of the situation that allow participants to attain an initial understanding of their mutual relations. That is, a definition of the situation provides information on rules for the use of that social place (see the discussion of definitions at the beginning of this chapter). An inaugural, relatively "context-free" definition of the situation gradually becomes more "context-bound" as the exact properties of the context become apparent (see McHugh, 1968: passim, on the process of "emergence"). The definition of the situation may be represented as a catalyst for participants' expectations and activity. As interaction evolves, the original definition may be modified, marred by inappropriate conduct, or even discarded in favor of another as might be indicated by the evidence of immediate experience.

Nonroutine, that is, problematic gatherings exist whenever the occasion itself is novel or the participants are naive (e.g., novices). A nonroutine gathering means that participants cannot apply typical definitions of the situation. Hence, the rules for the "correct" use of that place remain obscure. By default, as it were, the situation comes to be defined as an undefined situation; anomie prevails. Unlike the routine gathering, participants do not know who they are in relation to one another; or, that is, which identity to front. They are nervous without structure and uncomfortable in one another's presence (e.g., Sampson, 1971: 1−3). By defining the situation as undefined, participants are largely thrown back on their own biographies for guides to suggest activity (Wentworth, 1976: 23). A nonroutine, unfocused context of strangers will remain temporarily anomic. With no history or purpose, a gathering can produce little more than a sense of mutual presence and a scattering of personal realities.

The production of reciprocal relations out of anomie is not always the democratic process this discussion may have so far implied. Even the passing appearance of "leadership" can provide a simple structure and start the reduction of anomie. Purpose, commitment, values and authority bring people out of themselves and give different social weight to various lines of activity. Moreover, it would be exceedingly rare to find that all participants in a context are absolutely naive. Experienced members have achieved some competence in greeting strangers, bringing them into reciprocal relationships. In short, the organized world outside the context "leaks" in through its experienced participants.

Two notes of caution are in order at this juncture. First, the argument describing the context has thus far been implicitly directed against sociological determinism. Nevertheless, individual efforts should not be seen as the prime sources of social order, even if leadership and charisma are taken into account. The context separates itself from individual efforts, because when these are placed into the stream of history (ongoing interactions), the complex interplay of resources produces an unintended and unique reality. The creation of a sui generis reality occurs even in minimum complexity of two-person relationships (Berger and Kellner, 1970). The sociological history of a group is the history of negotiated meanings.

Second, the opposite of anomie is not necessarily consensus, when consensus means simple agreement or similar viewpoints. People may, in effect, "agree to disagree" (Scheff, 1970: 363). The key to grasping the difference between order and consensus lies in the parallel difference between *shared* and *common* reality. To share an apple, for example, cannot mean taking the same bites. What is merely convenient for the slaveowner can be a degrading task for the slave. Likewise, having shared rules or order, a shared definition of the situation or a shared reality does not declare a condition of common values, but instead may be best thought of as a kind of compatibility, a working relationship coordinating and containing differences in subjective vantage points. As an example, submitting to authority can well be *mere* reciprocity, either because no realistic alternatives exist, or because, "He who has the bigger stick has the better chance of imposing his definitions of reality" (Berger and Luckmann, 1966: 109). Assent does not prove similar and positive evaluation.

The Rules of Context Construction

That subjective perspectives and resources can be interrelated to achieve order among creatures of meaning, creatures whose every move is potentially ambiguous, requires that certain ground rules appear in their interaction. That is to say, a cultural substrate of rules emerges to define the present limits of the acceptable.

Next I want to give the rules of context construction, so that I can thereafter refer to them in a more defined form. They will be presented as "context-free" rules. Context-free in this case means that the rules are given in terms of four problem areas for *any* context (boundary formation, internal order, resource use and identity, and legitimacy) and not in terms of what interaction in a *specific* context produces. As each rule is given, it will be illustrated in terms of a specific context.

Many recent students of social life have written of the necessity of describing actors as rule-guided and therefore starting the understanding of society by seeing it as a system of rules (Goffman, 1961a, 1974; Garfinkel, 1967; McHugh, 1968; Cicourel, 1970a,b; Harré and Secord, 1973; Mehan and Wood, 1975; Giddens, 1976). Despite the popularity of the idea, almost no one has characterized the rules required to put life situations together. Erving Goffman (1961a) is an exception to this, but the rules he derives are incomplete, covering only the production of the situational "membrane." Others (e.g., McHugh, 1968; Cicourel, 1970a,b) might write as if they have come up with rules. However, what they actually attempt is the description of certain cognitive strategies (e.g., "searching for normal form"). That is, these authors are concerned with the subjective organization of experience, not the *social* organization of society.

Perhaps the best way to demonstrate these rules is to show how they come to life in situated behavior. In order to anchor the rules in this way, I will use the repeated observations of a single type of setting. An excellent study accomplished by Joan P. Emerson ("Behavior in Private Places: Sustaining Definitions of Reality in Gynecological Examinations," 1970) will be the source of the examples drawn upon to illustrate the rules of context construction.[2] The advantages of using a study, as opposed to a single observation or an anecdotal account of some setting, stem from more than a concern for validity and reliability. In reporting her observations, Emerson attempts to highlight the typical features of reality construction during pelvic examinations. Further, her theoretical perspective serves to highlight the precarious, ambiguous and negotiated qualities of reality. Her analysis thereby unwittingly indicates the presence of an underlying rule system that helps to sustain the respectable air of certain behaviors in spite of several strongly competing interpretations and requirements. Thus, the exam is already presented in typical form—the translation from multitudinous real-life details having been already performed by Emerson.

Emerson describes the pelvic exam as an attempt by participants, especially the medical staff, to sustain a medical definition of the situation in the face of a strongly competing sexual connotation that could easily be attached to man—woman intimate touching. The *ambiguity* of that act is highlighted, as its meaning is transformed—with some strain—from one context to another. In relation to these competing definitions and, moreover, out of a concern for the dignity of the woman, the exam situation requires that the physician maintain a shifting balance between purely *instrumental activity* and *expressive activity*. Here, instrumental activity easily becomes an offensive invasion of privacy if the person is ignored. "In short, the doctor must manage to convey an optimal combination of impersonality and hints of intimacy that simultaneously avoid the insult of undue sexual familiarity and the insult of unacknowledged identity" (Emerson, 1970: 85). The participants in the exam take space, time, objects and relationships and use them according to certain rules to produce understanding, activity and order in a respectable mix.

1. *The rules of context bounding.* These rules establish context duration, the range of appropriate subjects and activity, and the etiquette of recontextualization.[3]

---

[2]Emerson's study was based on the participant observation she carried forth in a general hospital as part of the work for her doctoral dissertation. Emerson's interpretations of the gynecological examination come primarily from 75 observations of male "physicians" (ranging from third-year medical students to senior doctors) on an obstetrics-gynecology ward.

[3]Goffman expresses boundary production activity in terms of three rules: (1) *The rules of irrelevance* consist in the systematic exclusion of perspectives, objects and actions from the sphere of interaction; these rules work to exclude from the participants' attention all those things that are not to be treated as situationally real (1961a: 19). (2) *Realized resources* are those things that rules of relevance treat as situationally real (1961a: 26). (3) Transformation rules are both inhibitory and facilitating of things that pass the membrane. They suggest what modifications will occur when external properties intrude upon and are given expression "inside" an encounter (1961a: 29). I group these three rules under one general heading, then go on to define aspects of context formation in addition to boundary production.

Every context begins with the sense of mutual presence; a focused encounter begins with mutual recognition—a greeting—including even purposefully ignoring one another. The context's ending is often signaled by various verbal and nonverbal cues that indicate the time is up. In between these temporal boundaries, the context unfolds. When people meet for a "gynecological examination," the ensuing interaction is bounded in various ways. Lay persons, and especially those intimately related to the patient, are excluded from the setting. There is often a nurse chaperon in the room to enhance the idea of the doctor and patient relationship and to downplay the possible connotation of "a man and a woman alone in a room." The exam takes place in "medical space" with all the appropriate equipment and clothing. The patient, too, is removed from her street clothes and "draped." The discussion is circumscribed to include only medical talk and what amounts to polite chatter. Sexual matters are not discussed unless they are directly pertinent to the details of the exam. Even doctor−patient eye contact is avoided to control its suggestive character. Any signs of sexual arousal on the part of the patient are either ignored or perhaps discounted as "ticklishness." The "seductive" patient may be controlled by humorously suggesting that she is not serious in her implications. In brief, the exam is cut off from the wider world where other definitions of the situation would interfere with isolating the gynecological reality.

2. *The rules of context ecology.* Ecological rules pertain to resource use, self-boundaries and identities, and the generation of appropriate deference and demeanor.

The bedside manner must shine through in order that the patient's identity as a patient remain clearly defined. A "patient" is *more* than an object of technical interest; a patient is a person who submits to medical procedure; he or she is a *someone* whose right to dignity is not denied by an examining gown. During the exam, it is primarily the responsibility of the medical personnel to convey propriety and technical efficiency. The doctor as a bearer of authority carries a particular obligation for directing the scene respectably. However, all participants accept some of the burden of producing the roles that contribute to respectability.

Thus, when an inexperienced third-year medical student finds some difficulty in balancing the professional and personal concerns, the nurse or an experienced patient might assert her responsibility to the context and cover for the student's lack of finesse. Routinely, the patient's responsibility includes deference to the cues projected by the staff and the maintenance of her poise. The doctor's authority to touch the patient intimately is tied specifically to the context of the gynecological examination and does not extend beyond the appropriate time-bounded zone. The patient's self is somewhat "eclipsed," as

Emerson put it, during the touching, almost as if in due respect for the highly precarious nature of this reality, "her facial expression should be attentive and neutral, leaning toward the mildly pleasant and friendly side" (Emerson, 1970: 83).

> 3. *The context grammar.* The contextual grammar governs the arrangement of objects and persons in space and time and the etiquette for generating themes, including the meshing of interactional and instrumental activity.

Modesty and willingness to expose oneself are both important ingredients of the exam context. According to the medical definition of the situation, medical personnel have "the right" to touch and view what others do not. However, the strict application of the medical definition threatens the precarious balance of expressive and instrumental activity. The medical definition is a task and time-bounded part of the entire context. There occurs a time when, if a patient remains modest and reluctant to uncover herself, she threatens the contextual "right" of the staff to view her. However, if she extends to period of exposure, then she is "immodest" and will be subject to control. Within the context, a conversation of cues modulates modesty and exposure.

A respectable exam smoothly meshes medical procedure with rituals to express a concern for the patient. "It is insulting to be entirely instrumental about instrumental contact" (Emerson, 1970:85). Some acknowledgment of the otherwise intimate connotations of gynecological touching must occur. The doctor accomplishes this more by radiating concern or occasionally sacrificing the task for the "requirement" of gentleness than by the lingering contact of hand and eye.

> 4. *The rules of context legitimacy.* Legitimacy rules aid in discovering the authenticity and morality of contextual themes by allowing the correlation of experience.

Much of the activity that, in the case of the gynecological examination, serves to generate the context boundary also gives off signs indicating the legitimacy and special place of this context among all others. It is this array of special signs that differentiates gynecological touching from an invasion of privacy related to rape and generally mutes the sexuality of the scene. Furthermore, the actions of the staff assure the patient that what happens to her is required by impersonal rules of procedure and is in no way related to the staff's personal pleasure. Medical jargon desexualizes the scene still further, while at the same time the doctor implies that this exposure and touching is what is done *here, other* people go through it all the time, and all this is done in the interest of the patient's health.

The preparation and draping of the patient prior to the doctor's entry into the examining room separates the doctor and patient during a possible suggestive activity. Use of the doctor's title of address is a constant reminder of the rightness of the activity he is performing. Further, the title is a means that diminishes the *man* occupying the role of examiner.

Whatever social tension that lingers during the exam is eased through bypassing direct and personal reference to exposed areas. Consequently, the doctor might use the definite article rather than a personal possessive pronoun when referring to sexually defined areas of the body. Patients in turn resort to euphemisms, saying for example, "It's so uncomfortable *down there*."

All in all the legitimacy of the context is sutained by the participants drawing upon the socially acceptable character of the exam and the personal distance each person maintains from the activity: "The man is a doctor performing his rightful duty"; "He is not examining me, he is looking at it"; "He is keeping me informed about my status as a patient"; "This is all respectable activity."

The four types of rules for context construction sketch the structure of culture. The structure of culture by itself is context-free. Together, the rules speak to the problems of interacting and reality construction found any time persons come to a sense of mutual presence. Within their framework one finds foundation for all of the traditional sociological concerns. Some of these concerns, implied by the material from Emerson's work, include the division of labor; latent and manifest social functions; member identification; the regulation of the capacity for collective activity; the idea of socialized conduct; membership control; socialization and the structural possibility for satisfying personal needs and purpose. In their context-free form, the rules clearly outline the simplicity of the cultural design that suggests what sometimes is the dazzlingly complex array of activity performed by actors.

It is precisely the simplicity of the design within, if you will, when associated with the world-limiting conception of the context, that contributes to the significance of the "context" for understanding interaction and socialization. The world may be entered at all by the novice because the combination is reasonably simple to the lock controlling its secrets. It is the grasp of the cultural design upon which social life is predicated—the mastery of a relatively small array of *types* of problems common to all contexts.

Outside of a specific context type, the rules do not produce suggestions for activity; they are abstract descriptions of activity, more suitable for the sociologist than for the budding member. The rules are, of course, not presented to the novice context-free. They organize, but are interwoven with the activity of life situations.

I will now turn to a discussion of the relationship between the superficial and the fundamental structures of society.

SUPERFICIAL AND FUNDAMENTAL STRUCTURE

The superficial structure of society consists of the persisting pattern of (meaningful) relationships that can be resolved into components called roles. The superficial structure is what sociologists conventionally call social structure. Theoretically, "social structure" is a descriptive concept. Manifestly, it is constituted by interaction. Each actor's part in the interaction utilizes (is composed of) a personal style of interactional and expressive competency. Further, each actor in a structure is typed. The social knowledge of that type or role is correlated with values, expectations and normative activity that reproduce that role, reproduce role relations, and hence, reproduce the social structure. This is the macrosociological view of society.

Social structure is real. The concepts of social structure and role are useful and powerful descriptors of the demonstrable persistence of beliefs and practices. Some difficulty arises when these concepts are pushed too far and asked to explain how people live. The definition of "role" is either too limited or too slippery to be of more than supplementary use to the observer of the microsociological scene.

There are virtually no limits to the number of roles that can be found in society. The list can go from male and female, to husband, wife, father, mother, and child, to the multitude of occupational roles, to positions in voluntary associations, to the thousands of further roles one could name. Within the medical establishment alone, in addition to doctor, nurse, hospital administrator, pink lady, and so on, the number of specialist technicians is so large and multiplying so rapidly as to literally defy accounting (Enos and Sultan, 1977). Therefore, in some respects the concept lacks parsimony.

The "front-stage—back-stage," "role—out of role" division presents perhaps the most serious difficulty to the theorist—observer. Closely connected to this is the differentiation of organizations into their formal and informal components. That is, every formal organization is accompanied by the shadow of an informal network of members. The problem is clear-cut. Even if there are *at least* these two ways of thinking about the performance of actors, is it not the case that actors continually slip into and out of their official roles during the day? Take as an instance the two office managers at the water cooler who are talking over the virtues of a football team. Are they doing front-stage business or have they lost their work roles? Again, does the mere act of a boss smiling at a secretary in a *friendly* way dissolve momentarily the role of boss? Or, does this sort of formal—informal division multiply the already existing and "limitless" number of roles by a factor of two? How does personal style really affect "role"? How do the wide-ranging topics of conversation, unrelated to strict role performance, affect the relationship of an individual to a role? Can more than one role be occupied and fulfilled simultaneously? If so, how many?

The questions grow absurd as the nice macrosociological concept begins to drown in the furious details of microsociological situations. (It was these details, remember, that fathered the neoindividualistic interpretive reaction to traditional sociology.) However, one more question remains: Where is the sociological unity of life to be found in real-life detail?

As already discussed, the context is the site of reality construction; it is also the medium of this constitutive activity (see Giddens, 1976: 121, for his concept "duality of structure"). When considered as the medium of intersubjectivity in microsociological gatherings, the context should be understood as a system of generative rules that unify the activity of participants. However, the context considered as a sociological place is the basic unit of the social order. The reality created in terms of its rules serves to mediate and organize interaction as it proceeds. The context serves as a framework for subjective meaning, objective reality and activity.

The rules of context construction are not generally explicit in life situations and are not consciously called upon. Internalized, they suggest a range of possibilities, some of which *may* be consciously weighed: Should I do what my mother told me or should I do like my grandfather used to do? Contextual rules are thus *constraining* and *enabling*, but they are not deterministic. It is upon the basis of the internalized and shared rules of context construction that surface activity is organized. Society is thus reproduced as rules; understanding and activity are continually brought to the shared context. For members the reproduction of society is natural; it cannot be too strongly emphasized that this reproductive process is routinely unapprehended. Routine reality reproduction is not the product of immediate creativity. Most situations and definitions preexist engaged actors; they need only "assess what the situation ought to be . . . and then act accordingly" (Goffman, 1974: 2). At any rate, creativity and situational uniqueness are more likely to occur in surface activity than in the fundamental structure of contexts.

The context is a *shared* reality production or reproduction. Strictly speaking, it is not a *common* experience. Individuals continue to participate in a context from their own subjective vantage point. The individual enters the context by coming to a sense of mutual presence. Thereafter, it is assessed and then defined on the basis of purpose, knowledge and the significant setting (see Burke, 1969).[4] From the time a sense of mutual presence is achieved, each participant contributes "intentions" to the context by activity (or "studied" inactivity). There ensues a conversation of activity among social

---

[4]Keep in mind that the context concerns the organization of society and not of experience. Therefore, the structure of the interpretive act itself is beyond the scope of this book. Only its briefest mention is necessary here to engage individual subjectivities with the context—a *social* construction.

objects. Motives, lines of activity and values arise in relation to the context of participant actors. Reality is "talked through" (Berger and Kellner, 1970: 61) in a mutually orienting fashion.

The subjective perspective of the context is externalized and objectified during interaction and through expressive and instrumental activity. What people do in their activity is mediated by the context in the form of "realized resources" (Goffman, 1961a: 26–29).

Realized resources are the sociological qualities of the context, that is, *things treated as "situationally real."* These *things* can include such qualities of the context as roles, authority, identities and reputation, threats, promises, favors, expertise (and knowledge in general), the past, the future, etc. The list is virtually endless, depending upon the degree of abstraction. I have mentioned some aspects of the context associated with traditional sociological analysis, things such as authority that have no existence outside a relationship, but nevertheless are very real.

The important idea here, in relation to the context, is that these qualities are part of a relationship. An actor does not possess authority as some inherent quality. Authority enters a context because of a shared recognition of it in a relationship. Authority cannot become a realized resource in the presence of skeptics. Likewise, a role may fade in and out of immediate contextual relevance as a conversation of activity is pursued. This refers to the *selective* nature of contexts, spoken of previously in this chapter and noted by earlier generations of sociologists (e.g., Znaniecki, 1925; Thomas and Thomas, 1932). In other words, the context does not hold all possible resources, whether they be the physical features of the setting, verbal and nonverbal activity, or sociological "things," as equally relevant at all times; only some become realized resources.

As society is being reproduced in interaction, elements of the macroworld such as roles, role relations, authority, the state of the economy, and so on, impinge on the context. Microworld qualities such as leadership, identities and activity also impinge. The context selectively incorporates and objectifies these potentialities in terms defined by its generative rules. The potential qualities of the world are merely resources drawn upon by actors in context construction.

Once again, it must be emphasized that context construction is natural for actors. It is a (background) given for members that does not require the special efforts of the actor as creator. We are, however, conscious, purposeful creators of reality who individually contribute our selves to society. Because of our reflexive ability, we can take hold of ourselves and attempt to be instrumental in the course of events. Again, however, we most often try to do so in familiar or routine ways. We negotiate our personal style into the context as one of many resources.

Problems, problematic situations and accident are the roots of creative world-building activity. Florence Nightingale created a new profession because of a dream. Thomas Edison invented the electrical future. The vision of Werner von Braun influenced the spending of billions of dollars in the United States space industry.

Creativity is deviance at worst—ignored at best—if its author cannot negotiate the creation to within the respectable limits of the world. The world prepares the author; the author must also prepare the world. Instances of independent codiscovery (e.g., the steam engine, the concept of internalization as discussed earlier) demonstrate that we are prepared by society. The Greek of 52 B.C. who deduced after observation that the earth was spherical and who could not prepare his world to accept even what was true illustrates the bounded nature of reality and the requirement that resources be negotiated into reality. Truth and necessity are not obvious. Creativity is sociological.

Primary Contexts

The advantages of the sociological explanation offered by the idea of culture as a design for living and the context as unit of culture are several. The context provides a way of thinking about the connection between what people do and their relations with others. Further, the concept places "mere" activity in relation to superficial social structures and their components. By the device of the context, we may see how activity receives its fundamental organization and how even creativity is context bound. Stated differently, the concept of the context explains how culture intrudes on behavior encouraging us to reproduce society. Even one of the most complete traditional statements of the relationship between culture and behavior fails to explain their nexus (Parsons, 1951, 1966; Parsons and Shils, 1951). The idea of the context allows for situational uniqueness and continuity. The critique of sociology by neoindividualistic interpretive sociology was very serious, almost reaching the heart; the "context" shores up sociology against such attacks from the microsociological level, providing a stronger place for the very central concepts of "social structure" and "internalization."

There is also the important addition of parsimony. All contexts face the same four possible "problem areas": (1) boundary formation in time and space; (2) the internal ordering of activity and artifacts; (3) resource use; and (4) legitimacy. Granting this significant degree of commonality and using concepts already discussed in this chapter, society can be portrayed by relatively few context types. Table 2 thus helps to summarize graphically the following: the relation of surface activity (expressive, instrumental) with actors' approaches to a context (play, seriousness); and further, it ties in the general type of gathering (focused, unfocused) with the sense of mutual presence (routine, problematic). All of these superficial qualities serve to frame conceptually the several context types. I will call them *primary contexts*. The context types are delimited by descriptions of surface activity. This description is what a sociological observer could see and represents the *display* of culture available to the novice during socialization. Thus, Table 2 represents the parsimony of explanation and the relative simplicity of depicting the cultural design made possible by the concept of context.

The simplicity of the world is important in understanding how the novice can quickly master the fundamentals of respectable social participation in the face of the myriad details of life situations—indeed, how it is possible to become a member at all. A novice needs to internalize from personal experience of society the four common "problem areas" as they apply in eight context types. Repeated observations on the part of the novice give the experience necessary to extract the cultural design from the superficial structure. The *particular* experiences of the novice's world provide the raw material for the repertoire of activity that will be expressed as a degree of cultural competence. Activity is the means to express culture and culture is the organizing principle behind activity.

Novices may *learn* words, behavior sequences and other discrete items of information and use them in interaction. If the novices' experience has been insufficient for them to have extracted the design from social life, their use of their learned repertoire will be disconnected and awkward. Further, the internalized design of culture helps novices retain learned information. (See Brown, 1965, on language acquisition; Berger and Luckmann, 1966, on "sedimentation"; and Becker et al., 1961, on the anchoring of medical school basic science facts in clinical experience.)

The major division in Table 2 is between Routine and Problematic mutual presence. That division is particularly germane to socialization theory. The routine world is the typical world of the member's everyday life. Mistakes, misunderstandings, ambiguity and problems occur, but within a known framework. Interpretational and interactional difficulty subsides in the wake of "aligning actions" (Stokes and Hewitt, 1976). The world is fundamentally a familiar place. Members are able to reproduce society from the cultural tools at hand.

The problematic world, by contrast, is unfamiliar; expectations and responsibilities are uncertain or changing. The qualities of reciprocity in relationships are yet to be negotiated into a stable objectivity. Society cannot be reproduced; it must first be produced.

For some or all of the reasons listed above (depending upon particular circumstances), the world of socialization is problematic. Surely, novices may become familiar with their socializing environment—the world constructed

TABLE 2. Primary Contexts

		TYPE OF GATHERING			
		FOCUSED		UNFOCUSED	
TYPE OF MUTUAL PRESENCE		expressive/ unspecialized	instrumental/ specialized	expressive/ unspecialized	instrumental/ specialized
ROUTINE	Play		THE REPRODUCTION OF SOCIETY		
	Seriousness				
PROBLEMATIC	Play		NORM-BUILDING OR SOCIALIZATION		
	Seriousness		(THE PRODUCTION OF SOCIETY)		

by socialization—but so long as the tension between the member and novice remains contextually relevant, the world presented by socialization remains problematic. The problematic world has the same range of context types (see Table 2). However, they remain opaque until novices have created their part in them, even if that part is one of rebel and destroyer.

The world of socialization is a minimum world when compared to the members' domain. Among members as a status there is a functional recognition of incompetence on the part of the novice. As a result, novices are led through a series of minimum worlds that they *can* produce with their limited degree of internalization and their small repertoire of activity, and with their subjective frame of reference out of symmetry with the historical institutions in their surroundings.

Novices are located in a minimum world and may pass through a series of them as their competence progresses. The novices are typed as eligible (competent) to be introduced to the experiences of various subworlds. Of course, all persons are typed, whether on the basis of ascribed or achieved status. Typing, or "selection" as it is often called, is significant in the socialization career of the individual and in achieving an economy of member production.

Selection functions to channel types of actors into types of socialization experience. For example, males are socialized to be men, peasant babies to be peasants, "selected" premed graduates to be doctors, and so on. Selection is an ordering and simplifying activity through which categories of nonmembers are deemed eligible to confront certain categories of socialization (see Etzioni, 1961: 154, for discussion of "selectivity"). By "ordering and simplifying" I mean that novices are selected according to some (achieved or ascribed) criteria in an attempt to match resources and resource potential. Matching novices in this way reduces the range of socialization activity expended in "remedial" work. This reduced expenditure of effort affects the resource allocation in society. And, on the interpersonal level, it means that assumptions and expectations about persons in either the status of novice or member are more easily institutionalized, thus allowing for an economy of effort in member—novice interactions.

SUMMARY

The cultural context of interaction shows a sociological environment naturally circumscribed, yet not strictly determinate of activity. All participants in a context, accordingly, possess a responsibility for the reality they produce. There are no second-class citizens in the production of human reality, only deviants in the *re*production of historical society. In keeping with this position, the socialization-as-interaction model gave the novice a role as a co-producer of socializing contexts. The model allowed further that the personal perspective of novices refracts their actual experiences of socialization.

Thus, an asymmetry exists between the cognitive frameworks of the member and the novice. Socialization reduces this asymmetry, helping to ensure that society will be reproduced. As the novice passes through the various minimum worlds of socialization, recruitment and selection act to constrain further the degree of asymmetry between member and novice to within expected limits.

The socializing context is a description of society as manifested during socialization. It is the means through which societal "demands" are conveyed to the novice, simplified by the various organizational and other tendencies to limitation in the resource structure of a socialization context. The medium of transfer is the set of rules for context construction. These rules are the fundamental structure that serves to organize and make intelligible surface activity.

The "context" offers a parsimonious means to penetrate society's complexity. Once again, in spite of the many social types or roles, in spite of the vast knowledge empirically available, for the novice (the member and the observer—theorist), life's social situations can be organized in terms of a few primary contexts, the ease with which the novice is able to penetrate through to a context's fundamental structure being facilitated by its character as a minimum world. Moreover, all contexts face the same few types of "problem areas" (outlined by the rules of context construction). It is postulated then that the novice, on the basis of an inherent "world-building" capacity, extracts the culture necessary for societal reproduction from the surface social structures demonstrated in interaction.

CHAPTER FIVE

CONTROL, POWER, AUTONOMY AND THE SELF IN SOCIALIZATION

INTRODUCTION

I will endeavor here to produce a social psychology equal to the anthropomorphic model of the individual suggested by the "context." The theme throughout concerns establishing sociological autonomy as the imprint left by society upon the person.

To accomplish this, the chapter will begin with an examination of power and control. The discussion will of course build upon the socialization-as-interaction model. Socializing interaction is but one kind of interaction. It shares the defining characteristics of all interaction: *mutual* influence. Furthermore, interaction is sustained and given content by the participants' use of social resources. At some times interaction is more problematic than at others. The emerging order in problematic interaction is a more concertedly negotiated order than that of routine situations. Mutual influence, resourcefulness and negotiations imply social control and power relations. *Control and power are fundamental and necessary in the description of all interaction.*

I intend to construct a theory of socialization compatible with a general account of human social life. It would make no sense theoretically to isolate "socialization." Therefore, the discussion of control and power in this chapter is general before it is specific. These concepts are first discussed as concepts. This part of the argument summarizes many of the qualities attributed to "power" in sociological literature. Then, in consideration of these attributes, the concepts of control and power are related to one another *as they appear in interaction*.

How do they appear? Weber provides a preliminary reply, "All conceivable qualities of a person and all conceivable combinations of circumstances may put him in a position to impose his will in a given situation" (1964: 153). In this statement Weber is essentially writing about the possible configurations of resources in social situations. It is during socialization that rules for the typical use of resources in control relations may become internalized. The less naive the novices, the wider the range of resources they may make available to a socialization context, and the greater the novices' (theoretical) potential to countervail and refract the presentation of historical "society."

Usually throughout these problematic negotiations the historical reality of the members' world remains integrated—in spite of the so-called generational invasion of barbarians. The novice may well command the resources to influence the content of socialization; however, the resources at hand are limited by the "minimal" quality of the socialization context. And in fact, those resources are derived from a preexisting society: socialization occurs in a perhaps reified context, held together by the imposing structures of historical realities.

We must then speak of a common asymmetry of resources between members and novices. Notwithstanding, it is merely an asymmetry and not the complete determination of a novice's experience. Purposefully and otherwise, novices establish their influence with the resources available to them. The argument in this chapter will hold that attributions of resources to novices during socialization (identity ascription), as instances of control and power relations, affect self-formation through a reflexive appraisal of identity. Control and power relations lead to social self-control—that is, an autonomy grounded in social experience. Socialization, then, develops primitive reflexivity into sociological autonomy, a characteristic necessary in "cultured" beings.

Such a psychology can be formulated without violating either the spirit or the letter of classic sociological theories. They were written, after all, in the very shadow of individualism. Using the perspectives of Erving Goffman and George Herbert Mead, along with some ideas from Karl Marx and Emile Durkheim, I will undertake to extend certain common ground among these theories in a way suitable to the requirements of the context. Durkheim will prove to be the theorist most concerned with showing the evolutionary and developmental place of autonomy in his theory of society.

In light of these matters, a social psychology might do well to start with the theory of control and power. The concepts of control and power easily bear further discussion. The present analysis will start by examining "social power" because what is said about power can be applied to social control. Furthermore, I have found definitions for power to be more forthcoming, clearly stated, and as a group, offering a rather complete picture of the various manifestations of power. This leaves the tasks of discovering what power (control) is; how it enters relationships; the sources of power (resource control); how power and control are related; the social psychological bases of control and power; the role of autonomy in control and power relations; and finally, how these concepts are related to socialization.

REALITY, STRUCTURE AND STRUCTURATION
A Summary of the Attributes of Power

We may begin to explain the link between control and power by first summarizing, in the following eight statements, various descriptions of power to be found in the literature (in addition to what follows, see Lukes, 1978: 633–676 for a thorough discussion of power):

1. Power is said to be the result of an at least temporarily held controlling interest in certain resources originating in the subjective, objective, material and symbolic realms (Weber, 1964: 153; for more detail on the Weberian resources for power relations see Figure 1). The "bluff" may well be the archetype of the *social* power relation.
2. Power can be said to be the property of social relationships per se rather than residing in one party to a relationship. This property has social psychological implications. The self has been imbued with meaning in terms of the generalized other. The self may be taken as an object: that is, a person may enter into a social relationship with the personal self and act toward the self in a willful way (Mead, 1962: 154 fn, 155 fn). From this it can be inferred that the individual may enter into power relations with the personal self when it is held in a (reflexive) relationship.[1]

---

[1] This is not a startling revelation if it is remembered that unconscious social *self-control* is the appropriating mechanism of socialization in the Parsonian scheme.

An example can still help to clarify the connection between resource control, social relations and power. For example, a person controls the awesome resource of a doomsday machine, but if that resource is concealed from others—that is, it does not enter into relations with others—then that person has no social power, only the power of death, which ends all actions rather than influencing their course. It may be, however, that this person has exerted extreme control over personal actions to hide all evidence of such a dangerous machine, in which case that person has used self-discipline (in a power relation with the self) to retain this fearful secret from the world.

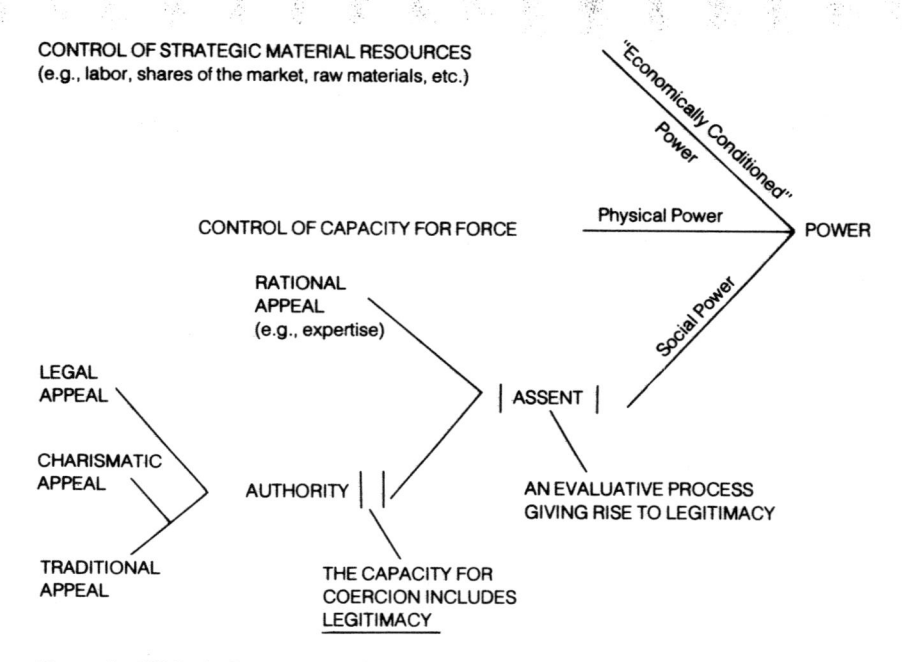

Figure 1. Weber's Conception of the Sources of Social Power

3. Power is said to arise in circumstances in which there is or has been a choice point: Weber (1958: 180) referred to the determination of one's will and Bierstedt (1950: 735–736) spoke of shifts and adjustments in social structure.
4. Power exists as a potential as well as arising in action. We might call this condition of potential "power by relevance," in which action is affected by the moral authority of an institution without any necessary threat of overt social control (with broad interpretation, see Rose, 1967: 47); Crespigny, 1968: 193; Marshall, 1969: 146–147; and Berger and Berger, 1975: 80). We may then act according to or be affected by our conscience. The social scientific equivalent of "conscience" is internalized social self-control.
5. Power is said to arise in and change the course of interaction and thereby affect future realities (Lasswell and Kaplan, 1950; Mills, 1956; Parsons, 1957; Weber, 1958). Power, therefore, is embodied in action affecting the "negotiation" of reality.
6. Power relations need not be exclusively hierarchical (in the sense of a permanent hierarchy) or unilateral (Wrong, 1968: 674). There can be rapid changes in the control of the resources for power and a "balance of power," which brings a stalemate or forms of reciprocal influence.

7. Either an individual (Weber, 1958: 180) or a corporate actor (Parsons, 1960: 180–183) may control the resources that bring power.
8. Conflict is not a necessary part of power relations; it is a contingent one (Giddens, 1976: 112; and compare Weber, 1958: 180, with Weber, 1964: 132).

These eight points may be brought together to describe *power appearing as a relative, potentially shifting control of resources which could affect the outcome of relations when nonroutine situations generate a choice point where action can be constructed.*

The position I am assuming in my understanding of power is basically Weberian, with some added refinements and a theoretical requirement to deal with social control. As such, what I have to say is quite the reverse of "An Analysis of Social Power," a famous paper written by Robert Bierstedt originally appearing in the *American Sociological Review* in 1950. Bierstedt permits himself to disagree with Weber's position with respect to the relationship between power and various resources for power (what Weber occasionally called the "means of power"), one of which is authority. I choose authority as an example because both Bierstedt and Weber have paid it considerable attention. Weber's position was that authority was a resource that when legitmated in a relationship (assented to) became the basis for imperative control—a specific type of power. For Bierstedt, on the other hand, force is the basic resource and "power is the ability to introduce force . . . ," or "Power symbolizes the force which may be applied" (1950: 733). Furthermore, in formal organizations power "dissolves" into authority; thus it becomes the role of authority to symbolize force or which has the ability to introduce force. Power is somehow transformed.

This point of difference with the Weberian scheme derives from two more basic dissimilarities. First, Bierstedt assumes that power "arises only in social opposition of some kind" (p. 735). Weber's position is that conflict always includes power relations, but that the exercise of power does not imply conflict or even resistance. (Compare Weber's definition of "power" (1958: 180) with his definition of conflict (1964: 132), paying special attention to the word "even" in the definition of power.) The second dissimilarity is that Bierstedt says that power ("hypostatized from the adjective potential") is "always potential: when it is used it becomes something else, either force or authority" (p. 736). That is to say, power is a capacity, and is never able to *appear* in interaction. For Weber, power itself arises in communal relations in the act of imposing one's will upon a situation.[2]

I accept the Weberian position as a fruitful starting point, but can only

---

[2]Translation is more art than rote technique and quibbles are always possible; let me assume this privilege of argument because Bierstedt seeks some legitimation for his position from the roots

agree with some of Bierstedt's peripheral insights. The idea of power proffered by Weber is etymologically and conceptually tied in with action, whereas Bierstedt has a small, closed semantic system built especially for "power," which cannot be connected immediately to a theory of human conduct.

An Overview of the Theoretics of Power

Power in functionalist sociology is the disembodied capacity of social structures, in particular societal and organizational systems. Power grows out of the dependence of individuals upon the system, but it may be exercised by agents of the system (see Olsen, 1968: 184; and Parsons, 1960). In this scheme, the basic role of power in the social system "is for the protection and perpetuation of boundaries and patterns of social relationships—or the ensuring of internal order" (Olsen, 1968: 185).

In other words the exercise of power gets things done; it accomplishes goals in accordance with the dominant and consensual value norm complex. This is simply a logical extension of the principle of interdependence upon which systems theory is built; that is to say, *social activity has consequences* in an action system, because it *is* a system of interrelated elements. It is the essential power of the system that constitutes selves and determines conduct—through socialization.

In a way strictly limited to the analysis of systems, this is a satisfactory use of "power." Power is, after all, frequently associated with the politics of societal and organizational interests. Nevertheless, the deficiencies in this approach are threefold. First, it is too restrictive of the circumstances in which power occurs. Social power is a more general concept (see Weber, 1958: 78–79, 180, 228–235; 1964: 153, 324–423). Control and power relations are simply the result of bringing social resources to bear upon the course of interaction (Rogers, 1974; Giddens, 1976: 53). Second, this use confuses a social resource—the status of being an agent for a societal or organizational system—with the role of a conduit through which the reified system's power flows toward some corrective end. The third shortcoming is the most serious; it harks back to the contradiction in the functional scheme wherein the completely determined person must also be the creator of society. In the case

---

of the English word, "power." "Power" is a translation of Weber's word "Macht." The ancient Latin origins of Macht are not "potential," but rather to crush or beat or repress. (A related word in Spanish, "macho," was originally defined as an ax or hammer; its present-day diminutive is "machete.") It seems then that Weber and we English speakers—if only strict, nonmetaphorical, nonidiomatic uses are counted as Bierstedt does—are talking about slightly varying conceptions. (It is interesting to note in this regard that the physical sciences use the concept of power as a rate of doing useful work. This once again links "power" with transformative motion.) Thus, while Weber can speak of "naked power," Bierstedt finds he must say "naked force," because in his lexicon only force can appear in interaction.

of an actor "wielding" power, the specific problem is the source of motivation.

Within the functionalist construct, the "system" has needs that it attempts to realize by imparting a (socialized) functional reliability to its wholly appropriated actor elements. Thus, the system's needs possess actors for the reason that they are part of the system. If the "dead" system is the fundamental reality, the actor an element in the system, and the system's "needs" are one and the same with the actor's need dispositions (the system's needs constituting the actor's), where then can the motivation come from to act with power for the system? Nowhere. As has been so often said, this is an anthropomorphic and reified view of a social structure and an emasculated version of the human actor.

The structure cannot truly have needs, interests or motivation; it is instead an ensemble of relations that presents certain opportunities, and in which the interests, needs and motivations of people take on form—even to the extent of motivations to destroy the structure itself. Simply, without the concept of sociological autonomy power cannot exist in a social system. For whatever sociological resources may be involved in power relations, it is at root a social psychological and interactional phenomenon.

What then of power in interpretive sociologies? In the first place, the concept is infrequently used. Offhand, this is a curious circumstance for analyses containing purposeful individuals and negotiated realities. The ideas of purpose and negotiation seem a fertile soil for inserting a discussion of social power and control. However, other parameters of this general approach virtually disallow the introduction of "power."

"Power" deals with the practical consequences of actions. In interpretive sociology action constructs a meaningful, rather than an objectively practical, reality. The analysis is always wedded to the "here and now" as a set of conditions for action on the part of an individual (or, how the world appears from the actor's viewpoint). Hence, a course of action is not examined insofar as it is a realization of will that affects social objects. "Purpose" is thus diluted and transformed to an inferred characteristic of others—a mere part of the total situation to be accounted for in an actor's interpretive process. (Refer again to the earlier discussion of "situational adjustment" and "commitment"; and compare Wilson, 1970: 700.) Likewise, "negotiation" is more like a throwing out of suggestions in a company of peers than a politics of interest and power (see Giddens, 1976: 31–32, 53). As a result, some theorists interested in the microecology of situations have introduced *conflict* as the fundamental principle of human action (Lyman and Scott, 1970; Collins, 1975). And although power and conflict require will (or autonomy) and resources, power does not imply conflict or even opposition (Giddens, 1976: 110–113). Further, "power" most assuredly does not require the theoretical necessity of reducing the multidimensionality of human relationships to the single dimension of conflict (Collins, 1975, attempts no such reduction);

control and power may become attached to relationships of cooperation, consensus, loyalty and competition.

Furthermore, consider the interpretationist's conceptualization of social structure—structuration. Structure pictured as an emerging order in unique situations makes it difficult to reconcile certain continuous properties of relationships—for example, authority. Authority, for a person in "a position of authority," is an important resource that can bring control and power into relationships with others. Although authority requires assent, it is not created of the moment, but rather it is drawn upon by situated actors to anticipate the responses of others and as a factor in interpreting the situation as a whole. Contrary to the interpretationist's view, but in keeping with the Meadian perspective, a great many relationships in the human world have a "preexisting" meaning insofar as people confront them with a particular preparedness to act in routine, familiar and unquestioned ways (Stokes and Hewitt, 1976: 841). The context of situated interaction may modify or simply verify these stable meanings; however, they persist because they are taken for granted.

The upshot of the biases in both sorts of sociology is that functionalist and related theories can describe power relations but cannot explain their creation without autonomous individuals to embody purpose and to mobilize resources; interpretive sociology, in at least some of its formulations, can neither describe nor explain power relations because of its lack of attention to the objective consequences of action and its inability to handle the long-term properties of relationships.

The expression of social resources is a universal feature of interaction, just as motivation must be present for an encounter to proceed. However defined in a specific context, it is the stability and conventionality of various resources in a culture that allow for truly *social* control or power to be a part of every relationship. In spite of the virtually omnipresent character of control and power phenomena and their overall importance as concepts, there has been little systematic and devoted effort toward grounding them in theory (Clark and Gibbs, 1965; Wrong, 1968; Marshall, 1969; Rogers, 1974). And while considerable effort has been granted to clarifying the issues surrounding power relations in particular, virtually nothing has been done to relate the two concepts. Two important concepts related to the very basis of the production and reproduction of social life have been left without sufficient explanation to account for them as phenomena. Available theory has produced some promising leads, but nothing really substantive has been accomplished since Max Weber provided his basic insights into the nature and sources of power.

"Aligning Actions" and Control

In both Weber (1958: 180) and Bierstedt (1950: 735–736) we can discern a preference for saying that power appears under certain conditions. Stated differently, the nature of the circumstances points to the nature of the control mechanism. Power and control are functions of the articulation of a social structure, but the presence of a structure is not a sufficient condition for the existence of social power. The common ground between these two statements appears to be that *power appears when relationships are not quite routine*. This does not mean that such nonroutine activity will be totally free from convention. It is simply that power relations per se appear only during problematic circumstances and adjustments in the emerging social structure. As will be elaborated upon presently *the existence of power relations in interaction depends on the level of human behavior*: distinguishing principally between whether behavior is habitual or contrived. However, we must first be able to discriminate the simple reciprocal influence occurring in interaction (that is, what in fact is usually meant by social interaction) from the exercise of social control, and then go on to distinguish social control from the particular modes of activity that contain power relations. The next major task is to develop the theoretical guidelines to generate a plausible relationship between "social control" and "power."

At the most general level, it might be said that social control is work done to produce and maintain a particular version of reality. Social control is work that sustains expectations. The concept of *aligning actions* (Stokes and Hewitt, 1976) can bring more precision to this very general description of social control. In the formulation of Stokes and Hewitt, aligning actions are of two varieties. First, they recognize and account for discrepancies between behavior and expectations; they explain a behavior in terms of expectations and thereby restore the mutual orientation (or alignment) of an interaction. Abstract examples of aligning actions include "motive talk" (Mills, 1940), "accounts" (Scott and Lyman, 1968), "remedial interchanges" (Goffman, 1971: 108) and "disclaimers" (i.e., verbal devices employed in advance of an action that the person thinks might be discrediting—Hewitt and Stokes, 1975). The second type of aligning action is essentially social control: "an actual effort of some kind to bring conduct more into line with normative culture" (Stokes and Hewitt, 1976: 847). This effort may be levied by the person whose behavior is "out of line" (social self-control) or by others in the situation where alignment occurs. Aligning actions therefore occur when ongoing lines of action become disrupted—or the situation becomes in some way problematic. As a consequence, either (1) participants attempt to explain the problematic event in terms of what had been expected, thus normalizing the situation (the first type of aligning action mentioned above); or (2) they might attempt to effect social control (the second type of aligning action mentioned above). The important conclusion can be reached from this discussion of aligning action that not all reactions to discrepant behavior can be classified as social control. The concept of aligning actions provides two categories of response to deviations from expectations. By contrast, and somewhat carelessly, Clarks and Gibbs (1965: 402) consider all social reactions to deviation to be social control.

In addition to the two types of aligning actions conceived of by Stokes and Hewitt, I wish to add a third. This third type does not concern itself with aligning action to *cultural* expectations, or is it *reactive* social control. Instead, I am speaking of imposing one's will onto a situation—asserting control over interaction to bring it into line with personal expectations and desires. When successful, this is the stuff of the confidence man's "scam," the teacher's most prized skill, the politician's stock in trade, and the seducer's coveted line. But also, it is the way each of us makes our meaning count and the way we manage to persuade others to do what we wish. These are aligning actions with respect to personal design; it is social control with individual purpose in mind.

The latter two conceptions of social control (the second and third types of aligning actions) intentionally do not take the perspective of the collective, thereby requiring that reality must belong to an anonymous "society" that offers only infallible, absolutized dicta untailored for concrete experience and untouched by autonomous human purpose. Social control itself must be understood to belong within a context. Moreover, social control must be associated with a set of expectations as to what counts as a "correct" version of some reality. It is simply because opinions vary regarding "correctness" that social control is a viable concept. From the sociological perspective, the matter is not so easy as saying, "Here are the standards and there is the activity; they do not match." Standards appear different from within different contexts. Values, norms, mores and laws vary in their relevance to a given context. Such features of reality operate in the background, as it were, to suggest the character of expectations we might apply. Of course, the *precise* meanings attached to rules of conduct are contextually generated—that is, their exact meaning arises only when persons translate them into interaction. Interaction is the prism through which institutionalized standards are refracted as they are contextually applied.

The Margin for Discretion, Respectability and Types of Deviation

Life as it is lived is too complex to be regulated by absolute (abstract) norms.[3] There is an associated margin for discretion or error that does not disrupt the routine nature of even highly ritualized activity. Part of the context is an

---

[3] Jack Douglas (1970: 18) makes the same point with considerable cogency when he says, "Is it not obvious from a consideration of the inevitable arguments even among judges, such as justices of the U.S. Supreme Court, who have the *greatest possible knowledge* of precedents—or previous moral definitions of analogous situations—and of legal reasoning?"

understanding of what counts as acceptable activity. Although the margin for discretion is variable across contexts, it may be quite small in highly ritualized performances. For example, audiences to a master pianist or to the plays presented in ancient Athens are not the sort to tolerate appreciable error. Similarly, a modern surgeon applying cryonic techniques in retinal surgery must act with extreme precision. But in other contexts, the natural or expected margin for error may be very high. For example, the conduct of children in a nursery school, the awkward behavior of a foreigner to our ways, or the mistakes of a novice to some occupation are not, as it is said, "measured by the same standards" as the performances of those who are deemed to have membership status.[4]

Activity that stays within the bounds set by context-generated expectations could be called "respectable." Respectable activity is produced by actors in interaction who combine relevant knowledge with the social skills necessary to participate in the construction of a reality appearing to those involved that "nothing unusual is happening here" or that "all is going well" (Ball, 1970; Douglas, 1970; Emerson, 1970).

Whatever the vernacular designations might be, it is possible now to see behavior as:

1. *respectable* that is, apparent conformity, being within the margin for discretion;
2. *postively connoted deviance* that is, mistakes or innovation accounted for as beneficial, jokes (see Zijderveld, 1968; Wentworth, 1976), charismatic performances (for example, outlaws who in their time were heroes, such as Billy the Kid or Pretty Boy Floyd), or allowances for greatness (as in Charles de Gaulle's leniency with the various unlawful, antigovernment activities carried on by the likes of Jean-Paul Sartre, etc.);
3. *negatively connoted deviance* that is, unacceptable behavioral nonconformity to personal or cultural expectations, including the overconformity norms: from boorishness to rape; or
4. *ambiguous* that is, behavior without either causal determinancy or contextual relevance (Garfinkel, 1967; McHugh, 1968; if continued it will be granted determinacy and relevance vis-à-vis one of the other three categories: for example, "crazy," category 3; "messenger of the gods," category 2; "Aw, that's just old Joe," category 1.

Whenever social control is extended, it is the result of a situation having been defined as warranting control. In other words, those persons with some

---

[4] It might be noted from these examples that more precise ("absolute") standards are available to judge "instrumental" as opposed to "interactional" competence. Clearly, this is a factor of goal (or step-by-step) expectations being more clearly defined for instrumental activity. However, there is often the possibility in many circumstances of covering up incompetence in one area by a dazzling display in the other.

commitment and the responsibility to uphold a version of reality have deemed certain behavior less than respectable. However behavior may be assayed, it is understood only in relation to the contexts available to the audience. Social control may occur within the context originating the behavior in question or later in a recontextualized version of a past event (for example, in a Catholic confessional or a court of law). In light of this discussion we should now lend more specificity to our former characterization of social control as reality maintenance and production activity.

Levels of Human Behavior and the Relationship of Control with Power.

How then can we distinguish power relations? As mentioned earlier in passing, it is the levels or modes of human behavior that allow a distinction between the two concepts. It is possible to label four levels of human behavior:

1. *Organismic or reflex behavior* refers to those activities that for the most part are controlled by the autonomic nervous system and that would go on whether or not the person is conscious.
2. *Socially learned, nonsocial behavior* is the effect of social life on the biological equipment as registered in private behavior, whether overt or covert. It refers to those activities such as hunger at noon, smoking according to habit, organismic arousal before certain stimuli and not others, and so on.
3. *Conduct* is the habitual performance of meaningful social routines, or the institutionalized activity that forms the background of the taken-for-granted world.
4. *Action* "is devised in advance" and "based upon a preconceived project" (Schutz, 1970a: 125). Action is here conceived of as specifically adaptive to situations perceived as problematic, and it is constructed from the cultural tools at hand with an awareness of probable consequences.

Social control pertains to the last three types of behavior while power relations pertain only at the action level. Power relations are a special case of social control. Therefore, social control (minus power relations) can be defined as the routine means of dealing with problematic situations or nonroutine circumstance. Power relations (a subtype of control activity), on the other hand, are nonroutine means of dealing with problematic situations or nonroutine circumstance. Therefore, I understand that *the concept of social control subsumes that of social power.*

The particular relationship between social control and social power suggested here was, I believe, inadvertently suggested by Bierstedt when he stated that "power stands behind every association" to be called forth in problematic circumstances (1950: 735–736). Social control activity is immediate evidence of socially pertinent and persuasive resources, not power.[5] The task of preserving humanly organized reality is an inherent and usually routine part of reality construction. However, there are situations that require "action" and control. At these times it is power that is relied on, whatever its basis in socially relevant resources.

Two definitions may now be posited that specifically illuminate the subsuming relationship between social control and social power: (1) social control is the possibility to affect social *activity* (with routine control measures); and (2) social power is the possibility to affect social *action* (with nonroutine control measures). Definitions of such broad scope are not unprecedented in the literature. Compare Talcott Parsons: "Power . . . is the generalized capacity of a social system to get things done in the interest of collective goals" (1960: 180–183). I have attempted to bring power into social action, to embody it in the human sphere rather than accepting it as a capacity of a reified system.

From this point, the discussion will now turn to ascertain the relations of the self to resources control and power.

A SOCIAL PSYCHOLOGY OF CONTROL AND POWER RELATIONS: THE BASIS OF AUTONOMY

Goffman and Mead: Identity, Resource Management and the Self

It could be said that people are tied to whatever social resources they have; that their identity is directly related to how they manage their resources in the presence of others. Erving Goffman (e.g., 1961a, 1971) has devoted considerable effort to sorting out the relationship among the situational specificity of resources, resource management and identity. Goffman's writings offer us one of the more sophisticated explications of face-to-face interaction in these terms. However, the commonly noted artificiality of Goffman's actors leaves them curiously empty. The sense that we get in reading Goffman is that there is nothing behind the mask of a social performance except another mask.[6]

---

[5] Let me give an example to help clarify the point. Some parents may consider spanking a matter of routine (conduct). When their children misbehave, a swat soon follows. Other parents, less liberal with spankings, but more liberal in their views of the parent–child relationship, may reserve their spanks for types of misbehavior deemed particularly hazardous or onerous. Here the spanking is *administered*, not merely given. It is an act of power, not merely control, although the vernacular may have it as control.

[6] I realize that this aspect of Goffman is more the result of the empirical quality of his work (he is describing what he observes) than a bona fide logical shortcoming in his theoretical position. As a result, the core of his work is quite compatible with that of George Herbert Mead and the social psychological ideas developed by Emile Durkheim.

The upshot is a species of people without a source for their reputed motivation to give off the best impression under the prevailing circumstances and no personal reasons to demand treatment with "ritual care" (Goffman, 1967: 95).

George Herbert Mead (1962) provides a motivational anchor—the self—to the human social performances described by Goffman. Mead's theory of the self indicates that our identity is a part of our social relations with others. Mead also understood that our self-monitoring behavior (reflexivity) allows us to adjust our performances as situations emerge. So far, this is no more than Goffman has said. Mead adds to this that the responses of others to our actions become organized within us. In fact, through social intercourse our very selves are formed. In other words, the self emerges from one's identity, if identity is understood as an assigned place in the world, a social location (Berger and Luckmann, 1966: 132–133).

As personal development progresses, the person becomes able to "take the attitude of the other" and to express identity in coordinated action with others. At this point, too, persons can act toward themselves, because the self has emerged as a relatively stable reference point: "It is, so to speak an eddy in the social current and so still a part of the current" (Mead, 1962: 182). References to our self, the "me" and the spontaneous eruptions of the social "I" become the motive force through which the identity can be maintained or changed (Mead, 1962: 174, 200, 204–205, 210). Within this scheme we can perform or intentionally produce an intended identity for a given situation. We manage our identities by relying on stable meanings and the ritual features of interaction—and by calling on our social resources.

"A resource is any attribute, circumstance, or possession that increases the ability of the holder to influence a person or group" (Rogers, 1974: 1425). An implicit idea in this definition is that a resource is only a resource when it appears to ourselves and to others as such; in other words, when the resource has in some way become part of a social relationship. After a person is reputed to control a resource (for example: authority, expertise or a foul temper), it is then a part of his or her identity. According to Mead, reflection upon such attributions affects the formation of the self. Now return for a moment to the statement made somewhat earlier: that people are tied to their resources.

The sense of that statement has been significantly modified by our brief discussion of Mead. His position on this matter might more nearly be that, in so far as they possess a developed self, *people are their own resources*; further, that they understand themselves in terms of how they can and do affect others. Such a perspective can only be understood in view of the interpenetration of the self and the social world. The question who we are is resolved through the responses of others to us, by the social expressions of our selves, and through the "internal dialogue" made possible by our self-monitoring capacity. The way we manage the presentations of the self is both a *use* of the resources attributed to us and an *expression* of a self that has been constituted by a (reflexive) appraisal of our resources.

We are what we do (and we do what we are), but only to the extent that we have first considered the attitudes of others toward us. Of this reciprocal and interpenetrating relationship among associates, Mead says that he wants:

> to avoid the implication that the individual is taking something that is objective and making it subjective. There is an actual process of living together on the part of all members of the community which takes place by means of gestures . . . . Now, all that has taken place in the appearance of the mind is that (the social) process has been in some degree taken over into the conduct of the particular individual (1962: 188).

The theoretical implication of a self in the situated performances of actors gives a source, or a reason, for the motivation of Goffman's actors to manage their identities. Our motivation to act in a certain way is an expression of the self. But we are not dealing with some solipsistic entity; the self is derived from society and is in constant conversation with others; motivation is also a preeminently social affair. This should not be considered the same as a deterministic relationship between social structure and behavior; the person we are contributes to who we are becoming. This degree of autonomy that the self possesses, this self-control, is the basis for our ability to manifest power and control in our relations with others. From a social psychological perspective, power and control relations can be seen as features of all interaction.

By elaborating and contrasting the theoretical position of George Herbert Mead with the more descriptive, empirical writings of Erving Goffman, a crucial bridge has been established between behavior and the pursuit of interests. This link can be elucidated by turning once again to a modification of Howard Becker's concept of commitment.[7]

From Mead we can understand how commitment (or, that is, the pursuit of interests) is possible; it grows from the relative stability of the self as a point of reference for social action. Resources, as elements of identity and constituents of the self, generate interests that are in turn pursued to maintain the self. It is not my intention to say that persons always know what is in their best interest or always understand the situation in which they find themselves or even that they are always serious. Nevertheless, they do mobilize their social resources

---

[7]In accepting Mead's theory of the self, we can also interpret "situational adjustment" with respect to Goffman's concept of role distance. A person may deny *self*-involvement in situations that cannot be satisfactorily negotiated toward self-expression, because such situations are inescapable and coercive for reasons external to the "real" person. During such times, people present themselves "as the situation demands," accepting some "short-term losses", while their role-distant perspective allows them to retain their self-conceptions. And so "situational adjustment" becomes one aspect of reflexive behavior.

in the attempt to understand their current condition and to pursue the complex of interests that appear relevant.

Commitment may be carried to the level of various degrees of separation from the ways of doing and attitudes of being that nurture mind and self. Mead tells us that the possession of a mind (the self in action) "enables human individuals to turn back critically, as it were, upon the organized social structure of the society to which they belong" (1962: 308). It is at first difficult, perhaps, to grasp how a mind derived from certain human relations can become relatively independent of that pattern. The problem is central to a fruitful understanding of interaction and socialization, warranting further explanation.

In addition to Mead, two other notable theorists, Marx and Durkheim, have postulated the possibility of sociological autonomy in their images of the person.[8] We will examine their contributions to the theory of autonomy as a step toward an understanding of the role of power and control relations in socialization.

Karl Marx: Rebellion and History

Karl Marx has written that autonomy is possible to the extreme of self-definition by rebellion (Marx, 1966: 150). Such an event occurs when people come to realize that the conceptions they hold of their historical form of existence are in contradiction to their actual life processes. Upon grasping this contradiction, a people's relationship to its society can never be the same: "Self-changing can only be comprehended and rationally understood as revolutionary practice" (from Karl Marx, *German Ideology*, quoted in Fromm, 1961: 22). Marx's position is more complex than I have stated, being bound up with his concept of work and his ideas of human nature. However, as far as it goes in detail, my portrayal is true to what Marx saw as a feasible theoretical interpretation of personal rebellion. For our immediate purposes, Marx is a clear reminder that it is idle to accuse the individual of being a passive object of circumstance.

With threats of revolution and intellectual power, Marx can shake us from the opinion, proferred by much of modern sociology, that socialization necessarily decreases individual creativity and autonomy. On the other hand, Marx can be held at bay as a radical to be used seriously only by radicals. He was an avid social critic, but he was also a serious theorist. True, these two facets of his work are not easily separated. We can, however, consider the richness and

---

[8]Bendix and Berger (1959) give brief discussion to the aspects of autonomy in the works of Georg Simmel and Max Weber. And as they say, "Apparently, this perspective is well-known in sociological theory. Yet . . . it runs counter to the 'sociological determinism' characteristic of much contemporary sociological literature" (1959: 96).

the constancy of his humanism in his massive critique of our historical conditions. Appreciated on these terms, his sociology is persuasive, if not without fault. Concerning the matters at hand, it may be that Marx was too restrictive in his allowances for the appearance of critical appraisal in human behavior. His position was certainly more circumscribed than that of Mead, who takes reflexiveness at the level of an anthropological condition (Mead, 1962: 133–134).

Mead is more difficult to understand accurately on this account because he does not seek definite parameters for reflexive or critical behavior. We know from him that such powers evolve and become more acute as the self develops. It is apparent, too, that Mead holds a position between the artful fluidity granted to actors by Becker and Goffman, and the strict historical limitations placed by Marx upon our critical faculties. Much more than Becker and Goffman, Mead's account of sociality gives the person an opportunity to rest upon habit and routine. Unlike in Marxian sociology, after a period of "rest," an actor need not come out fighting. However, locating Mead among such theorists does not really help us to identify the specific conditions leading to degrees of autonomy. Emile Durkheim can be of considerable usefulness in this matter.

Durkheim: Society, Complexity and Sociological Autonomy

Durkheim is a surprisingly compatible supplement to the social psychology of Mead. It is true that Durkheim's principal interests focused upon the domain of social organization. From his *The Division of Labor in Society* (1933) onward, however, he evinces a fascination with the social nature of the person.[9] His basic social psychological position in this work emphasizes the vital relationship between the individual and society. He saw that the individual, as a cultural being, was born of society (Durkheim, 1933: 279).

And similarly in *The Elementary Forms of the Religious Life* we find that

> the collective force is not entirely outside of us; it does not act upon us wholly from without; but rather, since society cannot exist except in and through individual consciousness, this force must also penetrate us and organize itself within us: it thus becomes an integral part of our being (1965: 240).

Durkheim is once again making his case for the priority and reality of society, but in a framework designed to include human agency in the authorship of society. What we now seek from Durkheim is the relationship between autonomy and the social bond.

First, we must understand that both the mind and society are considered as

---

[9]The original dates of publication for Durkheim's works can be found in the bibliography. They may be helpful in critically appraising the development of the ideas I will cite.

unique realities by Durkheim (1965: 471, 479; 1974: 3, 7, 9, 15, 33). Further, if the individual "has been able to escape, to free himself, to develop a personality, it is because he has been able to shelter under a sui generis force [society] (1947: 55). And generally, autonomy comes as a result of experience in society, or as Durkheim put it, "the personal ideal disengages itself from the social ideal in proportion as the individual personality develops itself and becomes an autonomous source of action" (1965: 471).

If a single variable had to be construed from the writings of Durkheim to account for the possibility of sociological autonomy, it would be "complexity." It is reflected in his composite of biological, social, political and historical antecedents to autonomy, and further, in his description of the genesis of the autonomy (the "relative indetermination") of the mind. Pertaining to complexity, Durkheim says that "when a sufficient number of representations are present"—a hypothesized take-off point—in the mind, creative synthesis is possible. In other words, the nature of the mind itself leads toward autonomous action (1974: 1–34).

A group of collateral conditions supplements this primary independence. These all fit into a kind of evolutionary scheme regarding social complexity; as social differentiation progresses in a society, the less its culture, ideas and sentiments reflect a particular structural origin. Thus, when the mind is being formed during an individual's participation in society, it can be said that the more complex the society, the less likely the mind will be derived from an easily delimited set of social conditions. The elements of this complexity are several; we will begin with the individual's biological equipment.

Durkheim manifested a belief in genetic predilection, or as he says in *The Division of Labor in Society* and again in *Suicide*, there is a distribution of "natural talent" (1933: 374–381; 1951: 251). Moreover, the body forms a point of reference; it is an individualizing force in social relations:

> as bodies are distinct from each other, and as they occupy different points in space and time, each of them forms a special center about which collective representations reflect and color themselves differently (1965: 305).

Social structure also plays a direct role. We occupy a unique social location; each person is therefore situated differently in relation to others, in relation to various intermediate groupings and associations and to the society at large (1951: 374–384, 390; 1957; 1965: 306). It is the case that Durkheim did not comprehend the moral force of society to be entirely restrictive, as he is so often construed. In fact, his consistent position is that the person's perception of social rules merely sets limits to the acceptable variation allowable in obeying social structures (Durkheim, 1951: 250; see also Nisbet, 1974: 210–212 for a similar interpretation). Beyond that, deviance is always a genuine possibility.

Thus far we have reviewed the relatively timeless facets of sociological autonomy that are to be found in the writings of Durkheim; those that are a part of any society at any time. In respect of this analysis, they are inherent qualities of man's existence. By his inclusion of personal autonomy or "relative indetermination," it is apparent that Durkheim was willing to accept a relatively difficult explanation of social life. There is no simple core of social structural determinism—that is, a materialistic explanation, to which we can turn for relief as we ponder society with Durkheim. He was against such overly simple pictures of society (e.g., 1965: 471) and was determined to carry out a program in which the complex was explained by the complex, and the whole was to be elucidated by characteristics of the whole (e.g., 1964, passim.; 1974: 29). The whole—society—was for him a historical entity that changed "by virtue of the inevitable causes that govern its evolution." What these historical engines might be, Durkheim did not systematically pursue, but that is another matter. However, the notion of change and his sensitivity to "history" are tied closely with the probability of the appearance of the personality *as a source of autonomous action*. Once again, he understood that such a probability was a function of complexity, something that developed in history (1933: 171; 1961: 52–54; 1964: 71–72; 1965: 471; see also "Durkheim and History" by Robert N. Bellah, 1959).[10]

Durkheim would say that social structure does not squeeze the individual into too narrow a path; it is not absolutely deterministic: "the determinism which reigns . . . [in the mind] . . . is much more supple than the one whose roots are in the constitution of our tissues and it leaves the actor a justified impression of the greatest liberty" (1965: 307). This statement should not be interpreted as a theoretical disjoining of the material and the cultural realms. Durkheim would vehemently oppose such an attempt. As he says, for example, inequitably distributed "vital necessities" may be the material basis for conflict; and yet, inasmuch as this underlying order is *mediated* by a system of representations, the sparks of actual conflict may not be struck (1965: 470–471). Elements of this system of representation might be feelings of solidarity or patriotism that can at times defer a critical negative evaluation of material conditions. Be these things as they may, Durkheim repeatedly insists that the structure of association generates these representations whereby we understand our relationships to others. It is just that the more differentiated the society, the more complex will be the nexus between a reality and its material source; in complex societies representations tend to "take on a life of

---

[10]"A man is far more free in the midst of a throng than in a small coterie." Durkheim is speaking here of the way the state unites disparate social units into a politically joined society. "And it is out of this conflict of social forces (in a political society) that individual liberties are born." (Durkheim, 1957).

their own." In fact, to demonstrate adequately the connection of the two realms Durkheim said in *The Elementary Forms of the Religious Life* that he was forced to study simple societies.

The potentially autonomous individual is not simply washed by the currents of history into blind conformation with a changing order.

> The individual can free himself partially from the rules of society if he feels the disparity between them and society as it is and not as it appears to be—that is, if he desires a morality which corresponds to the actual state of society and not to an outmoded condition (Durkheim, 1974: 65).

It is of crucial importance to understand that in this passage Durkheim is speaking about liberation from a felt sense of duty to an outmoded moral order. Durkheim is formally recognizing the possibility of a difference of opinion (cf. 1974: 63–64). This important interpretation points at once to the social sensitivity (relative determinism) of individuals and their moral independence (relative indeterminism or autonomy).

Additionally, the political structure of society can encourage or discourage expressions at variance with traditional opinion. Within a democratic heritage the "individual comes to acquire ever wider rights over his own person and over the possessions to which he has title; he also comes to form ideas about the world that seem to him most fitting and to develop his essential qualities without hindrance" (1957: 56). And Durkheim understood that it is the "State that creates and organizes and makes a reality of these rights" (1957: 60).

The seeds of autonomy and individuality are ever present in society; nevertheless, the structural reorganization associated with the modernization of Western societies offers increased opportunity for free thought. Durkheim realized that traditional, provincial constraints were disrupted by the wake of the industrial and democratic revolutions, and nothing had yet arrived to replace their governance. This condition constitutes a state of anomie that is conducive to a growing consciousness of an incongruity between the real and the ideal conceptions of society. So too, political and economic intercourse among hitherto-isolated social units opens the world still further to a variety of interpretations not in keeping with any one tradition.

The stresses of social change bring forth impassioned statements reflecting social origins and interests. Persons from "different parts" of the societal structure express their perspectives on issues; "they materialize and oppose abstractions," separate pieces of an entire mosaic not fully captured by any single perspective. The conflict thus engendered is not itself subjected to anything like an elaborate analysis by Durkheim. He says only that opposing views are an often not-too-accurate expression of a "collective ideal," anchored in some fashion by a particular "sphere of action" or set of "social conditions." Stated somewhat differently, there is a distribution of knowledge in society concerning the nature of social reality, particular "truths" being related to the different parts of society and to the individuals who express their opinions.

Even though the overall probability of individuality and critical thought is increased by modern structural relationships, Socrates and Christ are spectacular evidence of moral discordance occurring in ancient history (Durkheim, 1961:53). Generally, therefore, each individual "understands [collective ideals] after his own fashion and marks them with his own stamp; he suppresses certain elements and adds others" (Durkheim, 1965: 471). The single thread running through all of this is that development (increased complexity), whether of the personality or of society, leads to sociological autonomy. An immediate corollary is that socialization points the way to individuation and that subsequent personality formation at all stages provides the basis for autonomy.

Durkheim's conception of social causation was not at any point simple, unmitigated determinism. He described the individual as deeply affected by society as at the same time autonomous. However, even through his ideas on "collective representations" and the related concept of complexity, Durkheim never satisfactorily explained autonomy, but he always allowed for it and showed where it could appear. Durkheim's writing supplements the theory relating culture and the context to surface activity and social structures set forth in previous chapters that explains autonomy. The work of Durkheim and other early theorists acts as a constant reminder of the important place "autonomy" has in a sophisticated, fairly rigorous, highly sociological system of sociology. Durkheim writes of it often and everywhere intimates its place in society.

The preceding sections discussed the relationship of the identity and the self, of resources and creativity and of autonomy. All of these concepts have been mentioned in a framework suggesting that social control and social power were somehow related to them. The connection will now be made more substantial.

CONCLUSIONS: CONTROL AND POWER RELATIONS AND THE THEORY OF SOCIALIZATION
Context, Control and Autonomy

It is a fundamental and necessary proposition that society and person interpenetrate; consequently, a person gains both an identity and a self over the course of interaction with others. In other words, focused aspects of "society" come to life during interaction, supplying persons with the basic elements of self-formation and the content for further interaction. Using this content, persons engage one another in a conversation of activity that interrelates the subjective, social and physical environments. During interaction persons orient one another to this content, continually interpreting and judging the ensuing performance and the participating actors. Actors differ in the various resources they can bring to bear during interaction. Furthermore, not all resources have equal legitimacy or force in influencing the behavior of other people. This is a matter of culture.

The "society" that appears in interaction is a function of the particular resources available. These resources are sometimes aspects of fairly stable organizational roles, sometimes much more general cultural tools, and sometimes socially recognized skills and attributes belonging to individuals. By characterizing social encounters as the interaction of relatively resourceful individuals, the negotiated property of situations is brought to light. Another way of saying this is that human social activity has consequences. If the consequences of behavior are considered, then a formal recognition of social control and power relations is in order; these are the sociological concepts that are specially related to the consequences of various social conditions.

The concept of sociological autonomy is a necessary precursor for control and power. As Durkheim explained, autonomy does not indicate egoistic contrariness, but rather it is the result of a schooling in collective ideals that produces a judgmental sensitivity to the course of events (Bucher and Stelling, 1977: 270−277). The individual is a link between the collective ideals and the present moment when society is being created through interaction. Mead's succinct phrasing for this was that the self is an eddy in the social current.

There is always a degree of tension between the person and the situation. We do not *merely* adapt or react to whatever conditions have most recently appeared. Judgments of morality, or the recognition that certain behavior is somehow "out of place" can only come about as a consequence of the tension between the person and the moment. Such judgments, based on the autonomy of the individual, are at the heart of social control activity. Social control activity may be best explained by saying that the possession of autonomy allows for the discernment of what counts as discrepant behavior, and whether or not such activity happens to *matter* here and now.

Autonomy can also account for the fact of varying responses; that is, the decision of what, if anything, should be done in anticipation of (or response to) impropriety, and when and how a response should be made. Similarly, the concept of power is absurd without a "someone" to initiate and modulate the attempt to realize one's wishes and interests even against the resistance of others.

I have already indicated that power relations may occur between an institutionalized aspect of the environment and a person. The power relation per se arises when a person must make a choice of possible actions and bases that decision upon what would be expected of a responsible member. Put differently, a collective ideal is realized in the interests (the Weberian "will") of a person who is knowingly influenced by *its* (the collective ideal's) information rather than by the sway of immediate circumstance. The "power" of an institution reflects its psychological and contextual relevance (see above, this chapter). Such power may then be felt in ways other than the direct interaction of two or more people. Once again the relatively autonomous self is implicated as the source of an action. Behind every portrayal of social control and social power is the (often hidden) assumption of an autonomous individual.

It was stated earlier that control and power relations are a result of bringing resources to bear upon a situation. In my examination of Durkheim's views of sociological autonomy I quoted his view that the body acts as an individualizing force in the environment. The result of this focus is that personal qualities come to be attributed to individuals. These attributions are the constituents of our identities, and we know from Mead that attributions affect self-formation. We first come to understand ourselves in terms of our identities and then gradually assimilate representations of our identies into our very selves. Mead stresses that this is not a passive process. Instead, reflexive behavior modifies the effects of our relations with others so that self-expression is rooted in how we have understood our relations with others.

Whether by guile or error, our objective identity in a situation may be at variance with our personal understanding of that identity. So too, our interpretation of the situation may be marred for many reasons. Whatever interpretations are applied, however, persons manage their identities according to where they believe their interests lie (*something much more complex than just trying to make the best impression*) and according to the contextually relevant resources they can associate with their identities (Bucher and Stelling, 1977: 277).

The agents of socialization often have the resources to manipulate situations and contrive identities that limit the raw materials available for self-formation. Thus, social control and power are in one respect limiting features of a socializing environment. However, it should be clear from our discussion of autonomy that there are individual and sociological features inherent to any relationship that would refract a member's presentation of and a novice's response to historical values and norms. For one thing, the effort expended by the agents of socialization may be met by some form of resistance on the part of the novice. Counter-power and counter-control may be exerted. For it must be stressed that both members and novices utilize social resources for control.

Counter-Control, Resistance, Seekership and Autonomy

The "student culture" described by Becker and his colleagues (1961) is one example of the way novices can limit and channel the experiences they receive during socialization. Novices can, like members, conjure up power and social control in their socializing relationships. Even though novices might be seekers who willingly enter into socialization, they have interests that must be transformed in accordance with the identity for which they are being socialized. In the successful socializing process, members gradually negotiate the novice toward the identity stereotype of the new role (Collins, 1975: 98).

For contrast, it should be instructive to look briefly at a case where the outcome of adult socialization is likely to be unsuccessful, that is, not in keeping with the vaguely defined goals of the program (e.g., lowering recidivism rates).[11]

Prisoners are often quite resistant to the effort of negotiating them toward a legal identity. Surely part of the difficulty lies in the selection process. Prisoners are not usually made captive through their own desires, and too, a certain similarity in their backgrounds and their common plight encourages the formation of a "society of captives" (see Sykes, 1958). But this is merely saying that prisoners have their own interests.

The "society of captives" plays much the same role as the "student culture" described by Becker et al. (1961). However, a group of prisoners is more like a turn-of-the-century workers' union than an academic fraternity. Prisoner society provides resources for prisoners that, by appeals to the collective, may refract "rehabilitation." The society of captives acts to help prisoners absorb any invidious comparison between the morality of their lives and that degree of morality demanded by law. Even in respect to the powerful insistance of prisoner society and the constant vigilance possible in those confined quarters, some flexibility is possible. There are "lone wolves," not responsive to any group and there are model prisoners who genuinely wish to identify with official values. Not only do groups define common problems and construct their environmental niches, individuals work out certain personal accommodations as well (see also Bucher and Stelling, 1977).

We have looked at prisoner society as an example of resistance to socialization to emphasize that both members and novices, collectively and individu-

---

[11] It is usually easier to recognize "unsuccessful" socialization than "successful," unless it has been "very successful" socialization, as for example, when a poor peanut farmer becomes the President. Most of the time fine criteria are lacking and expectations are not long-range or precise.

ally, may have access to the resources necessary for social control and social power. Therefore, historical, collective (in this case, lawful and moral) ideals may be presented during socialization, but the interaction involved in presenting them leads to a negotiated order; that is, a reality emerges that is in many ways unique. For these reasons it can be said that internalization is not a psychological mirror of socialization and that *socialization not only presents a world, it constructs one.* It may well be the case that some of the ground rules of a negotiated order might include a resistance to personal change and an institutionalized unwillingness to submit to the demands of socialization.

The success of much, if not all, socialization is directly dependent upon the willingness of the novice to submit in some way to expected conduct, to be a seeker as it was just phrased. Thus, institutional resources may include even the commitment or seekership of the novice.

In one sense the notion of seekership can be translated into saying that autonomy is one resource members both have and depend upon in the novice. Here I refer not to autonomy as expressed in rebellion, but rather to the (growing) *responsibility* (social self-control) on the part of a novice to control personal behavior in accordance with members' expectations, even if often such expectations are from the standpoint of moment-to-moment activity. For instance, parents watch their children's abilities and make assumptions about when they can be allowed to play unchaperoned. There might be the nearby potential for the child's harm—a busy street, for example—but the child now "knows better" than to wander into the path of traffic. "Knowing better" means the child is sufficiently cognizant of its activities to monitor them in a respectable way. Similarly, the occupational trainee is gradually granted a greater degree of freedom in accordance with assessments of increasing competence. In general, however, the novice must see the legitimacy of the process in order to grow in autonomous responsibility.

Stress and Socialization[12]

In the first years of medical school, returning to that example, there is very little direct supervision of medical students because it is tacitly assumed that they already know how to attend lectures and that they will try to assimilate the material presented therein (*direct* supervision increases later as the socializing contexts become less "ordinary," then gradually decreases once again as students become accustomed to the clinician's role).

Student culture may well help them control the sheer volume of their workload as has been suggested; however, that they also *want* to become

---

[12]Chapter 4, the subsection, "Ritual, Seriousness and Play," is particularly pertinent here.

doctors is indicated by the telling competition just to get into medical school. As a result, we find medical students eagerly absorbed in their socialization. Their seekership notwithstanding, it can be seen that the nature of socialization is such that the member's world, as presented during socializing activity, makes at least cognitive impositions upon the novice. And too, he or she deals regularly in nonroutine, problematic situations and faces the stress attendant to producing *actions* to accommodate them (rather than routine *conduct*). Medical novices are thus confronted by the power of an institution that predates perhaps their very existence.

Insofar as they are constraining, power relations are by their nature stressful. When institutional resources are great and the tasks difficult and there is little chance for a change of contexts, and especially where there is either active resistance to power or a deep commitment to a personal goal in the organization, then the stress will be greatest.

In fact, the effects of stress management are quite apparent in socializing processes that call for almost total submersion in the relevant environment. Generally, such environments have been described, and quite aptly, as having a low level of natural "ventilation" (Etzioni, 1961: 162). Novices have little opportunity within the contexts of these total socializing organizations to "vent" the stress induced by the pressures of socialization, and because of the degree of submersion they have little chance for escape.

The medical school requires a high degree of submersion in its contexts (Coombs and Stein, 1971: 110). Furthermore, a wide variety of anecdotal and some systematic evidence indicates that medical students might be described as seekers, that is, highly committed to the successful completion of their medical training (Gough, 1971: 26; Rhoads et al., 1974). Both of these points are exemplified in the far from atypical words of one medical student:

> I spend (so much) time studying. There is no time to meet people and I don't know anybody. I don't get as much sleep, I don't do what I would like to do. I would like to travel more and maybe go to the mountains every weekend, but the time I take off makes me feel guilty.
>
> Since I don't have much free time, I would like to spend my vacations in some fantastic way. But I also feel like I should go home to see my parents. But when I go home I feel like I haven't done anything for myself (Field notes, *Developmental Study of Medical Socialization*, University of Virginia Medical School).

The context of medical education imposes its own idiosyncratic stress. A medical school presents contexts to its novices in an enormous and esoteric medical lexicon that must be mastered, and in addition, many of the institution's experiences are normally hidden to everyday life; there are the sights, sounds and smells of abnormal bodily conditions, surgical invasions, confrontations with death and stranger-to-stranger intimate touching—all of which must in some way be accommodated by the student. There are significant status changes (Coombs, 1971: 151) and "fréquent and rapid shifts in role playing" (Lief, 1971: 81). Medical students are faced daily with the impossible task of mastering more knowledge than can be acquired within available time (Coombs and Boyle, 1971: 93). All of these strenuous challenges occur in an environment where rationality and stoicism are *de rigueur*. As would be expected from high levels of action in an organization allowing little natural "ventilation," medical novices have unusually high rates of psychological disturbances among medical students (Lief, 1971: 58).

Medical schools are not unusual with respect to stress, and they do offer the heuristic advantage of having been thoroughly studied. It is not hard, for example, to imagine a Marine recruit risking harsh discipline or drowning to escape from the Parris Island Recruit Training Depot. The frequent disparity of socializing resources between the novice and the world of membership might be so great and the pressure so intense that only the resource of absolute nihilation can neutralize institutional power, but that is the painful antithesis of seekership and a difficult alternative, because it often means accepting a deviant identity.

In addition to their basic role in negotiating socialization realities in some regular fashion, social control and power relations may also be understood in several quite straightforward ways: (1) they are themselves a demonstration of the etiquette and techniques of social control and social power relations; (2) they are a display of some of the kinds of resources (e.g., authority, knowledge, etc.) available to members;[13] (3) they may be used with the function of stimulating stressful conditions the novice could experience as a member (e.g., "cops and robbers" role-playing in a police academy); (4) they may be used as a dreadful show of force to encourage the rapid breakdown and disappearance of former identities (This is part of the basic technique of brain-washing, see Hunter, 1951; but there are close parallels to any total institutional setting, see Goffman, 1961b.); (5) they may be used to establish the idea that failure is related to disadvantageous consequences (Goffman, 1961b: 51); and (6) they may be used simply in the immediate management of current behavior.

However problematic socialization might be, it would be unreasonable to assume that socialization always conjures up the need for action. After all, if the subjective apprehension of anomie were the constitutive condition of socialization, internalization might produce psychic disability more fre-

---

[13]In this respect, Sanford M. Dornbusch describes hazing in a military academy as a means of teaching the meaning of rank and position: "One is not being hazed because the upperclassman is a sadist, but because one is at the time in a junior status" (1955: 319).

quently than social competence. Power relations can become routinized or cast into a pattern. During this process action is recycled into conduct and power relations become routine control activity and stress is reduced.

Social control is not, of course, unique to the world presented in socialization. However, social control, and especially its subtype social power relations, are particularly salient features of a world like that of a socialization environment, which is problematic almost by definition. In addition to social control being a valuable descriptive feature of socialization, it may be understood as a motivational feature of the environment. Control and power are somewhat analogous to the carrot and the stick; they "encourage" novices through the stressful problematics of socialization.

SUMMARY

The rather long and complex argument contained in this and the previous chapters may best be summed up by listing the main points as four groups of suppositions. Each suppostion is descriptive of the social phenomenon implied by the title of the group to which it belongs. The four groups are themselves tied together by three fundamental postulates: (1) that society is nondeterministic; (2) that the ability to produce society is grounded in rules that suggest behavior; and (3) that person and society interpenetrate. Taken together, what I understand to be the implications of these three postulates generate the descriptive statements under the several headings.

A. The Social Order:
   1. Social acts have consequences.
   2. Each social act modifies, amends or confirms a reality.
   3. Reality is a (social and cultural) construct arising during interaction.
   4. Interaction is a conversation of activity; that is, a structured expression of meanings through speech, actions and use of space.
   5. Activity is produced in a current conversation vis-a-vis its meaning to participants.
   6. The basis of current conversations is typically historical society.
   7. Therefore, there are elements of continuity and discontinuity in the construction of reality (from 5 and 6).
   8. Meaning is relative to a structure of implications.
   9. Therefore, meanings both preexist and arise in a given conversation of activity (from 1, 2, 5, 6, 7 and 8).
   10. Therefore, acts are inherently ambiguous (from 7, 8, and 9).
   11. Therefore, reality is a negotiated order.
   12. Negotiations tend to (re)produce rules for living (culture).

13. Continued negotiations are on the basis of historically created rules for living.
14. Those rules tend to circumscribe the sphere of "respectable" activity (the context).
15. Social resources are the fundamental sociological constituents of the negotiated order.
16. Social resources may have stable or emergent meanings, but in either case they are made consequential in the conversation of activity of specific contexts (from 3, 6 and 10).
17. A typical aspect of human social activity is social control (from 1, 5, 11 and 13).

B. Aspects of the Nature of Individuals and Their Relations to the Social Order:
18. There is a degree of tension between the individual and the situation (from A. 3, 9, 10 and 16).
19. This tension may be characterized as a degree of asymmetry between subjective and objective versions of reality.
20. Therefore, socially the individual is a localizing agent in the environment.
21. Actors attribute qualities to one another during interaction.
22. The identity is made up of social attributes or resources.
23. Social interaction leads to identity formation (from 20 and 21).
24. Identity is an indication of the individual's contextually relevant resources.
25. During socialization members attribute particular context-related identities to novices.
26. The agents of socialization have the resources to construct particular contexts that limit the raw materials at hand for identity formation on the part of the novice.
27. Identity affects self-formation.
28. Reflexive ability allows individuals to take an active part in the self-formation process from selected aspects of the identity (creativity).
29. Interaction (and *ipso facto* socialization) affects, and tends to decrease, the asymmetry between subjective and objective versions of reality (from 23, 25, 26 and 27).
30. Person and society interpenetrate in self-formation, but each remains a reality sui generis.
31. The selved individual can take an active part in the situated expression of that self (from 18 and 29).
32. Persons can contribute to their own identity (from 18 and 30).
33. The individual has interests vis-à-vis self (and identity).

34. The self represents an internalized version of culture as experienced by the actor.
35. Internalized culture becomes the basis for organizing identity and interests.
36. The person is capable of conduct and action in social relationships.
37. Self-formation changes egocentric independence (mere reflexivity) into autonomy.

C. Social Control Activity:
38. The notion of the autonomous individual is a necessary assumption behind the portrayal of social control.
39. The ability to perform social control activity (whether conduct or action-oriented) has its basis in the autonomy of the individual.
40. Autonomy is at root social self-control (from B. 37).
41. *Social* control is first self-control before it can be the control of others.
42. The ability to use and express social resources is the interactional basis of social control and social power relations.
43. The expression and use of resources in problematic situations in order to effect lines of activity constitutes an instance of social control.
44. *Social* control occurs where there is a shared design for activity, that is, where identity and society interpenetrate (from A. 17).

D. Social Control and Socialization:
45. The novice is by definition unfamiliar with the members' world (from B. 18 and 19).
46. Socialization in the interactional presentation of the members' world to the novice.
47. Therefore, the world presented during socialization is problematic.
48. Socialization constructs a minimum world.
49. Members and novices negotiate a reality and an order among themselves.
50. Socialization not only presents a world (the members'), it also constructs one (the order negotiated by members and novices in interaction).
51. Therefore, both the novice and the agents of socialization are in control of the resources necessary for social control and social power relations (from C. 42, 43 and 44).
52. Therefore, social control activity is a basic mode of behavior during socializing interaction (but socialization is not identical with social control) (from B. 16 and 19; D. 45, 46 and 47).
53. The socialization context contains the minimum world, while drawing upon the larger historical world for content and legitimacy (from A. 4, 5 and 7; C. 43 and 44).

54. The sheer weight and relative completeness of members' resources tend to ensure the production of expected socialization contexts (from B. 26).
55. The sheer weight and relative completeness of members' resources tend to ensure the eventual reproduction of their world by new initiates.
56. The context is the human legacy of "world-openness."
57. Cultural closure is not complete (deterministic).
58. The (historical) world is not one possible world and the most likely world to be reproduced.
59. Objectively, the world retains its openness.
60. Therefore, world-building, maintenance and reproduction require creativity and control.
61. Sociological autonomy replaces primitive creativity during socialization and internalization.
62. Social control and social self-control, as manifested in sociological autonomy, serve to maintain even an open world.
63. Therefore, the concepts of structure and internalization (pointing to continuity and conduct) can be theoretically consistent with creativity (pointing to situational uniqueness, action and sociological autonomy).
64. The socialization context is the parsimonious means of entry in a nondeterministic, complex world.

APPENDIX I

A LOGIC OF DEFINITIONS

As a concise statement of a relationship, a definition is both a representative element in and the active agent of a perspective more inclusive than itself. Charles Lachenmeyer claims in *The Language of Sociology* that

> any science can be conceptualized as a dual information transfer. The first information transfer is between men and the events that are the subject matter of their science. The second is between men as scientists about these events (1971: 1).

Definitions are the gateways through which this information must pass. Individuals qua scientists do not speak a language filled with definitions. Instead, and extrapolating from Lachenmeyer's insight, definitions orient us, giving us some coordinates in the world of our subject matter and pointing to particular aspects of that world. A venerable, somewhat frightening adage is apropos here: physical reality is inexhaustible; the possible descriptions of it are infinite. For scientists this means orienting devices are necessary because the significant aspects of the subject field are not obvious until they become community property. It is necessary, then, to construct a definition structure as free as possible from vagueness, ambiguity, opacity and contradiction. The scientific utility of a definition derives from the precision with which it reproduces the intended semantic, grammatical and contextual correlations among a set of referents, the concept and observers. Particularly in the social sciences where the "subject matter" produces its own semantic fields, definitions must be constructed with care. (Unfortunately, there is no commonly agreed upon procedure for the writing of definitions.)

Many efforts have been made to state the logical criteria for a good definition (see, for example, Russell and Whitehead, 1910; Carnap, 1942, Ayer, 1946; Hempel, 1952; Robinson, 1954). These and other attempts at defining correct definitions are quite varied, are often stated in esoteric language and grandly seek criteria that are independent of particular needs or intentions. The latter is more a desire than a fact. Usually a given set of parameters for definition is quite strictly limited to the author's approach to philosophy. Penetrating the language and making sense of the variety are somewhat difficult.

Raziel Abelson (1967) is helpful in organizing and criticizing the positions taken by various philosophers. Abelson divides these positions into a schema of three types: essentialism, prescriptivism (these two are similar to, but more general than, the realist–nominalist division suggested by Bierstedt, 1974b: 156–187) and linguistic theories (which bring attention to the logical grammar of a term, but equate use with usage). Because of the order Abelson sees in what at first appears as an undifferentiated whole, it becomes apparent that the independent contributions are not elaborating some central thought and that, accordingly, there is no single convention in philosophy (or elsewhere) for the formulation of definitions. Another aspect of this inconclusiveness is that an ethic does not exist for judging good from bad definitions. Furthermore, each of these types suggests rules for definition too constricted for general use.

Abelson tries to provide some pragmatic, general guidelines for judging and constructing definitions. He tries to be more concrete where others have been abstract, while at the same time transcending the narrower interpretations of definition provided by essentialism, prescriptivism or linguistic theories. His first suggestion is that *a definition is a prescription for the use of a term* (see also Giddens, 1976: 124). In other words, a definition conveys the special knowledge of how (or when) we should employ a term (see also Lachenmeyer, 1971: 19–59). Behind a definition, therefore, is some perspective or purpose that draws our attention to a particular aspect of that which is being defined. A good definition, simply put, is very closely in keeping with the perspective or purpose of its author. This very general stricture is qualified by the following rules of thumb (adapted from Abelson, 1967: 322):

1. A definition should give the essence or nature of the thing defined, rather than its accidental properties.
2. A definition should indicate, or not contradict, the logical grammar of a term.
3. One should not define by synonyms.
4. A definition should be concise.
5. One should not define by metaphors.
6. One should not define by negative terms or by correlative terms (e.g., one should not define north as opposite of south, or parent as a person with one or more children). This last rule does not apply in the formal deductive systems of mathematics or logic where p may properly be defined as "the negation of p."

Before going ahead and constructing a new definition for socialization, keeping my purpose and the six rules of thumb in mind, I want to offer an interpretation of number 1. I want to interpret it in a way that will offend neither the realist nor the nominalist (Bierstedt, 1974b: 156—187). In its present form, by virtue of the phrase "the essence or nature of the thing defined," it appears to favor a realist definition, although I believe this is not necessarily the case. A more balanced interpretation of the relationship between the "essence of a thing" and "its accidental properties" will be obtained if we examine the meaning of "context-free" and "context-bound" definitions (cf. Giddens, 1976: 105, passim.).

Sociology has as one task the systematic translation of life's variety into the more concise form of theoretical knowledge. Following the venerable wisdom of Adam Ferguson, the sociological perspective should facilitate our seeing differences in similar events and similarities in different events.[1] A sociological concept is useful precisely because it can be "found" in many superficially different social occasions. For this reason, as we do sociology and reconceptualize the world, a certain level of that work should include the attempt to disengage concepts from a slavery to particularistic contexts of the life-world. Thus, the sociological perspective becomes a stable reference point; it is, or should be, a theoretical attitude stripped of the multitude of purposes playing upon events of the lived-in world. A value-free definition is an essay in the interpretation of some social phenomenon apart from its many live contexts. It is context free. This is not so impossible as it might initially appear (Berger, 1974: 124). And certainly, the production of context-free concepts is not a form of speculation. Instead, it follows from extensive experience. I will try to clarify this notion of context freedom in the following paragraphs.

The terms "context-free" and (its opposite) "context-bound" refer to two

---

[1] *Essay on the History of the Civil Society*, 1767.

types of definitions and so are related to rules for the use of a term. A context-free definition is maximally generic and parsimonious while still retaining the power to differentiate. A context-bound definition is ostensive and particularistic in that it identifies a concept in fewer contexts than does its context-free counterpart. A context-bound definition is minimally powerful if it identifies a concept in only one context. A context-free definition will be hereafter called simply a *definition*. Context-bound definitions will be called *descriptions*.

Description as a form of definition in sociology is narrow and terribly vulnerable to contradiction because it relies so heavily upon the point of view and the frame of reference of the concrete context to which it is tied. A definition, on the other hand, allows for a larger range of denotations and is thus more parsimonious and powerful than a description. For example, we can find the definition of a word in the dictionary. Such a meaning is often not exactly clear in and of itself. The word and its definition gain in meaning and take on a particular meaning only as they relate to a context; that is, as they relate to some sentence or to some other ideas (Wittgenstein, 1958: 181).

The definition (the "proper" use, pointing to the "nature of the thing defined") and the usage (the customary, habitual or "accidental properties of the thing defined") help to clarify one another; each gives significance to the other, and meaning emerges. And again, using the following definition: an _____ is a motor- or engine-propelled, wheeled, passenger platform designed for traveling on streets or roads.[2] That was a farily nonhistorical and relatively context-free definition of the term "automobile." However, we understand what "automobile" *really* means (given the *denotative* limits of the definition, which thereby make an automobile distinguishable from jeeps, pickup trucks, aircars, airplanes, etc., but not from buses) by seeing it as "my car," a taxi, a means to mobility, or to freedom, or to prestige, an instrument for suicide, or of pollution, and so on. Each description points to a context that limits the connotation of the word "automobile" and elicits the specific purpose behind the human use or understanding of (an) the automobile. *The definition of a concept cannot stand apart from its elaboration by a description.* It should be too general, and therefore possessed of the flexibility necessary to provide a connotative orientation toward many contexts. Conversely, a description is too narrowly bound to the context, or point of view, to serve as a general way of organizing meaning. The description, nevertheless, lends precision to the definition (perhaps allowing us to differentiate, as the above definition of automobile will not, between a car and a bus). A definition may

---

[2]This definition was adapted from *Webster's New World Dictionary of the American Language*, 1972.

well be fully comprehensible only when accompanied by a description. And yet, the definition itself must remain separate from that or other particular contexts. In this way the definition can be used to identify a concept in a variety of human contexts that bear only a "family resemblance" (Wittgenstein, 1958: 119, 123; see also Burke, 1969: 24—29, on contextual and familial definitions).

APPENDIX II

THE THEORIST AS SOCIOLOGICAL OBSERVER:
A METHOD FOR THEORY

ANALYTICAL FRAMEWORK

This appendix is an attempt to describe the particular perspective I attempted to sustain in formulating an understanding of socialization theory, whether historic, current or that in my own approach. Appendix II concerns the historical and methodological component that enters into the design of specific theories.

It has been pointed out in numerous places that every theory is formulated from the ideas, values, facts and hypotheses that permeate the biography of the theorist. Stated in another way, a theorist at work is not equally susceptible to all perspectives or all data; some historically located means are employed in accepting what seems real, what seems to fit, or in resolving an apparent dilemma. Transforming these tacit presuppositions into explicit assumptions, to the extent it is possible, simultaneously produces the perspective or matrix of thought that allows a theorist to arrive at a particular vision of the world.

Elaborating on a theoretical perspective has several benefits. First, it is a worthwhile sociological endeavor in its own right (cf. "Theorizing" by Alan Blum, 1970). Second, an author's systematic attention to a perspective assists in the achievement of a consistent perspective throughout a work. Third, an explicit perspective increases the reader's relative depth of understanding of a theory, thereby aiding critical reply. For example, to suspect that Max Weber was in some way writing a reply to Karl Marx, or to read that Emile Durkheim had serious epistemological concerns needing expression in terms of sociological theory, or to know that Talcott Parsons was motivated to import a systems theory scheme (a metatheory) for use upon the data and concepts of sociology—each of these things gives us immediately deeper insight into the work of the author. Examples could be multiplied, but the point is not obscure; such insights are interpretive tools that shed more light upon an author's work than provided by the actual argument alone. From an array of such insights we can partially reconstruct the "context of discovery" (Kaplan, 1964: 13), a concept apparently very similar to the idea of a method for theory. I understand the relationship in the following terms: *when the context of discovery is purposively constructed and used toward some end, it becomes a method for theory.* Let me go on to explain more about theoretical methodology and its relation to theory.

In the sense that the term is most frequently understood, a method may serve as a means for replicating another's inquiry and conclusions. A method for theory has no such purpose although public knowledge of it can aid in the appraisal of a work. *A theoretical method is an explication of the stipulations that form the basis for what the theorist deems to be a plausible (existentially comfortable) rendering of the subject.* The function of methods in general is to limit the raw biographical effect upon observation. By contrast, a theoretical method is an attempt to render the "biographical effect" more visible. Once visible, it can be more systematically reflected in the substance of a theory.

The central and most interchangeable feature of the theoretical method I describe is the attitude taken by the theorist, the attitude of the "sociological observer." I will apply a stricter definition to the role of the observer a little later, but for now it must be stipulated that, however one's perspective is technically analyzed, the theorist is an observer—but in a different way from those who are immediately engaged in gathering facts. Accordingly, there are considerable differences in the methodology of each activity. The methodology of theory formulation is not so elaborate or finely drawn as are the formal techniques adapted to fact-collecting. The "biographical effect," as we have called it, is given more freedom. In physics, for instance, we find a subjective and community reliance upon such loosely defined criteria as elegance, symmetry, parsimony and fruitfulness.

These guidelines hold for sociology just as they do for physics. However, there are some extra dangers that exist in sociology. Within sociology it is not always clear whether a theorist is speaking from the perspective of some metatheory, as a "sociological observer," as a generalized (or quite specific) member might see the world, as a special kind of voyeur, as a doubter or critic of some state of affairs (debunker) or from a position composed from multiple perspectives.[1] Inasmuch as there is more involved here than simple perspectives, I will go on with my explanation. I want to generate some analytical categories to portray the "cognitive style" with which a theorist may approach work and which effectively shaped the product. This will give me a framework in which to couch my own theoretical method a few pages hence.

Theory itself might simply be described as a workable knowledge of a subject field *from some perspective* (Einstein, 1961: 123–124). With all it entails by way of attitude, it is the perspective that guides the mind of the theorist. However, there are other active agents within the consciousness of a theorist. I consider the theorist at work to be in dialogue: (1) with some *concrete situations* at least partially defined by the subject field; (2) with a range of *abstractions* (aggregate data or "social facts" and ideas); and (3) with an *unfolding logic* of conceptualization. The theorist is an observer, aware of being an observer. It is because of this state of awareness that it is possible for the theorist to exert a particular discipline specific to a defined *purpose* (problems, questions), as the "dialogue"—the act of formulating theory—is carried forward and a "theory" is subsequently concretized in speech or writing. This act of discipline may be understood as the fourth party in the internal dialogue of the theorist. In other words, the theorist constantly refers to the standards set by a chosen *methodological stance*.

Method, concrete situations, abstractions and unfolding logic are four "participants" in an internal dialogue. Each exerts its own force. It becomes too descriptive (or one step up in abstraction, too conceptual without being "theoretical"), too speculative, too carried away along a deductive path, or, finally, too much a technique vaguely in search of a theoretical content. Any of these excesses may be the typical style of a theorist or the approach of a certain school. C. Wright Mills gave extended discussion to some specific instances of theoretical imbalance in his book *The Sociological Imagination* (1959). We now all have a certain knowledge of the lopsided emphases in "Grand Theory" and "Abstracted Empiricism." Going beyond Mills, perhaps even the so-called theories of the middle range (Merton, 1949) or "substantive theory" (Glaser and Strauss, 1970) could be called the "Joy of Concepts." Be these things as they may, within the context of an entire discipline there is room for a variety of designs, if these three camps are not exhaustive of the membership.

By way of a clarification and summary, in rather gross analytical fashion I

---

[1] Each of these several perspectives has a valid role in sociology. There has been, I think, a problem of explicitness and of consistency—not brought on by scientific negligence, but by an absorption in the job of getting on with the work of sociology.

am taking a theoretical method to mean a representation of the subjectively powerful matrix formed by the interaction of the *theoretical perspective* (whether of the metatheoretician, the sociological observer, the member, the voyeur, or the debunker) and the *theoretical balance* (among abstractions, the unfolding logic or quality of emergence in one's writing, and method), plus the direction given by a specific *purpose*. Let us now turn to the task of outlining the historical and methodological component that informs this book.

THEORETICAL METHODOLOGY SPECIFIED

I have chosen in this book to remain within the perspective of the sociological observer. This perspective is not assumed in the haughty belief that this is, after all, where the sociologist belongs. Instead, assuming that role is a reaction to a criticism made by Matthew Speier (1973: 138–142). In his insightful but somewhat belligerent allegation, he declares that sociologists have simply employed and extended what is actually an adult member's commonsense viewpoint of socialization. He claims that our present conceptual apparatus channels our thoughts into a "broad time sweep" as if an "adult" were contemplating the development of a child. Inkeles makes essentially the same criticism, but with different intentions:

> In their interaction with the child, parents and other socialization agents generally have in mind some conception of what the child is "supposed to become" and of the role which any particular child rearing practice may play in achieving or hindering the desired outcome. In other words, *both the practice and the study* of child socialization are inherently "forward looking" (1968: 76–77, emphasis added).

Now, returning to Speier's criticism, backed by Inkeles' observations on the present state of the concept: what they call faults may seem irrelevant or minor. Inkeles claims that this form of definition takes our attention away from the sociology of what is done to the novice. Speier sees that in studying socialization, the routine interactional events of everyday life have been overlooked. By comparing what both men say and then considering the historical nature of the prevalent conceptualization, the apparent innocence of their criticisms begins to fade. Sociologists have been culturally induced by the conventions of their paradigm to ignore a need for the theoretical apprehension of socialization activity. This, as it happens, is where the theorist qua observer becomes an important role. This attitude is in part as appeal to observables as the basic data for theory formulation. Quite simply, I refer to the sociological observation of natural human settings. This is intended as a contrast to the primary reliance upon *reports* of behavior, collected for example by survey research, or theory derived from evidence obtained in the artificial atmosphere of experimentally controlled situations. However, what I mean by the attitude of the sociological observer is more than the already tired appeal for sociologists to notice what people actually do; it is a particular interpretive scheme.

Fortunately, there are precedents in the attempt to define what it means to take on the role of the observer during the theoretical interpretation of human events. I say fortunately because even when on guard, people inevitably theorize. Observation and theory cannot be readily divorced. The two words are really just tags for different emphases in the single task of making sense out of the world. Furthermore, as Durkheim pointed out, observation and theorizing are common prescientific events (1965: 21). We do, however, readily acknowledge that the scientific practice of these activities is different from their everyday manifestations. The hallmark of this distinction lies in the conscious attempt by the scientific observer to guide what is observed.

Several authors have tried to explain what this implies about the relationship of the observer to what is being observed. These are epistemological accounts. However, my immediate concern is not epistemological. The primary interest here is in creating a description of what the observer does. I will give four descriptions of observer activity, in order from the general to the specific, ending with my own position.

Abraham Kaplan (1964: 127) expresses the motivation of the observer in a satisfactory way. He says that surely there is the gratification of discovering what has been hidden (*the voyeur*), but that the mature observer is primarily moved to "facilitate an intimate, sustained, and productive relationship with the world."

In the eyes of Peter Berger (1963), the observer is not so pure and virtuous. Berger discusses sociology as a specific form of consciousness ideally transcending the inclinations of the individual sociologist. All of what Berger means by the role of sociological observer is compressed into one very quotable sentence; to wit, "It can be said that the first wisdom of sociology is this—things are not what they seem" (1963:23). For Berger, that maxim summarizes the four motifs that constitute the sociological vision: (1) the debunking motif, the attempt to apprehend the latent as well as the manifest functions of social events; (2) the theme of unrespectability, in which "the goggles of respectability" are shed to search behind official or routine definitions of reality; (3) the recognition of relativity, understanding that all motives and knowledge are grounded in specific historical social configurations; and (4) the idea of cosmopolitan concern, or the effort expended to attain an objective appraisal (1963: 37–53). Berger also maintains that "methodological atheism" (1969: 180) is an essential and specific perspective employed when theorizing about religion. This may be generalized to say that sociologists must stick by their own class of determinants and not assume the subjects' explanatory system. Berger would like us to see through the unconvinced eyes of *the critic.*

And, earlier, C. Wright Mills described an agile form of observer assessment he labeled the "sociological imagination." His conception demands that an observer maintain an understanding for the many personal milieux, while looking beyond them in an awareness of the way institutional linkages embrace and affect the real lives of people. This requires the capacity to shift effectively one's intellectual attention from "the most impersonal and remote transformations to the most intimate features of the self—and to see the relations between the two." (1959: 7).

Mills and Berger are telling us that the sociological perspective seeks *understanding that can be independent of specific contexts or data.* Their interpretations of the theorist as an observer on the sociological scene may be summarized by the slogan words: *doubt, distance* and *discipline*— appropriately modulated by a "mobile sensibility" (Lerner, 1958).[2]

I agree with these portrayals but I think the position can be made more specific. First, theories are our knowledge, but they are only the latest correction in a series of imperfect statements about the world. Theories help us learn to see differences in similar events and similarities in different events. A theory should not be reified: it should be understood as a *useful* way of viewing the world for the sociologist.

Second, the sociological theorist qua observer should differentiate between the way folk explanations lend logic to the situation and the way events and processes must appear to an outsider *(the observer).* Put differently, there are some aspects of social events visible to the observer that are not part of the routine attitudes taken by the *members.* Moreover, there is other information that can come to the observer only second-hand from members' interpretations. Theoretical account must be taken of the ultimate source of observations. This filtering process can be only relatively well done because, as Alvin Gouldner put it, "In practice, the sociologist's role realities and his personal realities interpenetrate and mutually influence one another" (1970: 42). This entwining of perspectives cannot be unraveled. To be able to do so would eventually lead to an alien formulation of an implausible theory—*a metatheory* too dissociated from life as we know it (Wentworth, 1975; 15–16). Nevertheless, this interpenetration of perspectives can be used:

---

[2] It seems to me that the agility of the sociological imagination is but a specially focused case of Lerner's description of modern consciousness as a "mobile sensibility" or "mobile personality." In other words, Mills is in fact speaking of a general capacity whose performance is aided by a rootedness in modern society and by a disciplined mind in control of sociological knowledge.

Husserl's notion of reflexiveness captures this moment. The reflexive turn which essentially characterizes theorizing treats the ordinary formulation of objects in the world as concrete insofar as the method of formulating is itself unheeded in the formulation of the object. The concrete grasp of the world does not include itself (its act of grasping) as a topic of inquiry. Thus, reflexiveness is not a mere suspension of the natural attitude; rather it constitutes an expansion of the possibilities inherent in ordinary looking in order to include such ordinary looking within its purview (Blum, 1970: 315).

Finally, the theorist must attend to and account for the events of concrete relationships; observation is now; there is no past and future except as they affect the present. This point can be expressed more clearly by adding that

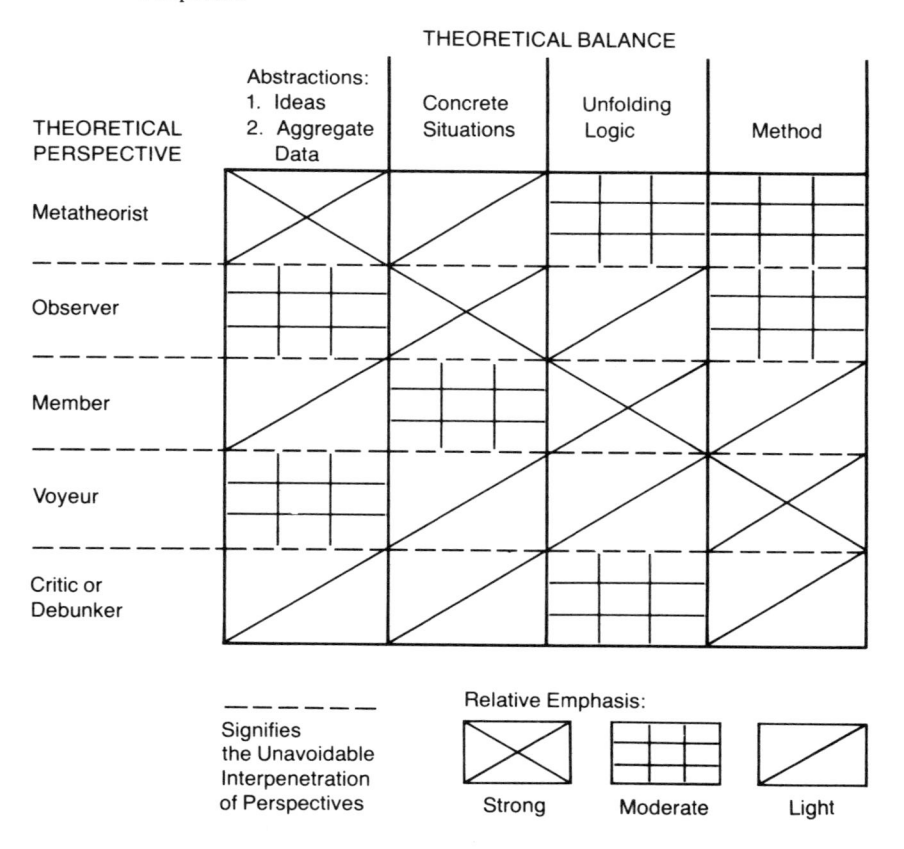

Figure 2. A Heuristic Comparison of the Likely Theoretical Balance According to Perspective

interactional events are what is held in the "imagination." We methodically create such examples "for the purpose of deciding whether or not they are true in all possible worlds. The theorist's method can then be seen as one of inventing, collating, and excluding possibilities" (Blum, 1970: 316).

To conclude, this appendix has been developed around the theme of explicating somewhat the context of discovery, or that is, a method for theory relevant to the theorist as a sociological observer. It was indicated earlier that this can never be finally accomplished: the appendix was not intended as a phenomenology of the creative experience. And indeed, by presenting what I have said couched in an analytical framework in terms of purpose, perspective and theoretical balance, I have precluded any such descriptive journey. Let me now continue within that framework. My *purpose* is to address and balance the social psychological bias of most previous socialization studies by assuming the role of the sociological observer. Taking on this perspective for the purposes of empirical research tends to stress attention to the details of concrete situations. When this perspective is approached by a theorist, this emphasis remains but is continually reconciled with the other elements of theoretical balance mentioned in this appendix (see Figure 2). Observation becomes an affair carried on in the imagination, but it is nonetheless based on experience. This method of perspective has been used in this book and is tied into what I have to say about socialization. In this respect a constant vigil must be kept to attend to the distinctions and relationships among the *concept* of socialization, the empirically occurring socializing *processes* and the *theory* of socialization.

REFERENCES

Abelson, Raziel
  1967 "Definition." Pp. 314–324 in Paul Edwards (Editor-in-Chief), *The Encyclopedia of Philosophy*, Vol. II. New York: Macmillan and the Free Press.

Aberle, David F.
  1961 "Culture and Socialization." In Francis L. K. Hsu (ed.), *Psychological Anthropology*. Homewood, IL: Dorsey Press.

Allport, Floyd H.
  1924 "The Group Fallacy in Relation to Social Science." *Am. J. Sociology* 29 (May): 688–703. With discussions by Emory Bogardus, pp. 703–704, and Alexander A. Goldenweiser, pp. 704–706.
  1927a "The Nature of Institutions." *Social Forces* 6 (December): 167–179.
  1927b " 'Group' and 'Institution' as Concepts in a Natural Science of Social Phenomena." Pp. 83–99 in Ernest W. Burgess (ed.), *The Relation of the Individual to the Community*. Vol. XXII of Publications of the American Sociological Society.

Almack, John C.
 1925 "Efficiency in Socialization." *Am. J. Sociology* 31 (September): 241–250.
Alwin, Duane F.
 1974 "College Effects on Educational and Occupational Attainments," *Am. Sociological Rev.* 39 (April): 210–223.
Anderson, Charles H.
 1971 *Toward a New Sociology.* Homewood, IL: Dorsey Press.
Ariès, Philippe
 1962 *Centuries of Childhood: A Social History of Family Life.* Tr. Robert Ballick. New York: Vintage Books.
Ashcroft, Norman and Albert E. Scheflen
 1976 *People Space.* Garden City, NY: Anchor Books.
Astin, Alexander W.
 1971 *Predicting Academic Performance in College.* New York: The Free Press.
Attewell, Paul
 1974 "Ethnomethodology Since Garfinkel," *Theory and Society* 1 (Summer): 179–210.
Ayer, A. J.
 1946 *Language, Truth, and Logic.* London: Routledge and Kegan Paul.
Baldwin, James Mark
 1902 *Social and Ethical Interpretations.* New York: Macmillan.
 1911 *The Individual and Society.* Boston: Gorham Press.
Ball, Donald W.
 1970 "The Problematics of Respectability." Pp. 326–373 in Jack D. Douglas (ed.), *Deviance and Respectability.* New York: Basic Books.
 1973 *Microecology: Social Situations and Intimate Space.* Indianapolis: Bobbs-Merrill.
Banton, Michael
 1970 *Socialization: The Approach from Social Anthropology.* New York: Tavistock Publications.
Barnes, Harry Elmer
 1948a "The General Character of American Sociology." Pp. 739–743 in Harry Elmer Barnes (ed.), *An Introduction to the History of Sociology.* Chicago: Univ. of Chicago Press.
 1948b "Albion Woodbury Small: Promoter of American Sociology and Expositor of Social Interests." Pp. 766–792 in Harry Elmer Barnes (ed.), *An Introduction to the History of Sociology.* Chicago: Univ. of Chicago Press.
Barrett, William
 1961 "Determinism and Novelty." Pp. 46–54 in Sidney Hook (ed.), *Determinism and Freedom in the Age of Modern Science.* New York:
Becker, Howard S.
 1964 "Personal Change in Adult Life." *Sociometry* 27 (March): 40–53.
Becker, Howard S., Blanche Geer, Everett C. Hughes and Anselm L. Strauss
 1961 *Boys in White.* Chicago: Univ. of Chicago Press.
Bellah, Robert N.
 1959 "Durkheim and History." *Am. Sociological Rev.* 24 (August): 1–15.

Bendix, Reinhard and Bennett Berger
   1959   "Images of Society and Problems of Concept Formation in Sociology." Pp. 92–118 in Llewellyn Gross (ed.), *Symposium on Sociological Theory.* New York: Harper and Row.

Bengtson, Vern L.
   1975   "Generation and Family Effects in Value Socialization." *Am. Sociological Rev.* 40 (June): 358–371.

Bengtson, V. L. and K. D. Black
   1973   "Intergenerational Relations and Continuities in Socialization." Chapter 9 in P. Baltes and W. Schaie (eds.), *Personality and Socialization.* New York: Academic Press.

Berger, Peter L.
   1961   *The Noise of Solemn Assemblies.* New York: Doubleday.
   1963   *Invitation to Sociology: A Humanistic Perspective.* Garden City, NY: Doubleday.
   1969   *The Sacred Canopy.* Garden City, NY: Doubleday.
   1974   *Pyramids of Sacrifice.* New York: Basic Books.

Berger, Peter L. and Brigitte Berger
   1975   *Sociology: A Biographical Approach.* New York: Basic Books.

Berger, Peter L. and Hansfried Kellner
   1970   "Marriage and the Construction of Reality." Pp. 50–72 in Hans Peter Dreitzel (ed.), *Recent Sociology No. 2.* New York: Macmillan.

Berger, Peter L. and Thomas Luckmann
   1967   *The Social Construction of Reality.* Garden City, NY: Doubleday.

Berger, Peter L. and Stanley Pullberg
   1965   "Reification and the Sociological Critique of Consciousness." *History and Theory: Studies in the Philosophy of History* 4: 196–211.

Berne, Eric
   1964   *Games People Play.* New York: Grove Press.

Bernstein, Basil
   1966   "Elaborated and Restricted Codes: An Outline." *Sociological Inquiry* 36 (Spring): 254–261.

Bershady, Harold J.
   1973   *Ideology and Social Knowledge.* Oxford: Basil Blackwell.

Bidney, David
   1967   *Theoretical Anthropology.* New York: Schocken Books.

Bierstedt, Robert
   1950   "An Analysis of Social Power." *Am. Sociological Rev.* 15 (December): 730–738.
   1957   *The Social Order.* New York: McGraw-Hill.
   1974a   *The Social Order*, 4th Ed. New York: McGraw-Hill.
   1974b   *Power and Progress.* New York: McGraw-Hill.

Blackmar, Frank W.
   1905   *Elements of Sociology.* New York: Macmillan.
   1929   "The Socialization of the American Indian." *Am. J. Sociology* 34 (January): 653–670.

Blackmar, Frank W. and John Lewis Gillin
    1916   *Outlines of Sociology.* New York: Macmillan.

Blau, Peter M. and Otis Dudley Duncan
    1967   *The American Occupational Structure.* New York: Wiley.

Blaug, Mark
    1975   "Kuhn versus Lakatos, or Paradigms versus Research Programmes in the History of Economics." *History of Political Economy* 7 (Winter): 399–433.

Blum, Alan
    1970   "Theorizing." Pp. 301–319 in Jack D. Douglas (ed.), *Understanding Everyday Life.* Chicago: Aldine.

Blum, Alan F. and Peter McHugh
    1971   "The Social Ascription of Motives." *Am. Sociological Rev.* 36 (February): 98–109.

Blumer, Herbert
    1954   "What Is Wrong with Social Theory?" *Am. Sociological Rev.* 19 (February): 3–10.
    1962   "Society as Social Interaction." Pp. 179–192 in Arnold M. Rose (ed.), *Human Behavior and Social Processes: An Interactionist Approach.* Boston: Houghton Mifflin.
    1967   "Sociological Analysis and the Variable." Pp. 84–94 in Jerome G. Manis and Bernard N. Meltzer (eds.), *Symbolic Interaction.* Boston: Allyn and Bacon.
    1969   *Symbolic Interactionism: Perspective and Method.* Englewood Cliffs, NJ: Prentice-Hall.

Bogardus, Emory S.
    1924   *Fundamentals of Social Psychology.* New York: Century.
    1934   *Sociology.* New York: Macmillan (original copyright 1913).
    1954   *Sociology* 4th Ed. New York: Macmillan.

Bourdieu, Pierre and Jean-Claude Passeron
    1977   *Reproduction in Education, Society and Culture.* Beverly Hills, CA: Sage Publications.

Bowden, Witt
    1929   "Are Social Studies Sciences?" *Social Forces* 7 (March): 367–378.

Brim, Orville G.
    1960   "Personality Development as Role Learning." Pp. 127–159 in Ira Isco and Harold W. Stevenson (eds.), *Personality Development in Children.* Austin, TX: Univ. of Texas Press.

Brim, Orville G. and Stanton Wheeler
    1966   *Socialization After Childhood: Two Essays.* New York: Wiley.

Broadhead, Robert S.
    1974   "Notes on the Sociology of the Absurd." *Pacific Sociological Rev.* 17 (January): 35–45.

Broom, Leonard and Philip Selznick
    1955   *Sociology: A Text with Adapted Readings.* Evanston, IL: Row, Peterson.
    1968   *Sociology: A Text with Adapted Readings*, 4th Ed. New York: Harper and Row.

Brown, Richard H.
  1976   "Social Theory as Metaphor: On the Logic of Discovery for the Sciences of Conduct." *Theory and Society* 3 (Summer): 169–197.
Brown, Roger
  1965   *Social Psychology.* New York: Free Press.
Bucher, Rue and Joan G. Stelling
  1977   *Becoming Professional.* Beverly Hills, CA: Sage Publications.
Burgess, Ernest W., Herbert Blumer and Louis Wirth (eds.)
  1939   *Am. J. Sociology* 44 (May).
Burke, Kenneth
  1969   *A Grammar of Motives.* Berkeley, CA: Univ. of California Press.
Burtt, E. A.
  1954   *The Metaphysical Foundations of Modern Science.* Garden City NY: Doubleday-Anchor Books.
Caplow, Theodore
  1971   *Elementary Sociology.* Englewood Cliffs, NJ: Prentice-Hall.
  1975   *Sociology.* Englewood Cliffs, NJ: Prentice-Hall.
Carnap, Rudolf
  1942   *Introduction to Semantics.* Cambridge, MA: Harvard Univ. Press.
Carter, Hugh
  1927   "Research Interests of American Sociologists." *Social Forces* 6 (December): 209–212.
Chapin, F. Stuart
  1928   "A New Definition of Social Institutions." *Social Forces* 6 (March): 375–377.
Charon, Joel M.
  1979   *Symbolic Interactionism.* Englewood Cliffs, NJ: Prentice-Hall.
Chomsky, Noam
  1965   *Aspects of the Theory of Syntax.* Cambridge, MA: MIT Press.
  1968   *Language and Mind.* New York: Harcourt, Brace and World.
  1975   *Reflections on Language.* New York: Pantheon.
Cicourel, Aaron V.
  1970a "The Acquisition of Social Structure: Toward a Developmental Sociology of Language and Meaning." Pp. 136–168 in Jack D. Douglas (ed.), *Understanding Everyday Life.* Chicago: Aldine.
  1970b "Basic and Normative Rules in the Negotiation of Status and Role." Pp. 4–45 in Hans Peter Dreitzel (ed.), *Recent Sociology No. 2.* New York: Macmillan.
Clark, Alexander L. and Jack P. Gibbs
  1965   "Social Control: A Reformulation." *Social Problems* 12 (Spring): 398–415.
Clarke, Michael
  1975   "Survival in the Field: Implications of Personal Experience in Field Work." *Theory and Society* 2 (Spring): 95–123.
Clausen, John A.
  1968   "A Historical and Comparative View of Socialization Theory and Research." Pp. 18–72 in John A. Clausen (ed.), *Socialization and Society.* Boston: Little, Brown.

Clegg, Stewart
    1976   "Power, Theorizing and Nihilism." *Theory and Society* 3 (Spring): 65–87.

Cochrane, Carl M.
    1971   "Successful Medical Trainees and Practitioners." In Robert H. Coombs and Clark E. Vincent (eds.), *Psychosocial Aspects of Medical Training*. Springfield, IL: Charles C. Thomas.

Collins, Randall
    1971   "Functional and Conflict Theories of Stratification." *Am. Sociological Rev.* 36 (December): 1002–1019.

Collins, Randall
    1975   *Conflict Sociology: Toward an Explanatory Science*. New York: Academic Press.

Collins, Randall and Michael Makowsky
    1972   *The Discovery of Society*. New York: Random House.

Cook-Gumperz, Jenny
    1973   *Social Control and Socialization*. London: Routledge and Kegan Paul.

Cooley, Charles Horton
    1964   *Human Nature and the Social Order*. New York: Schocken Books
    (1902)

Coombs, Robert H.
    1971   "The Medical Marriage." In Robert H. Coombs and Clark E. Vincent (eds.), *Psychosocial Aspects of Medical Training*. Springfield, IL: Charles C. Thomas.

Coombs, Robert H. and Blake P. Boyle
    1971   "The Transition to Medical School: Expectations Versus Realities." In Robert H. Coombs and Clark E. Vincent (eds.), *Psychosocial Aspects of Medical Training*. Springfield, IL: Charles C. Thomas.

Coombs, Robert H. And Louis P. Stein
    1971   "Medical-Student Society and Culture." In Robert H. Coombs and Clark E. Vincent (eds.), *Psychosocial Aspects of Medical Training*. Springfield, IL: Charles C. Thomas.

Crespigny, A.
    1968   "Power and Its Forms." *Political Studies* 16 (June): 192–205.

Cuber, John F.
    1947   *Sociology*. New York: Appleton-Century-Crofts.
    1951   *Sociology*. New York: Appleton-Century-Crofts.
    1959   *Sociology*. New York: Appleton-Century-Crofts.

Dahrendorf, Ralf
    1958   "Out of Utopia: Toward a Reorientation of Sociological Analysis." *Am. J. Sociology* 44: 115–127.

Danziger, Kurt
    1971   *Socialization*. Baltimore: Penguin Books.

Davis, Fred
    1968   "Professional Socialization as Subjective Experience: The Process of Doctrinal Conversion Among Student Nurses." Chapter 17 in Howard S.

Becker, Blanche Geer, David Riesman and Robert S. Weiss (eds.), *Institutions and the Person*. Chicago: Aldine.

Davis, Kingsley
1949 *Human Society*. New York: Macmillan.

Davis, Michael Marks
1909 *Psychological Interpretations of Society*. New York: Longmans, Green and Co., Agents (Columbia University).

Dawson, Carl A. and Warren E. Gettys
1948 *An Introduction to Sociology*. New York: Ronald Press.

Dealey, James Quayle
1909 *Sociology: Its Simpler Teachings and Applications*. New York: Burdett.
1920 *Sociology: Its Development and Application*. New York: D. Appleton.

DeFleur, Melvin, William V. D'Antonio and Lois B. DeFleur
1971 *Sociology: Man in Society*. Glenview, IL: Scott, Foresman.

Denzin, Norman K.
1970 "Symbolic Interactionism and Ethnomethodology." Pp. 259–284 in Jack D. Douglas (ed.), *Understanding Everyday Life*. Chicago: Aldine.

Dewey, John and James H. Tufts
1908 *Ethics*. New York: Henry Holt.

Diamond, Norman
1976 "Generating Rebellions in Science." *Theory and Society* 3 (Winter): 583–599.

Disco, Cornelius
1976 "Wittgenstein and the End of Wild Conjecture." *Theory and Society* 3 (Summer): 265–287.

Dollard, John
1935 *Criteria for the Life History, with Analyses of Six Notable Documents*. New Haven, CT: Yale Univ. Press.
1939 "Culture, Society, Impulse and Socialization." *Am. J. Sociology* 45 (July): 50–63.

Dornsbusch, Sanford M.
1955 "The Military Academy as an Assimilating Institution." *Social Forces* 33 (May): 316–321.

Douglas, Jack D.
1970 "Deviance and Respectability: The Social Construction of Moral Meanings." Pp. 3–31 in Jack D. Douglas (ed.), *Deviance and Respectability*. New York: Basic Books.

Duncan, O.D.
1966 "Path Analysis: Sociological Examples." *Am. J. Sociology* 72 (July): 1–16.

Durkheim, Emile
1933 *The Division of Labor in Society*. New York: Macmillan.
(1893)
1951 *Suicide*. New York: Free Press.
(1897)
1957 *Professional Ethics and Civil Morals*. London: Routledge and Kegan Paul.
(1900)

1961   *Moral Education: A Study in the Theory and Application of the Sociology of Education.* New York: Free Press.
(1902–
1906)
1964   *The Rules of Sociological Method.* New York: Free Press.
(1895)
1965   *The Elementary Forms of the Religious Life.* New York: Free Press.
(1912)
1974   *Sociology and Philosophy.* New York: Free Press.
(1898–
1911)

Einstein, Albert
1961   *Relativity: The Special and General Theory.* New York: Crown.

Ellis, Desmond P.
1971   "The Hobbesian Problem of Order: A Critical Appraisal of the Normative Solution." *Am. Sociological Rev.* 36 (August): 692–703.

Ellwood, Charles A.
1913   *Sociology and Modern Social Problems.* New York: American Book Co.
1923   "What Is Socialization?" *J. Applied Sociology* 8 (September): 5–10.
1931   "Scientific Methodology in Sociology." *Social Forces* 10 (October): 15–21.

Emerson, Joan P.
1969   "Negotiating the Serious Import of Humor." *Sociometry* 32 (June): 169–181.
1970   "Behavior in Private Places: Sustaining Definitions of Reality in Gynecological Examinations." Pp. 73–101 in Hans Peter Dreitzel (ed.), *Recent Sociology No. 2.* New York: Macmillan.

Enos, Darryl D. and Paul Sultan
1977   *The Sociology of Health Care.* New York: Praeger.

Etzioni, Amitai
1961   *A Comparative Analysis of Complex Organizations.* New York: Free Press.

Eubank, Earle Edward
1932   *The Concepts of Sociology.* Boston: D. C. Heath.
1937   "Errors in Sociology." *Social Forces* 16 (December): 178–201.

Faris, Robert E. L.
1967   *Chicago Sociology 1920–1932.* Chicago: Univ. of Chicago Press.

Featherman, David L.
1972   "Achievement Orientations and Socio-economic Career Attainments." *Am. Sociological Rev.* 37 (April): 131–143.

Fichter, Joseph H.
1972   "The Concept of Man in Social Science: Freedom, Values and Second Nature." *J. Scientific Study of Religion* 11: 109–121.

Fite, Warner
1911   *Individualism.* New York: Longmans, Green.

Frank, Arthur W., III
1976   "Making Scenes in Public: Symbolic Violence and Social Order." *Theory and Society* 3 (Fall): 395–416.

Frank, Lawrence K.
  1928 "The Management of Tension." *Am. J. Sociology* 33 (March): 705–736.
  1962 "The Beginnings of Child Development and Family Life Education in the Twentieth Century." *Merrill-Palmer Q.* 8 (October): 207–227.
Freud, Sigmund
  1939 *Moses and Monotheism.* New York: Knopf.
  1961 *Civilization and its Discontents.* New York: W. W. Norton.
  (1930)
Fromm, Erich
  1961 *Marx's Concept of Man.* New York: Frederick Ungar.
Fuller, John Scott and Jerry Jacobs
  1973 "Socialization." Pp. 168–208 in Jack D. Douglas (ed.), *Introduction to Sociology: Situations and Structures.* New York: Free Press.
Gardiner, Patrick
  1961 *The Nature of Historical Explanation.* London: Oxford Univ Press.
Garfinkel, Harold
  1967 *Studies in Ethnomethodology.* Englewood Cliffs, NJ: Prentice-Hall.
Geertz, Clifford
  1974 "The Impact of the Concept of Culture on the Concept of Man." In Yehudi A. Cohen (ed.), *Man in Adaptation.* Chicago: Aldine.
Giddens, Anthony
  1976 *New Rules of Sociological Method.* New York: Basic Books.
Giddings, Franklin Henry
  1896 *The Principles of Sociology: An Analysis of the Phenomena of Association and of Social Organization.* London: Macmillan.
  1897 *The Theory of Socialization.* New York: Macmillan.
  1910 *Elements of Sociology.* New York: Macmillan.
  1922 *Studies in the Theory of Human Society.* New York: Macmillan.
Gillin, John Lewis and John Philip Gillin
  1948 *Cultural Sociology.* New York: Macmillan.
Glaser, Barney G. and Anselm L. Strauss
  1967 "Awareness Contexts and Social Interaction." *Am. Sociological Rev.* 29 (October): 669–679.
  1970 "Discovery of Substantive Theory: A Basic Strategy Underlying Qualitative Research." Pp. 268–304 in William J. Filstead (ed.), *Qualitative Methodology.* Chicago: Markham.
Goffman, Erving
  1961a *Encounters.* Indianapolis: Bobbs-Merrill.
  1961b *Asylums.* Garden City, NY: Anchor Books (Doubleday).
  1964 "The Neglected Situation." Pp. 133–136 in John J. Gumperz and Dell Hymes (eds.), *The Ethnography of Communication.* A special issue of the *American Anthropologist* 66 (December, Part 2).
  1967 *Interaction Ritual.* Garden City, NY: Doubleday.
  1971 "The Insanity of Place." An appendix to *Relations in Public.* New York: Harper and Row.
  1974 *Frame Analysis.* New York: Harper and Row.

Gonos, George
    1977   " 'Situation' Versus 'Frame': The 'Interactionist' and the 'Structuralist' Analyses of Everyday Life." *Am. Sociological Rev.* 42 (December): 854–867.

Goslin, David A.
    1969   *Handbook of Socialization Theory and Research.* Chicago: Rand McNally.

Gough, Harrison G.
    1971   "The Recruitment and Selection of Medical Students." In Robert H. Coombs and Clark E. Vincent (eds.), *Psychosocial Aspects of Medical Training.* Springfield, IL: Charles C. Thomas.

Gouldner, Alvin
    1970   *The Coming Crisis of Western Sociology.* New York: Basic Books.

Groves, Ernest R.
    1932   *An Introduction to Sociology.* New York: Longmans, Green.

Habermas, Jurgen
    1970   "Toward a Theory of Communicative Competence." Pp. 115–148 in Hans Peter Dreitzel (ed.), *Recent Sociology No. 2.* New York: Macmillan.
    1975   *Legitimation Crisis.* Boston: Beacon Press.

Hadden, Jeffrey K. and Theodore E. Long
    1978   *A Study of Physician Socialization.* Hyattsville, Md.: Department of Health, Education, and Welfare, Public Health Service, Health Resources Administration, Bureau of Health Manpower.

Hall, Edward T.
    1959   *The Silent Language.* Greenwich, CT: Fawcett.
    1969   *The Hidden Dimension.* Garden City, NY: Anchor Books.

Handel, Warren
    1979   "Normative Expectations and the Emergence of Meanings as Solutions to Problems: Convergence of Structural and Interactionist Views." *Am. J. Sociology* 84 (January): 855–881.

Hanson, Todd and Ted Long
    1976   "Thinking About Medical Education: Working from the Classics." Working paper for the Developmental Study of Medical Socialization, Univ. of Virginia School of Medicine (unpublished).

Harré, R. and P. F. Secord
    1973   *The Explanation of Social Behavior.* Totowa, NJ: Littlefield, Adams.

Harrington, Michael
    1977   *The Twilight of Capitalism.* New York: Simon and Schuster.

Harris, James F., Jr.
    1976   "A New Look at Austin's Linguistic Phenomenology." *Philosophy and Phenomenological Res.* 36 (March): 384–390.

Hart, Hornell
    1923   "Research Possibilities with a Socialization Test." *J. Applied Sociology* 8 (March–April): 163–166.

Hawthorn, Horace Boies
    1926   *The Sociology of Rural Life.* New York: Century.

Hayes, Edward Cary
    1921a   *Sociology and Ethics: The Facts of Social Life as the Source of Solutions*

            for the Theoretical and Practical Problems of Ethics. New York: D. Appleton.
1921b "The Sociological Point of View." Pp. 1–16 in Ernest W. Burgess (ed.), *Factors in Social Evolution*, 16. Publications of the American Sociological Society.

Hempel, C. G.
1952 *Fundamentals of Concept Formation in Empirical Science*. Chicago: Univ. of Chicago Press.

Hewitt, John P.
1976 *Self and Society*. Boston: Allyn and Bacon.

Hewitt, John P, and Peter M. Hall
1973 "Social Problems, Problematic Situations, and Quasi-Theories." *Am. Sociological Rev.* 38 (June): 367–374.

Hewitt, John P. and Randall Stokes
1975 "Disclaimers." *Am. Sociological Rev.* 40 (February): 1–11.

Hinkle, Roscoe C., Jr. and Gisela J. Hinkle
1954 *The Development of Modern Sociology*. New York: Random House.

Hofstadter, Richard
1959 *Social Darwinism in American Thought*. New York: G. Braziller.

Homans, George C.
1958 "Social Behavior as Exchange." *Am. J. Sociology* 62 (May): 597–606.
1964 "Bringing Men Back In." *Am. Sociological Rev.* 29 (December): 808–818.
1970 "The Relevance of Psychology to the Explanation of Social Phenomena." In Robert Borger and Frank Cioffi (eds.), *Explanations in the Behavioural Sciences*. Cambridge, MA: Cambridge Univ. Press.

Horton, Paul B. and Chester L. Hunt
1972 *Sociology*. New York: McGraw-Hill.

House, Floyd N.
1929 *The Range of Social Theory*. New York: Henry Holt.
1936 *The Development of Sociology*. New York: McGraw-Hill.

Hsu, Francis L. K. (ed.)
1961 *Psychological Anthropology*. Homewood, IL: Dorsey Press.

Hunter, Edward
1951 *Brainwashing in Red China*. New York: Vanguard.

Inkeles, Alex
1968 "Society, Social Structure, and Child Socialization." Pp. 73–129 in John A. Clausen (ed.), *Socialization and Society*. Boston: Little, Brown.

James, William
1950 *The Principles of Psychology*, Vol. 1. New York: Dover.
(1890)

Johnson, Harry N. (General Editor, Robert K. Merton)
1960 *Sociology: A Systematic Introduction*. New York: Harcourt, Brace and World.

Jones, Edward W. and Harold B. Gerard
1967 *Foundations of Social Psychology*. New York: Wiley.

Judd, Charles H.
1931 "The Nature of Social Institutions." *Social Forces* 10 (October): 1–4.

Kamens, David H.
  1971 "The College 'Charter' and College Size: Effects on Occupational Choice and College Attrition." *Sociology of Education* 44 (Summer): 270–296.
Kaplan, Abraham
  1964 *The Conduct of Inquiry: Methodology for Behavioral Science.* San Francisco: Chandler.
Karpf, Fay B.
  1926 "The Development of Social Psychology." Pp. 71–81 in Ernest W. Burgess (ed.), *The Progress of Sociology*, 21. Publications of the American Sociological Society.
Katz, Jack
  1972 "Deviance, Charisma and Rule-Defined Behavior." *Social Problems* 20 (Fall): 186–202.
Kilpatrick, William
  1975 *Identity and Intimacy.* New York: Dell.
Klein, D. B.
  1930 "The Psychology of Conscience." *Int. J. Ethics* 40 (January): 246–262.
Kluckhohn, Clyde
  1949 *Mirror for Man.* New York: McGraw-Hill.
  1967 "The Concept of Culture." Pp. 74–93 in Peter I. Rose (ed.), *The Study of Society.* New York: Random House.
Kroeber, A. L. and Talcott Parsons
  1958 "Concepts of Culture and of Social System." *Am. J. Sociology* 23 (October): 582–583.
Kuhn, Thomas
  1970 *The Structure of Scientific Revolutions.* Chicago: Univ. of Chicago Press.
Lachenmeyer, Charles W.
  1971 *The Language of Sociology.* New York: Columbia Univ. Press.
  1973 *The Essence of Social Research.* New York: Free Press.
Lemert, Charles C.
  1979 "Language, Structure, and Measurement: Structuralist Semiotics and Sociology." *Am. J. Sociology* 84 (January): 929–957.
Landis, Judson R.
  1971 *Sociology: Concepts and Characteristics.* Belmont, CA: Wadsworth.
Lasswell, Harold and Abraham Kaplan
  1950 *Power and Society.* New Haven, CT: Yale Univ. Press.
Lavine, Thelma Z.
  1942 "Sociological Analysis of Cognitive Norms." *J. Philosophy* 39: 342–356.
Lenneberg, Eric H.
  1967 *Biological Foundations of Language.* New York: Wiley.
Lenski, Gerhard and Jean Lenski
  1974 *Human Societies: An Introduction to Macrosociology.* New York: McGraw-Hill.
Lerner, Daniel
  1958 *The Passing of Traditional Society.* New York: Free Press.

Levinson, Daniel J.
    1967   "Medical Education and the Theory of Adult Socialization." *J. Health Soc. Behav.* 8: 253–265.

Lichtenberger, James P.
    1923   *Development of Social Theory.* New York: Century.

Lief, Harold I.
    1971   "Personality Characteristics of Medical Students." In Robert H. Coombs and Clark E. Vincent (eds.). *Psychosocial Aspects of Medical Training.* Springfield, IL: Charles C. Thomas.

Lief, Harold I. and Renee C. Fox
    1963   "Training for 'Detached Concern' in Medical Students." In Harold I. Lief, et al. (eds.), *The Psychological Basis of Medical Practice.*

Lockwood, David
    1956   "Some Remarks on 'The Social System' " *Br. J. Sociology* 7 (June): 134–146.

Lowry, Ritchie P. and Robert P. Rankin
    1969   *Sociology: The Science of Society.* New York: Scribner's.

Luckmann, Thomas
    1967   *The Invisible Religion.* New York: Macmillan.
    1975   *The Sociology of Language.* Indianapolis: Bobbs-Merrill.

Lukes, Steven
    1973   *Individualism.* New York: Harper and Row.
    1978   "Power and Authority," Pp. 633–676 in Tom Bottomore and Robert Nisbet (eds.), *A History of Sociological Analysis.* New York: Basic Books.

Lull, H. G.
    1919   "Socializing School Procedure." *Am. J. Sociology* 24 (May): 681–691.

Lundberg, George A., Clarence C. Schrag and Otto N. Larsen
    1954   *Sociology,* New York: Harper and Row.

Lyman, Stanford and Marvin Scott
    1970   *A Sociology of the Absurd.* New York: Appleton-Century-Crofts.

McClendon, McKee J.
    1977   "Structural and Exchange Components of Vertical Mobility." *Am. Sociological Rev.* 42 (February, 56–74.

McHugh, Peter
    1968   *Defining the Situation.* Indianapolis: Bobbs-Merrill.

MacIver, Robert M.
    1924   *Community: A Sociological Study.* London: Macmillan.
    1947   *The Web of Government.* New York: Macmillan.

Malinowski, Bronislaw
    1923   *The Meaning of Meaning.* New York: Harcourt, Brace and World.

Manning, Peter K.
    1970   "Talking and Becoming: A View of Organizational Socialization." Pp. 239–256 in Jack D. Douglas (ed.), *Understanding Everday Life.* Chicago: Aldine.

Marshall, T. H.
    1969   "Reflections on Power." *Sociology* 3 (May): 141–155.

Martland, T. R.
    1975   "On 'The Limits of My Language Mean the Limits of My World." *Rev. Metaphysics* 29 (September): 19—26.
Marx, Karl
    1966   *The Poverty of Philosophy.* Moscow: Progress Publishers.
Maus, Heinz
    1962   *A Short History of Sociology.* New York: Philosophical Library.
Mead, George Herbert
    1925   "The Genesis of the Self and Social Control." *Int. J. Ethics* 35 (April): 251—277.
    1930a   "Cooley's Contribution to American Social Thought." *Am. J. Sociology* 35 (May): 693—706.
    1930b   "The Philosophies of Royce, James, and Dewey in Their American Setting," *Int. J. Ethics* 40 (January): 211—231.
    1962   *Mind, Self, and Society.* Charles W. Morris (posthumous ed.), Chicago: University of Chicago Press.
Mead, Margaret
    1928   *Coming of Age in Samoa.* New York: William Morrow.
Mehan, Hugh and Houston Wood
    1976   *The Reality of Ethnomethodology.* New York: Wiley.
Merton, Robert K.
    1949   *Social Theory and Social Structure.* New York: Free Press.
Merton, Robert K., George G. Reader and Patricia L. Kendall
    1957   *The Student Physician.* Cambridge, MA: Harvard Univ. Press.
Merton, Robert K. and Elinor Barber
    1963   "Sociological Ambivalence." Pp. 91—120 in Edward A. Tiryakian (ed.) *Sociological Theory, Values, and Sociocultural Change.* New York: Harper Torchbooks.
Meyer, John W.
    1972   "The Effects of the Institutionalization of Colleges in Society." Pp. 109—126 in K. A. Feldman (ed.), *College and Student.* New York: Pergamon Press.
Miller, Walter B.
    1959   "Two Concepts of Authority." Pp. 93—115 in James D. Thompson, et al. (eds.), *Comparative Studies in Administration.* Pittsburg: Univ. of Pittsburg Press.
Mills, C. Wright
    1940   "Situated Actions and Vocabularies of Motive." *Am. Sociological Rev.* 5 (October): 904—913.
    1956   *The Power Elite.* New York: Oxford Univ. Press.
    1959   *The Sociological Imagination.* New York: Oxford Univ. Press.
Milner, Murray, Jr.
    1972   *The Illusion of Equality.* San Francisco: Jossey-Bass.
Monod, Jacques
    1971   *Chance and Necessity.* New York: Knopf.

Mulligan, Glenn and Bobbie Lederman
    1977   "Social Facts and Rules of Practice." *Am. J. Sociology* 83 (November): 539–550.
Nisbet, Robert A.
    1969   *Social Change and History.* New York: Oxford Univ. Press.
    1974   *The Sociology of Emile Durkheim.* New York: Oxford Univ. Press.
North, Cecil C.
    1933   The Report of a Special Committee of the American Sociological Society: The Introductory Course in Sociology in Colleges and Universities. "Summary of Findings on the Present Status of the Introductory Course in Sociology, and Conclusion." *J. Educational Sociology* vii (October): 66–82.
Nygren, Anders
    1972   *Meaning and Method.* London: Epworth Press.
Odum, Howard
    1929   "The Scientific-Human in Social Research." *Social Forces* 7 (March): 350–362.
Ogburn, William F.
    1937   "Culture and Sociology." *Social Forces* 16 (December): 161–169.
Ogburn, William F. and Meyer F. Nimkoff
    1940   *Sociology.* Boston: Houghton-Mifflin.
    1946   *Sociology.* Boston: Houghton-Mifflin.
    1950   *Sociology*, 2nd Ed. (extensively revised). Boston: Houghton-Mifflin.
Olsen, Marvin E.
    1968   *The Process of Social Organization.* New York: Holt, Rinehart and Winston.
Orum, Anthony M. and Roberta S. Cohen
    1973   "The Development of Political Orientations among Black and White Children." *Am. Sociological Rev.* 38 (February): 62–71.
Orum, Anthony M., Roberta S. Cohen, Sherri Grasmuck and Amy W. Orum
    1974   "Sex, Socialization and Politics." *Am. Sociological Rev.* 39 (April): 197–209.
Panunzio, Constantine
    1939   *Major Social Institutions.* New York: Macmillan.
Park, George
    1974   *The Idea of Social Structure.* Garden City, NY: Anchor Books.
Park, Robert E.
    1927   "Human Nature and Collective Behavior." *Am. J. Sociology* 32 (March): 733–741.
Park, Robert E. and Ernest W. Burgess
    1921   *Introduction to the Science of Sociology.* Chicago: Univ. of Chicago Press.
Parsons, Talcott
    1937   *The Structure of Social Action.* New York: Free Press.
    1951   *The Social System* (1964 edition). Glencoe, IL: Free Press of Glencoe.
    1957   "The Distribution of Power in American Society." *World Politics* 10 (October): 123–143.

1960 *Structure and Process in Modern Societies.* New York: Free Press.
1966 *Societies: Evolutionary and Comparative Perspectives.* Englewood Cliffs, NJ: Prentice-Hall.
1967 *Sociological Theory and Modern Society.* New York: Free Press.
1977 *Social Systems and the Evolution of Action Theory.* New York: Free Press.

Parsons, Talcott and Robert F. Bales
1955 *Family, Socialization and Interaction Process.* Glencoe, IL: Free Press.

Parsons, Talcott and Edward A. Shils
1951 *Toward a General Theory of Action.* Cambridge, MA: Harvard Univ. Press.

Peabody, Francis
1913 "The Socialization of Religion." *Am. J. Sociology* 18 (March): 694–705.

Perry, John and Edna Perry
1976 *The Social Web: An Introduction to Sociology.* San Francisco: Canfield Press.

Peters, Charles C.
1924 *Foundations of Educational Sociology.* New York: Macmillan.

Piaget, Jean
1948 *The Moral Judgment of the Child.* Glencoe, IL: Free Press.
1967 *Six Psychological Studies.* New York: Random House.
1971 *Biology and Knowledge.* Chicago: Univ. of Chicago Press.

Poole, Roger
1972 *Towards Deep Subjectivity.* New York: Harper and Row.

Porter, James M.
1974 "Race, Socialization and Mobility in Education and Early Occupational Attainment." *Am. Sociological Rev.* 39 (June): 303–316.

Reinhardt, James N.
1932 *Principles and Methods of Sociology.* New York: Prentice-Hall.

Rhoads, John M., J. Gallemore, Jr., D. Granturco and S. Osterhout
1974 "Motivation, Medical School Admissions, and Student Performance." *J. Med. Education* 49 (December): 1119–1127.

Rice, Stuart A.
1932 "What Is Sociology?" *Social Forces* 10 (March): 319–326.

Rieff, Philip
1961 *Freud: The Mind of the Moralist.* Garden City, NY: Doubleday.

Riesman, David
1950 *The Lonely Crowd.* New Haven, CT: Yale Univ. Press.

Robinson, Richard
1954 *Defintions.* Oxford: Oxford Univ. Press.

Rogers, Mary F.
1974 "Instrumental and Infra-Resources: The Bases of Power." *Am. J. Sociology* 79: 1418–1433.

Rose, Arnold M.
1967 *The Power Structure.* New York: Oxford Univ. Press.

Ross, E. A.
   1896   "Social Control." *Am. J. Sociology* 1: 513–535.
   1919   "Socialization." *Am. J. Sociology* 24 (May): 652–671.
   1920   *Principles of Sociology.* New York: Century.
Rossi, Peter H.
   1957   "Community Decision Making." *Admin. Sci. Q.* 1 (March): 425–431.
Russell, Bertrand and Alfred North Whitehead
   1910   *Principia Mathematica* Vol. I. Cambridge, England: Cambridge Univ. Press.
Sampson, Edward E.
   1971   *Social Psychology and Contemporary Society.* New York: Wiley.
Sargent, S. Stansfeld
   1950   *Social Psychology: An Integrative Interpretation.* New York: Ronald Press.
Scharr, John H.
   1970   "Legitimacy in the Modern State." Pp. 276–327 in Philip Green and Sanford Levinson (eds.), *Power and Community*, New York: Pantheon.
Scheff, Thomas J.
   1968   "Negotiating Reality: Notes on Power in the Assessment of Responsibility." *Social Problems* 16 (Summer): 3–17.
   1970   "Toward a Sociological Model of Consensus." Pp. 348–365 in Gregory P. Stone and Harvey A. Farberman (eds.), *Social Psychology Through Symbolic Interaction.* Waltham, MA: Ginn-Blaisdell.
Scheler, Max
   1973   *Man's Place in Nature* (originally published in German under the title *Die Stellung des Menschens im Kosmos*, 1928). Tr. H. Meryhoff. New York: Noonday Press.
Schellenberg, James A.
   1978   *Masters of Social Psychology.* New York: Oxford Univ. Press.
Schutz, Alfred
   1963a   "Concept and Theory Formation in the Social Sciences." Pp. 231–249 in Maurice Natanson (ed.), *Philosophy of the Social Sciences.* New York: Random House.
   1963b   "Common-Sense and Scientific Interpretation of Human Action." Pp. 302–346 in Maurice Natanson (ed.), *Philosophy of the Social Sciences.* New York: Random House.
   1970a   *On Phenomenology and Social Relations.* (Edited with introduction by Helmut Wagner.) Chicago: Univ. of Chicago Press.
   1970b   *Reflections on the Problem of Relevance.* New Haven, CT: Yale Univ. Press.
Schwartz, Barry
   1971   "Critique of the Sociology of the Absurd." *Am. J. Sociology* 77 (July): 153–156.
Scott, Marvin and Stanford Lyman
   1968   "Accounts." *Am. Sociological Rev.* 33 (February): 46–62.
Sewell, William H.
   1970   "Some Recent Developments in Socialization Theory and Research." Pp.

566–583 in Gregory P. Stone and Harvey A. Farberman (eds.) *Social Psychology Through Symbolic Interaction*. Waltham, MA: Ginn-Blaisdell.

Sewell, William H., A. O. Haller and G. W. Ohlendorf
1970 "The Educational and Early Occupational Attainment Process: Replication and Revision." *Am. Sociological Rev.* 35 (December): 1014–1027.

Sewell, William L. and V. Shah
1968 "Social Class, Parental Encouragement and Educational Aspirations." *Am. J. Sociology* 73 (March): 559–572.

Shipman, Gordon D.
1931 "Science and Social Science." *Social Forces* 10 (October): 38–48.

Skidmore, William L.
1975 *Sociology's Models of Man*. New York: Gordon and Breach.

Skolnick, Arlene
1978 "The Myth of the Vulnerable Child." *Psychology Today* (February).

Small, Albion W.
1905 *General Sociology*. Chicago: Univ. of Chicago Press.
1907 "The American Sociological Society." *Am. J. Sociology* 12 (March): 579–580.
1916 "Fifty Years of Sociology in the United States—1865–1915." *Am. J. Sociology* 21 (May): 721–862. Reprinted in Index to Volumes I–LII: 177–269.
1920 *General Sociology*. Chicago: Univ. of Chicago Press.
1924 *Origins of Sociology*. Chicago: Univ. of Chicago Press.

Smelser, Neil J.
1973 *Sociology: An Introduction*, 2nd Ed., New York: Wiley.

Snedden, David
1924 *Educational Sociology*. New York: Century.

Sorokin, Pitirim A.
1931 "Sociology as a Science." *Social Forces* 10 (October): 21–27.
1943 *Sociocultural Causality, Space, Time: A Study of Referential Principles of Sociology and Social Science*. Durham, NC: Duke Univ. Press. Reissued, 1964, by Russell and Russell, New York.

Spaeth, Joe L. and Andrew Greeley
1970 *Recent Alumni and Higher Education*. New York: McGraw-Hill.

Speier, Matthew
1970 "The Everyday World of the Child." Pp. 188–217 in Jack D. Douglas (ed.), *Understanding Everday Life*. Chicago: Aldine.
1973 *How to Observe Face-to-Face Communication: A Sociological Introduction*. Pacific Palisades, CA: Goodyear Publishing.

Stokes, Randall and John P. Hewitt
1976 "Aligning Actions." *Am. Sociological Rev.* 41 (October): 838–849.

Stone, Gregory P. and Harvey A. Farberman
1970 "On the Edge of Rapprochement: Was Durkheim Moving Toward the Perspective of Symbolic Interaction?" Pp. 100–112 in Gregory P. Stone and Harvey A. Farberman (eds.), *Social Psychology Through Symbolic Interaction*. Waltham, MA: Ginn-Blaisdell.

Strauss, Anselm L. (ed.)
    1964   "Introduction." Pp. vii–xxv in George Herbert Mead: *On Social Psychology*. Chicago: Univ. of Chicago Press.

Stryker, Sheldon
    1973   "Fundamental Principles of Social Interaction." Pp. 495–547 in Neil J. Smelser (ed.), *Sociology: An Introduction*. New York: Wiley.

Sutherland, Robert L. and Julian L. Woodward
    1937   *Introductory Sociology*. Chicago: Lippincott.
    1940   *Introductory Sociology*. Chicago: Lippincott.

Swanson, Guy E.
    1953   "The Approach to a General Theory of Action by Parsons and Shils." *Am. Sociological Rev.* 18 (April): 1–10.
    1974   "Family Structure and the Reflective Intelligence of Children." *Sociometry* 37 (December): 459–490.

Sykes, Gresham M.
    1958   *The Society of Captives*. Princeton: Princeton Univ. Press.

Thomas, W. I. and Dorothy Swaine Thomas
    1932   *The Child in America*. New York: Knopf.

Toulmin, Stephen
    1961   *Foresight and Understanding: An Enquiry into the Aims of Science*. New York: Harper and Row.

Tumin, Melvin M.
    1973   *Patterns of Society*. Boston: Little, Brown.

Turner, Ralph H.
    1962   "Role-Taking: Process vs. Conformity." Pp. 20–40 in Arnold M. Rose (ed.), *Human Behavior and Social Process: An Interactionist Approach*. Boston: Houghton-Mifflin.
    1976   "The Real Self: From Institution to Impulse." *Am. J. Sociology* 81 (March): 989–1016.

Wallis, Wilson D.
    1928   "The Problems of an Empirical Sociology." *Social Forces* 7 (September): 46–49.

Ward, Lester Frank
    1911   *Pure Sociology*. New York: Macmillan.

Warriner, Charles K.
    1956   "Groups Are Real: A Reaffirmation." *Am. Sociological Rev.* 21 (October): 549–554.

Weber, Max
    1958   *From Max Weber: Essays in Sociology*. H. H. Gerth and C. Wright Mills (eds. and trans.). New York: Oxford Univ. Press.
    1964   *The Theory of Social and Economic Organization*. Talcott
    (1947)   Parsons (ed.). New York: Free Press.

Webster, Murray, Jr.
    1973   "Psychological Reductionism, Methodological Individualism, and Large-Scale Problems." *Am. Sociological Rev.* 38 (April): 258–273.

Weinstein, Eugene A. and Paul Deutschberger
   1963   "Some Dimensions of Altercasting." *Sociometry* 26 (December): 454–466.
Weizenbaum, Joseph
   1976   *Computer Power and Human Reason.* San Francisco: Freeman.
Wentworth, William M.
   1972   The Role of Stimulus-Bound Context on the Evaluation and Comprehension of a Communication (unpublished).
   1975   The Sociology of Knowledge and Plato's Ideal Society (unpublished).
   1976   "Becoming a Doctor: The Analysis of Medical Reality." Working paper for the Developmental Study of Medical Socialization, the Univ. of Virginia School of Medicine (unpublished).
Wheeler, Stanton
   1966   "The Structure of Formally Organized Socialization Settings." Pp. 53–116 in Orville G. Brim and Stanton Wheeler (eds.), *Socialization After Childhood: Two Essays.* New York: Wiley.
Whiting, John W. M.
   1968   "Socialization: Anthropological Aspects." In David L. Sills (ed.), *International Encyclopedia of the Social Sciences.* New York: Macmillan and Free Press.
Wieder, D. Lawrence
   1970   "On Meaning by Rule." Pp. 107–135 in Jack D. Douglas (ed.), *Understanding Everyday Life.* Chicago: Aldine.
Wiese, Leopold von
   1932   *Systematic Sociology.* (Adapted and amplified by Howard Becker.) New York: Wiley.
Willer, David and Murray Webster, Jr.
   1970   "Theoretical Concepts and Observables." *Am. Sociological Rev.* 35: 748–757.
Wilson, Everett K.
   1971   *Sociology: Rules, Roles and Relationships.* Homewood, IL: Dorsey.
Wilson, Thomas P.
   1970   "Conceptions of Interaction and Forms of Sociological Explanation." *Am. Sociological Rev.* 35: 697–709.
Winch, Peter
   1958   *The Idea of a Social Science and Its Relation to Philosophy.* London: Routledge and Kegan Paul.
Winch, Robert F.
   1973   "Family and Kinship." Pp. 193–246 in Neil J. Smelser (ed.), *Sociology: An Introduction.* New York: Wiley.
Wirth, Louis
   1947   "American Sociology, 1915–47." *Am. J. Sociology.* Index to Volumes I–LII: 273–281.
Wittgenstein, Ludwig
   1958   *Philosophical Investigations.* Tr. G. E. M. Anscombe. New York: Macmillan.

Wolfenstein, Martha
    1955   "Fun Morality: An Analysis of Recent American Child-Training Literature." Pp. 168–174 in Margaret Mead and Martha Wolfenstein (eds.), *Childhood in Contemporary Cultures*. Chicago: Univ. of Chicago Press.

Wright, Charles R.
    1964   "Success or Failure in Earning Graduate Degrees." *Sociology of Education* 38 (Fall): 73–97.

Wrong, Dennis
    1961   "The Oversocialized Conception of Man in Modern Sociology." *Am. Sociological Rev.* 26 (February): 183–193.
    1968   "Some Problems in Defining Social Power." *Am. J. Sociology* 73 (May): 673–681.
    1970   *Max Weber*. Dennis Wrong (ed.). Englewood Cliffs, NJ: Prentice-Hall.

Yinger, J. Milton
    1965   *Toward a Field Theory of Behavior*. New York: McGraw-Hill.

Young, Kimball
    1934   *An Introduction to Sociology*. New York: American Book Co.
    1942   *Sociology*. New York: American Book Co.
    1944   *Personality and Problems of Adjustment*. New York: F. S. Crofts.
    1956   *Social Psychology*. New York: Appleton-Century-Crofts.

Zijderveld, Anton C.
    1968   "Jokes and Their Relation to Social Reality." *Social Research* 35, 2: 286–312.
    1970   *The Abstract Society*. Garden City, NY: Doubleday.

Zimmerman, Don H.
    1970   "The Practicalities of Rule Use." Pp. 221–238 in Jack D. Douglas (ed.), *Understanding Everyday Life*. Chicago: Aldine.

Zimmerman, Don H. and D. Lawrence Wieder
    1970   "Ethnomethodology and the Problem of Order: Comment on Denzin." Pp. 287–298 in Jack D. Douglas (ed.), *Understanding Everyday Life*. Chicago, Aldine.

Znaniecki, Florian
    1925   *The Laws of Social Psychology*. Chicago: Univ. of Chicago Press.

INDEX

A

Abelson, Raziel, 142
Accounts, 118
Action, 121
Adler, Alfred, 23
Adult socialization, 133; *see also* Secondary socialization
Aligning actions, 106, 118−119
Alwin, Duane F., 74
Ambiguous behavior, 120
American Journal of Sociology, 20
American Sociological Society, 20
Analogy
 socialization and pregnancy, 69
 society and the game, 56−59
"Analysis of Power, An," 114
Anomie, 34, 96, 129, 136
Anthropology, 23−24
Anthropomorphic model of the person, 2, 68−70, 78−79
Anticipatory socialization, 36−37
Ariès, Philippe, 71
Assimilation, 27
Astin, Alexander W., 74
Attentional ray, 95
Authority, 5, 97, 104, 114, 117
Autonomy, 5, 50, 55, 57, 69−72, 79, 111, 116, 122−134
Ayer, A. J., 142

B

Bacon, Francis, 26
Baldwin, James Mark, 21, 25, 30, 92, 93
Bales, Robert F., 36, 70
Ball, Donald W., 120
Barber, Elinor, 3
Barrett, William, 3
Becker, Howard S., 9, 42, 50, 51, 52, 53, 54, 106, 124, 126, 133

"Behavior in Private Places: Sustaining Definitions of Reality in Gynecological Examinations," 97–101
Behaviorism, 23, 42
Bellah, Robert N., 128
Bendix, Reinhard, 33, 125n
Bengston, Vern L., 73, 76
Berger, Bennett, 33, 125n
Berger, Brigitte, 113
Berger, Peter L., 6, 34, 38, 57, 71, 85, 88, 88n, 96, 97, 104, 106, 113, 123, 143, 151, 152
Bernstein, Basil, 55
Bershady, Harold J., 25, 32, 34
Bidney, David, 23, 24
Bierstedt, Robert, 6, 35, 47, 48, 76, 113, 114, 114n, 115, 117, 121, 142, 143
Black, K. D., 73
Blau, Peter M., 75
Blum, Alan, 56, 147, 153
Blumer, Herbert, 4, 42
Bogardus, Emory S., 20
Boyle, Blake P., 136
Boys in White, 42, 51, 52, 53, 54, 55
Breaching activity, 67
Brim, Orville G., 37, 38
Broadhead, Robert S., 43
Broom, Leonard, 38
Brown, Roger, 67, 88, 106
Bucher, Rue, 6, 76, 84, 131, 132, 133
Burgess, Ernest W., 17, 27
Burke, Kenneth, 103, 145

C
Carnap, Rudolf, 142
Carter, Hugh, 20
Centuries of Childhood, 71
Change
 personal, 36
 social, 35, 129
Charisma, 89, 96, 120
Charon, Joel M., 4, 42
Chess analogy. *See* Analogy, society and the game
Child socialization, 63; *see also* Primary socialization
Childhood
 diminished responsibility of, 88
 experience, and personality, 22–23, 24, 25, 26n
Chomsky, Noam, 55
Cicourel, Aaron V., 42
Clark, Alexander L., 117, 119
Clausen, John A., 18n, 22, 23, 24, 31n
Cognition, 66
Cohen, Roberta S., 76
Collins, Randall, 19, 74, 88, 116, 133
Coming of Age in Samoa, 24
Commitment, 51, 116, 121, 124, 125
Complexity, 84, 127, 128, 130
Conduct, 121
Conflict, 15, 45, 114, 116, 129–130
Conscience, 113
Consensus, 96
Context, 8, 84–85, 90–108, 109; *see also* Culture
 concepts related to, 92–95
 construction, 90, 97–101, 103, 104, 109
 definition of, 92
 primary, 105–108, 109
 as unit of culture, 8, 92, 94
Context-bound definition, 144
Context-free definition, 144
Control, 5, 33, 110, 111, 115, 117, 118–119, 120–122, 136–137, 139–140
 relation of control and power, 118, 121–122, 131–132, 139–140
 social psychology of, 122–130
 and theory of socialization, 130–137
Cooley, Charles Horton, 15, 21, 25, 30, 35
Coombs, Robert H., 135, 136
Counter-control, 132, 133
Creativity, 3, 6, 50, 56–59 *passim*, 87, 103, 105
Crespigny, A., 113
Cuber, John F., 31
Culture, 8–9, 65–70, 78–79; *see also* Context
 limits of, 91–92
Culture and personality, 24, 35

D
Dahrendorf, Ralf, 33
Danziger, Kurt, 74, 76
Davis, Fred, 77

Dawson, Carl A., 31
Dealey, James, 17
Definitions, 7, 141–145
Descartes, René, 26
Description, 144–145
Determinism, 2, 3, 44, 45, 59, 60, 70, 73–74, 78, 96, 128
Deviance, 127
 and breaching, 67
 negatively connoted, 120
 positively connoted, 120
Differential association, 73–74
Disclaimers, 118
Division of Labor in Society, The, 126, 127
Dornbusch, Sanford M., 136
Douglas, Jack, 42, 119n, 120
Dramaturgical school, 42
Dreitzel, Hans Peter, 76
Duncan, Otis Dudley, 75
Durkheim, Emile, 6, 22, 25, 35, 58, 61, 67, 86, 88, 91, 111, 122n, 125–132 *passim*, 148, 151
"Durkheim and History," 128
Dynamic Sociology, 14n

E
Ego, 25
Einstein, Albert, 48n, 149
Elementary Forms of Religious Life, The, 126, 129
Ellis, Desmond P., 42
Ellwood, Charles A., 20
Emergence, 4, 5, 6
Emerson, Joan P., 97, 98, 100, 101, 120
Emotion, 88
Enos, Darryl D., 102
Essentialism, 142
Ethnomethodology, 42
Etzioni, Amitai, 108, 135
Eubanks, Earle Edward, 18
Expressive activity, 98, 104, 105, 107
Expressive competence, 89–90
External institution, 49

F
Faris, Robert E. L., 20
Featherman, David L., 75
Ferguson, Adam, 143

Fichter, Joseph H., 35, 44
Focused gathering, 93–94, 99, 106, 107
Fox, Renee C., 90
Frank, Lawrence K., 15, 22, 26, 26n, 29, 74
Free will, 3
Freedom, 2–3, 60, 84, 95
Freud, Sigmund, 22–27 *passim*, 38, 39, 45, 46; *see also* Psychology, Freudian
Fromm, Erich, 125
Fuller, John Scott, 44
Functionalism, 41, 44–45, 50, 53–55, 59, 60, 70, 73, 115–116

G
Game analogy, 56–59, 61
Game strategy, 56–59
Garfinkel, Harold, 58, 97, 120
Geertz, Clifford, 19, 66
Generalized other, 5, 49, 61, 71, 112
German Ideology, 125
Gettys, Warren E., 31
Gibbs, Jack, 117, 119
Giddens, Anthony, 42, 45, 58, 91, 97, 103, 114, 115, 116, 142, 143
Giddings, Franklin, 15, 17, 20, 28
Glaser, Barney G., 94, 149
Goffman, Erving, 42, 51n, 56, 57, 58, 88, 93, 94, 97, 98n, 103, 104, 111, 118, 122, 123, 124, 124n, 126, 136
Gonos, George, 3, 9
Gough, Harrison G., 135
Gouldner, Alvin, 44, 152
Greeley, Andrew, 74
Group hypothesis, 18–19, 21
Groups, reality of, 48–50

H
Hall, Edward T., 94
Hall, Peter M., 42
Handel, Warren, 42
Hanson, Todd, 54
Harré, R., 2, 42, 56, 97
Harrington, Michael, 45n
Hart, Hornell, 28
Hayes, Edward, 28

Hempel, C. G., 142
Hewitt, John P., 4, 42, 58, 106, 117, 118, 119
Hinkle, Gisela J., 20
Hinkle, Roscoe C., Jr., 20
Hobbes, Thomas, 45
Hofstadter, Richard, 14n
Homans, George C., 40, 42
House, Floyd N., 14n, 18n, 20, 26n
Human behavior, levels of, 121–122
Human nature, 19, 25, 26, 30–31, 33, 35, 38, 39, 78
Hunter, Edward, 136
Husserl, Edmund, 95

I
Id, 25, 33
Identity, 122–125
Inadequate socialization, 17
Incidental socialization, 86
Individual, 17–19, 26, 27, 30–32, 37, 39, 44
  anthropomorphic model of, 2, 68–70, 78–79
Individualism, 1, 2, 41–42
  neo-, 3, 45, 60; see also Interpretive sociologies
Induction, 74–75
Inkeles, Alex, 9, 29, 36, 38, 63, 64, 65, 76, 150
Institution
  external, 49
  norm-building, 85–86
Institutional process, 57
Instrumental activity, 98, 100, 104, 105, 107
Instrumental competence, 89–90
Interactional competence. See Expressive competence
Intergenerational transfer, 28
Internalization, 5, 8, 23, 24, 25, 26, 45–46, 50, 54, 59, 60, 67–68, 78, 90, 106, 134, 136; see also Socialization-as-internalization model
Interpretative sociologies, 42–43, 44–47, 50, 54, 59–60, 116–117
  example of, 50–53
Introduction to the Science of Sociology, 27

J
Jacobs, Jerry, 44
James, William, 21, 25
Joking, 87–88, 120
Jung, Carl, 23

K
Kamens, David H., 74
Kaplan, Abraham, 113, 148, 151
Kellner, Hansfried, 85, 96, 104
Knowledge, stock of, 45–46
Kroeber, A. L., 66
Kuhn, Thomas, 14, 18, 48n, 76

L
Labeling theory, 42
Lachenmeyer, Charles, 141, 142
Language, sociology of, 55–56
Language of Sociology, The, 141
Lasswell, Harold, 113
Leadership, 96
Learning, 31, 38, 67–68
Lederman, Bobbie, 58
Lerner, Daniel, 152, 152n
Lief, Harold I., 90
Linguistic theories, 142
Lockwood, David, 34
Long, Ted, 54
Luckmann, Thomas, 38, 57, 71, 85, 88, 88n, 97, 106, 123
Lukes, Steven, 112
Lyman, Stanford, 42, 46, 47, 58, 116, 118

M
McClendon, McKee J., 76
McHugh, Peter, 42, 56, 95, 97, 120
MacIver, Robert M., 22
Makowsky, Michael, 19
Malinowski, Bronislaw, 92
Margin for discretion, 119–120
Marshall, T. H., 113, 117
Marx, Karl, 35, 45, 111, 125, 126, 148
Marxian theory, 34
Maus, Heinz, 20
Mead, George Herbert, 4, 5, 6, 7, 15, 21, 22, 25, 30, 31, 33, 35, 45,

51, 52, 86, 88, 111, 112, 122n, 123, 124, 124n, 125, 126
Mead, Margaret, 24
Meaning, 59, 89–90, 91, 117, 119, 137, 138, 144
  shared, 90
Medical education, 51, 52, 53, 54, 55, 134–136
Mehan, Hugh, 42, 44, 45, 47, 97
Member and novice, relationship of, 69, 84, 85, 86, 108
Merton, Robert K., 3, 36, 37, 42, 43, 47, 53, 54, 65, 75, 90, 149
Methodological atheism, 151–152
Meyer, John W., 74
Mills, C. Wright, 113, 118, 149, 152, 152n
Milner, Murray, Jr., 74
Mobile sensitivity, 152
Mobility, 70, 75, 76
Morality, 6, 28, 29, 30, 47, 131, 133
Motive talk, 118
Mulligan, Glenn, 58

N
"Neglected Situation, The," 51n
Neoindividualism, 3, 45, 60
Nimkoff, Meyer F., 30
Nisbet, Robert A., 127
Nonroutine gatherings. See Problematic gatherings
Norm-building institutions, 85–86
Norms, 56, 57
Novice
  and member, relationship of, 69, 84, 85, 86, 108
  peers of, 85

O
Observer, sociological. See Sociological observer
Ogburn, William F., 30
Olsen, Marvin E., 115
Organismic behavior, 121
Orum, Anthony, 76
Oversocialized person, 34, 44, 78

P
Paradox of mutual indeterminism, 4–6

Park, Robert E., 17, 27
Parsons, Talcott, 25, 32–38 passim, 45, 66, 67n, 70, 105, 113, 114, 115, 122, 148
Peers, of novice, 85
Performance, 55–59 passim
Perry, Edna, 38
Perry, John, 38
Personal change, 36
Personality formation, 22–27 passim, 39, 78
Perspective, 51, 52
Piaget, Jean, 66, 88
Play, 87–88, 105, 107
Polish Peasant, The, 18n
Poole, Roger, 47
Porter, James M., 76
Power, 5, 6, 110, 111, 117–118, 121–122
  balance of, 113
  conflict and, 116
  descriptions of, 112–115
  relationship of, and controls, 118, 121–122, 131–132, 139–140
  social psychology of, 122–130
  theoretics of, 115–117
  and theory of socialization, 130–137
Power by relevance, 113
Prescriptivism, 142
Primary Socialization, 32, 36, 37–38, 70–72; see also Child Socialization
  definition of, 71
Principles, 55–59 passim; see also Rules
Problematic gatherings, 96, 106, 107, 108, 110, 118, 121
Psychology
  experimental, 23
  Freudian, 22–27, 33, 39
Pullberg, Stanley, 6, 34
Punishment, 73, 87
Pure Sociology, 20

R
Realism, 142, 143
Reality, 85, 87, 91, 96–97, 103
Rebellion, 125–126
Reciprocal relations, 96
Reference group theory, 37
Reflex behavior, 121

Reflexivity, 5, 6, 45, 111, 112, 123–132 *passim*, 138, 139, 153
Remedial interchanges, 118
"Research Possibilities with a Socialization Test," 28
Resources, 104, 111, 113, 114, 115, 122–125, 131, 134, 136
Respectable activity, 120
Rhoads, John M., 135
Rieff, Philip, 25
Ritual, 87–88
Ritual purity, 87, 88
Robinson, Richard, 142
Rogers, Mary F., 115, 117, 123
Role distance, 124n
Role learning, 33, 36, 37, 38, 52
Roles, 32, 56, 102–103, limits of, 91
Rose, Arnold M., 113
Ross, E. A., 17, 20
Routine gatherings, 95, 106, 107
Rules, 56–59 *passim*, 61, 66–67, 69, 70; *see also* Principles
Russell, Bertrand, 142

S

Sampson, Edward E., 96
Sanctions, 73, 87
Sargent, S. Stansfeld, 31, 32
Scheff, Thomas J., 96
Scheler, Max, 90
School effects, 73–74
Science, 48
  philosophy of, 3, 49
Schutz, Alfred, 95, 121
Schwartz, Barry, 42
Scott, Marvin, 42, 46, 47, 58, 116, 118
Secondary socialization, 32, 36, 70–72; *see also* Adult socialization
Secord, P. F., 2, 42, 56, 97
Seekership, 134, 135, 136
Self, 5, 17, 21–22, 31, 39, 78, 112, 123–125
Selznick, Philip, 38
Seriousness, 87–88, 105, 107
Sewell, William H., 22, 23, 24, 75, 76
Shah, V., 75
Shils, Edward A., 32, 33, 105
Simmel, Georg, 125n
Simplification, 84, 91, 106, 108, 109
Situation, 50–53, 92–96 *passim*

definition of, 51, 57, 95–96
Situational adjustment, 50–53, 57, 116, 124n
Situational continuity, 52–55 *passim*, 56, 60, 105
Situational uniqueness, 53, 54, 55, 103, 105
Skidmore, William L., 4, 42
Skolnick, Arlene, 73, 84
Small, Albion W., 14n, 15, 17, 19, 20
Smelser, Neil J., 38
Social change, 35, 129
Social order, 15, 34, 58
  conflict, consensus, and, 58
Social psychology, 4, 30, 36, 39, 110, 112, 122–130
Social self-control, 6, 111, 113, 118, 134
Social structure, 18, 21, 56, 78, 127; *see also* Society, superficial structure of; Structuration
  definition of, 56
  and personal needs, 116
Social System, The, 33, 35
Social Theory and Social Structure, 37
Socialization
  analogy to child, in womb, 69
  anticipatory, 36–37, 47
  changing concept of, 13–40
  as charicature of life, 54
  definition of, new, 85–86
  inadequate, 17
  incidental, 86
  as learning, 31, 38
  as minimum world, 108, 109
  outcome of, 29–30
  passivity of, 30–32
  primary. *See* Primary socialization
  research, criticism of, 72–77, 79
  resistance to, 133–134
  secondary. *See* Secondary socialization
  and stress, 87–88, 134–137
  superficial activity in, 86–90
  as teaching, 38
Socialization, 76
Socialization-as-interaction model, 83–109 *passim*
Socialization-as-internalization model, 31, 38, 62, 63–70, 78
Socialization failure, 34
Socialization theory
  central tenet of, 8

and control and power relations, 130–137
Socially learned nonsocial behavior, 121
Society, 14–15, 17, 18, 19, 39, 45, 78
 fundamental structure of, 102–108
 superficial structure of, 102–108; see also Social structure
Society of captives, 133–134
Sociological autonomy, 5, 50, 55, 57, 69–72, 79, 111, 116, 122–134
Sociological Imagination, The, 149
Sociological observer, 9, 64–65, 79, 85, 148, 150–153
Sociology and Ethics, 28
Sociology of the Absurd, A, 46
Sociologism, 1, 2, 13, 43
Socius, 21–22
Solidarity, 15
Spaeth, Joe L., 74
Speier, Matthew, 9, 44, 76, 150
Stein, Louis P., 135
Stelling, Joan G., 6, 76, 84, 131, 132, 133
Stokes, Randall, 42, 58, 106, 117, 118, 119
Strauss, Anselm, 94, 149
Stress, and socialization, 134–137
Structuration, 117
Structure of Scientific Revolutions, The, 18
Structure of Social Action, The, 35
Student Physician, The, 36, 37, 42, 53, 54, 55
Studies in the Theory of Human Society, 28
Subjective experience, 94–95
Sumner, William Graham, 20
Suicide, 127
Sultan, Paul, 102
Superego, 22, 23, 25
Sutherland, Robert, 30
Swanson, Guy E., 33, 76
Sykes, Gresham M., 133
Symbolic interactionism, 4–6, 42, 52
Systems theory, 34–35, 115–116

T
Technological competence. See Instrumental competence
Theory, method for, 9, 147–153

Toward a General Theory of Action, 32, 35
Thomas, Dorothy Swaine, 92, 104
Thomas, W. I., 18n, 21, 30, 92, 104
Turner, Ralph H., 42, 58
Toulmin, Stephen, 48n, 63

U
Undersocialized conception of the individual, 43–50, 78
Unfocused gathering, 93, 95, 96, 106, 107

V
Ventilation of stress, 135
Verstehen, 89
Vygotsky, L. S., 66

W
Ward, Lester Frank, 14n, 20
Weber, Max, 88, 89, 90, 111–115 *passim*, 117, 125n, 148
Webster, Murray, Jr., 42
Weizenbaum, Joseph, 56
Wentworth, William M., 87, 96, 120, 152
Wheeler, Stanton, 37, 76
Whitehead, Alfred North, 142
Whiting, John W. M., 24
Wilson, Thomas P., 42, 116
Winch, Robert F., 38
Wirth, Louis, 18n
Wittgenstein, Ludwig, 56, 144, 145
Wolfenstein, Martha, 26n
Wood, Houston, 42, 44, 45, 47, 97
Woodward, Julian, 30
World-building, 90–92, 105, 109
World openness, 90–91
Wright, Charles R., 74
Wrong, Dennis, 22, 33, 34, 40, 44, 113, 117

Y
Young, Kimball, 31, 32

Z
Zijderveld, Anton C., 120
Znaniecki, Florian, 18n, 21, 92, 93, 104